THE DEVIL'S FOOTPRINTS

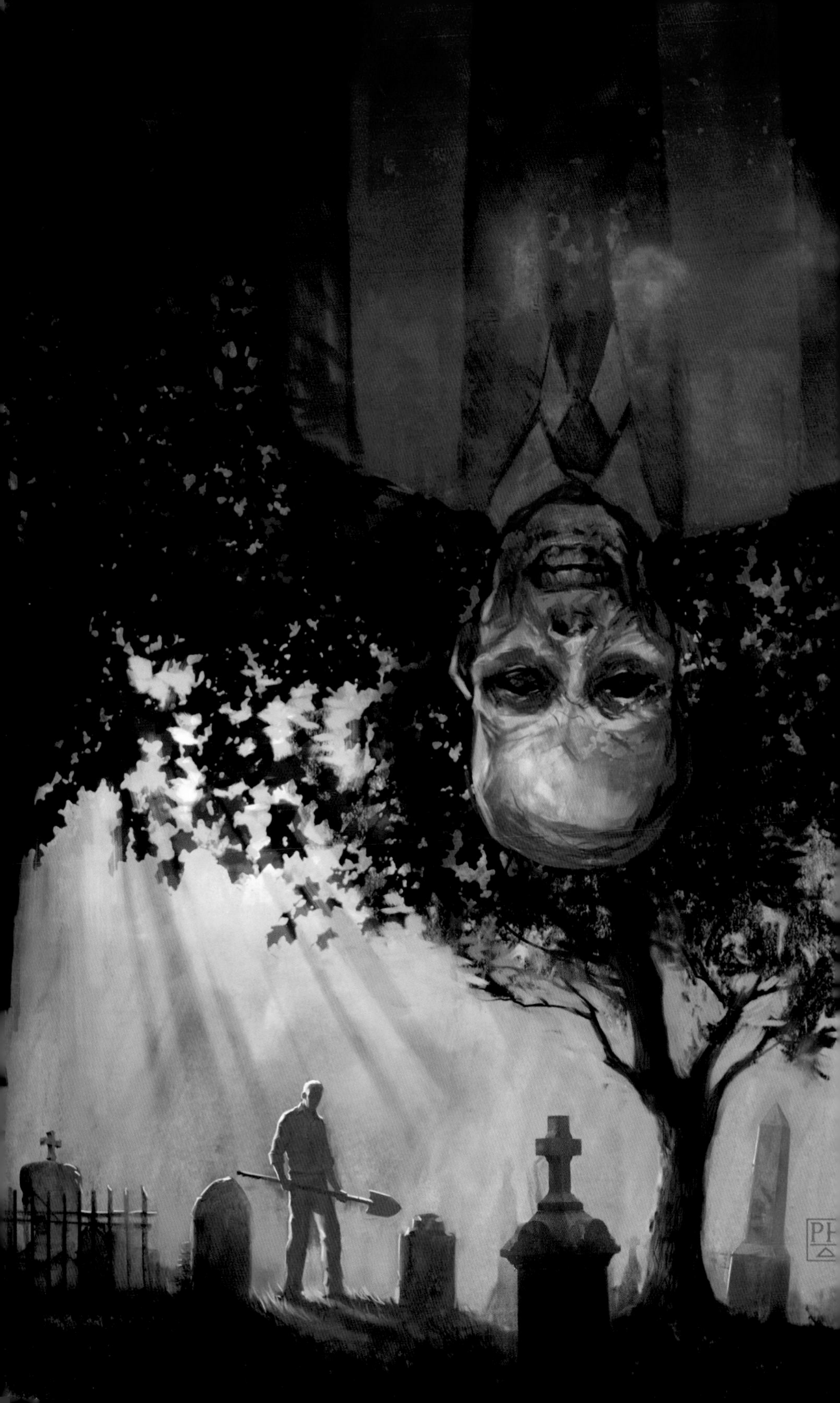

The DEVIL'S FOOTPRINTS ™

Story
Scott Allie

Art
Paul Lee and Brian Horton

Colors
Dave Stewart

Dark Horse Books™

Editor Shawna Ervin-Gore
Designer Amy Arendts
Publisher Mike Richardson

This book collects the four-issue series The Devil's Footprints, as
well as short stories from Dark Horse Presents #142 and Reveal,
published by Dark Horse Comics.

Published by Dark Horse Books,
A division of Dark Horse Comics, Inc.
10956 SE Main Street
Milwaukie, OR 97222

November 2003
First edition
ISBN: 1-56971-933-0

10 9 8 7 6 5 4 3 2 1
Printed in China

A powerful rain along the New England coast had broken the early summer heatwave of 1969. Three Dog Night, Elvis, and the Beatles topped the request list on WRKO in Boston. The men of *Apollo 10* returned from their lunar orbit, while in Viet Nam, U.S. troops scored an important victory at Hamburger Hill. For the moment, Lyndon Johnson believed things would be all right.

In the small town of Ipswich, Massachusetts a terrible debt had come due.

Dedicated to
the whole family—
Melinda, Wendy,
Susan, and Michelle,
and to
Ethan Alexander Lee and
Victor Harrison Horton,
both born during the telling
of this story.

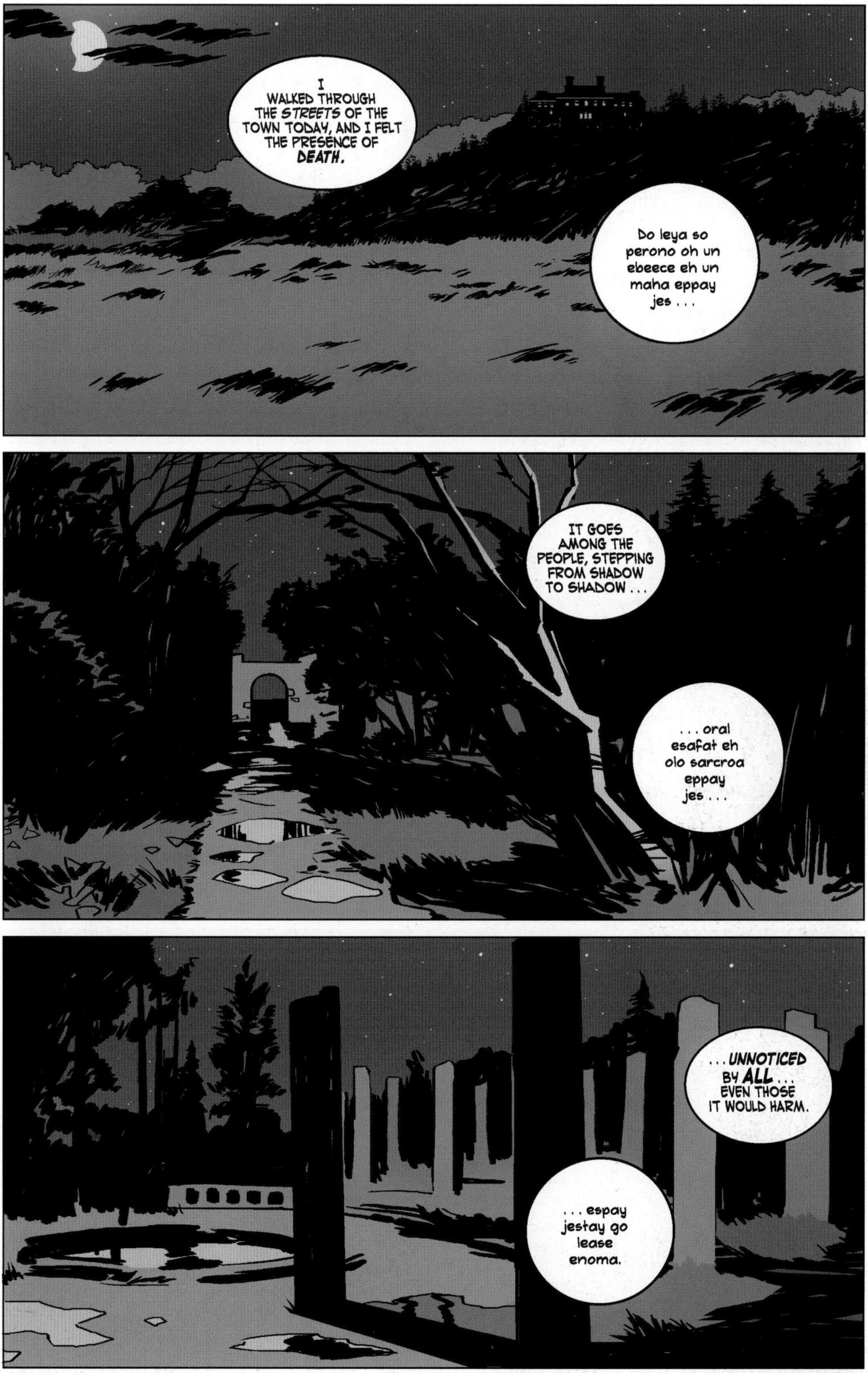

I WALKED THROUGH THE STREETS OF THE TOWN TODAY, AND I FELT THE PRESENCE OF DEATH.
Do leya so perono oh un ebeece eh un maha eppay jes . . .
IT GOES AMONG THE PEOPLE, STEPPING FROM SHADOW TO SHADOW . . .
. . . oral esafat eh olo sarcroa eppay jes . . .
. . . UNNOTICED BY ALL . . . EVEN THOSE IT WOULD HARM.
. . . espay jestay go lease enoma.

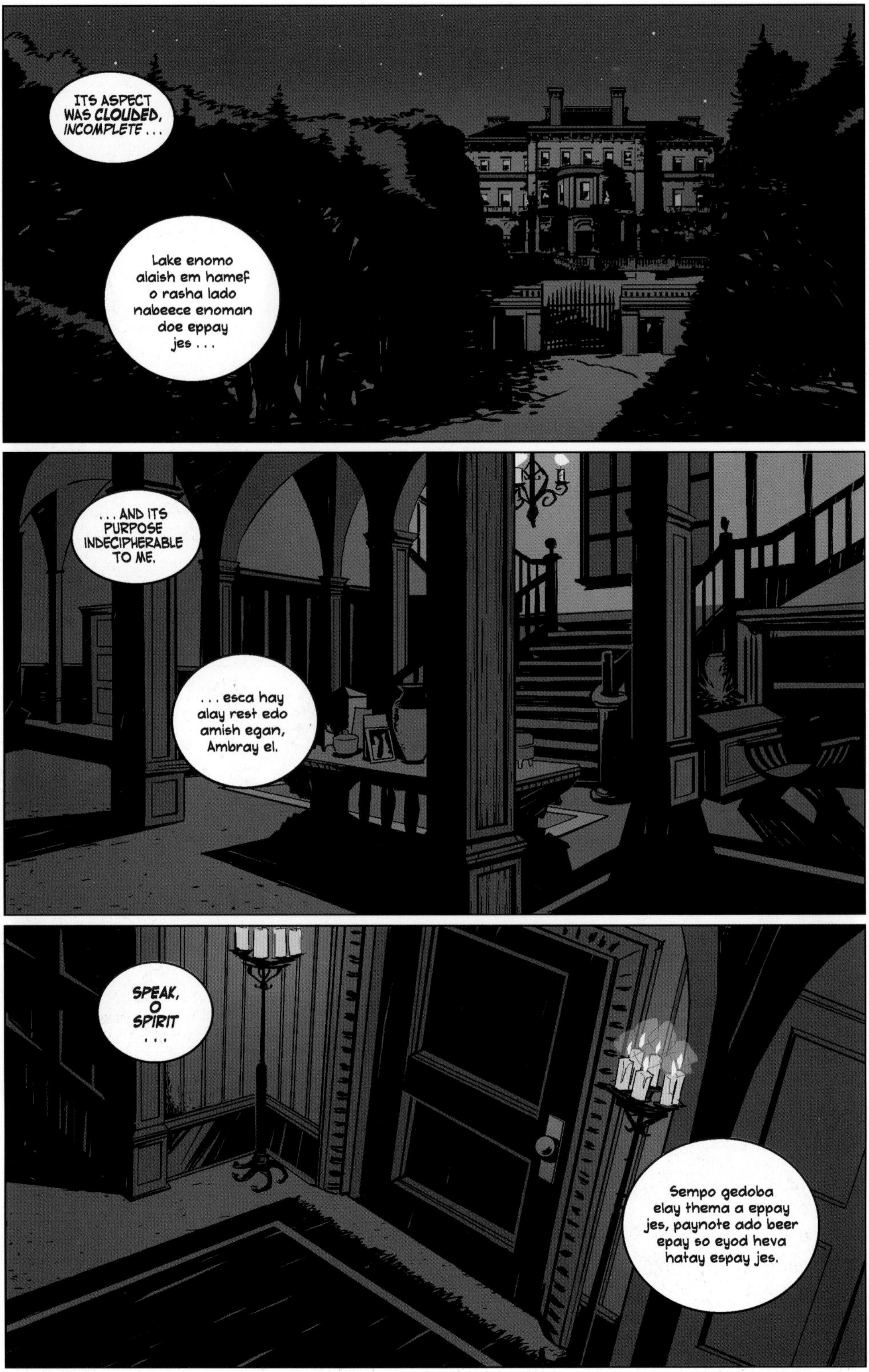
ITS ASPECT WAS CLOUDED, INCOMPLETE . . .
Lake enomo alaish em hamef o rasha lado nabeece enoman doe eppay jes . . .
. . . AND ITS PURPOSE INDECIPHERABLE TO ME.
. . . esca hay alay rest edo amish egan, Ambray el.
SPEAK, O SPIRIT . . .
Sempo gedoba elay thema a eppay jes, paynote ado beer epay so eyod heva hatay espay jes.

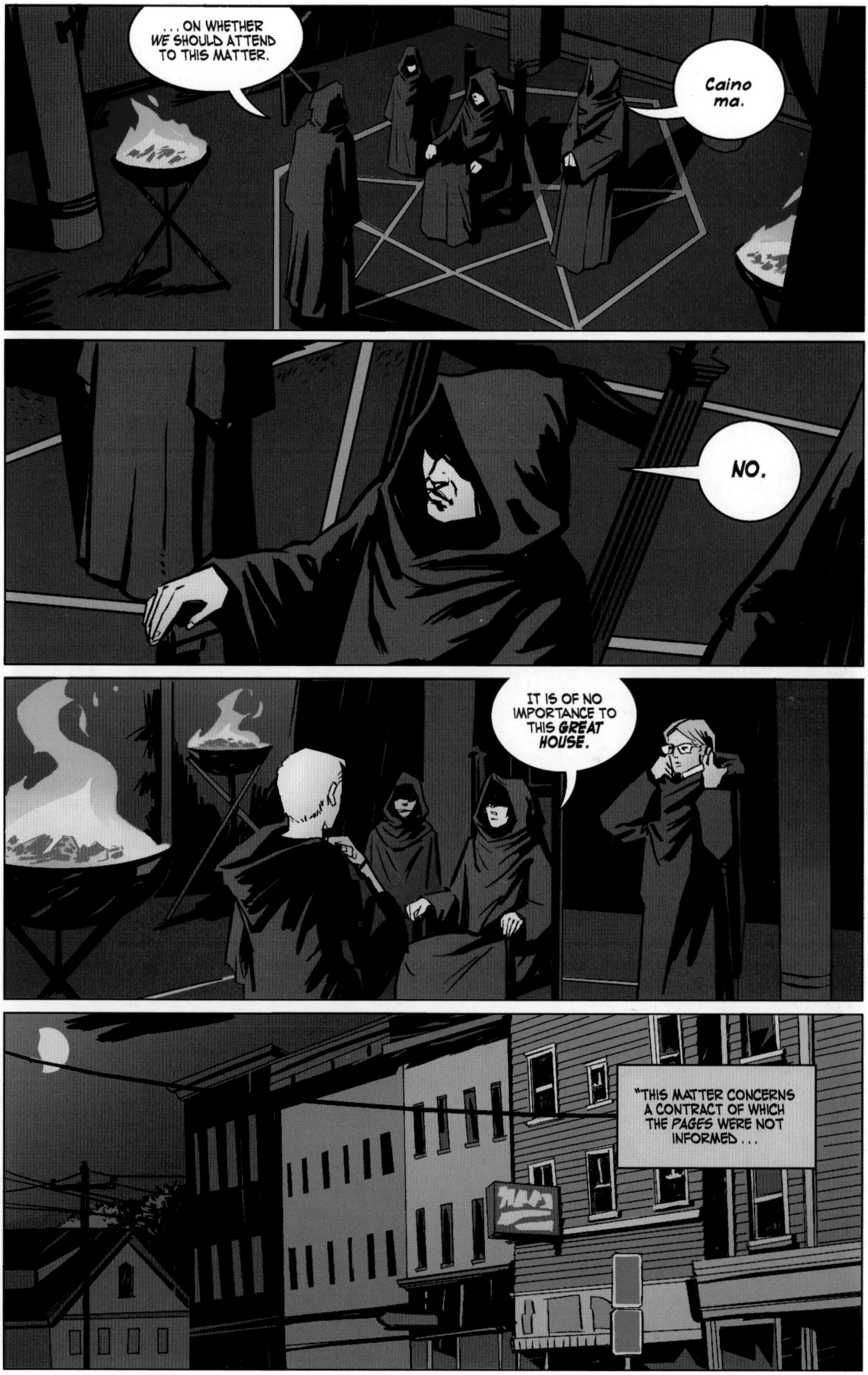

. . . ON WHETHER WE SHOULD ATTEND TO THIS MATTER.
Caino ma.
NO.
IT IS OF NO IMPORTANCE TO THIS GREAT HOUSE.
"THIS MATTER CONCERNS A CONTRACT OF WHICH THE PAGES WERE NOT INFORMED . . .

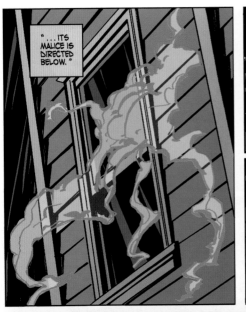

"...ITS MALICE IS DIRECTED BELOW."

snif

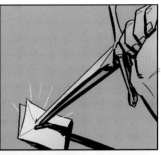

METATRON OVER *DAATH*, AND BY THE *CHAIOTH HA QADESH*-- LET THERE BE UNTO THE VOID *RESTRICTION*, AND FIX WITH THE *VOLATILE FLAME* AN ANSWER.

HISSSS-SSS

BY THE *FOURTH PENTACLE OF MERCURY,* ALLATORI . . .

. . . WHY DOES THE *WAITE FAMILY* SUFFER?

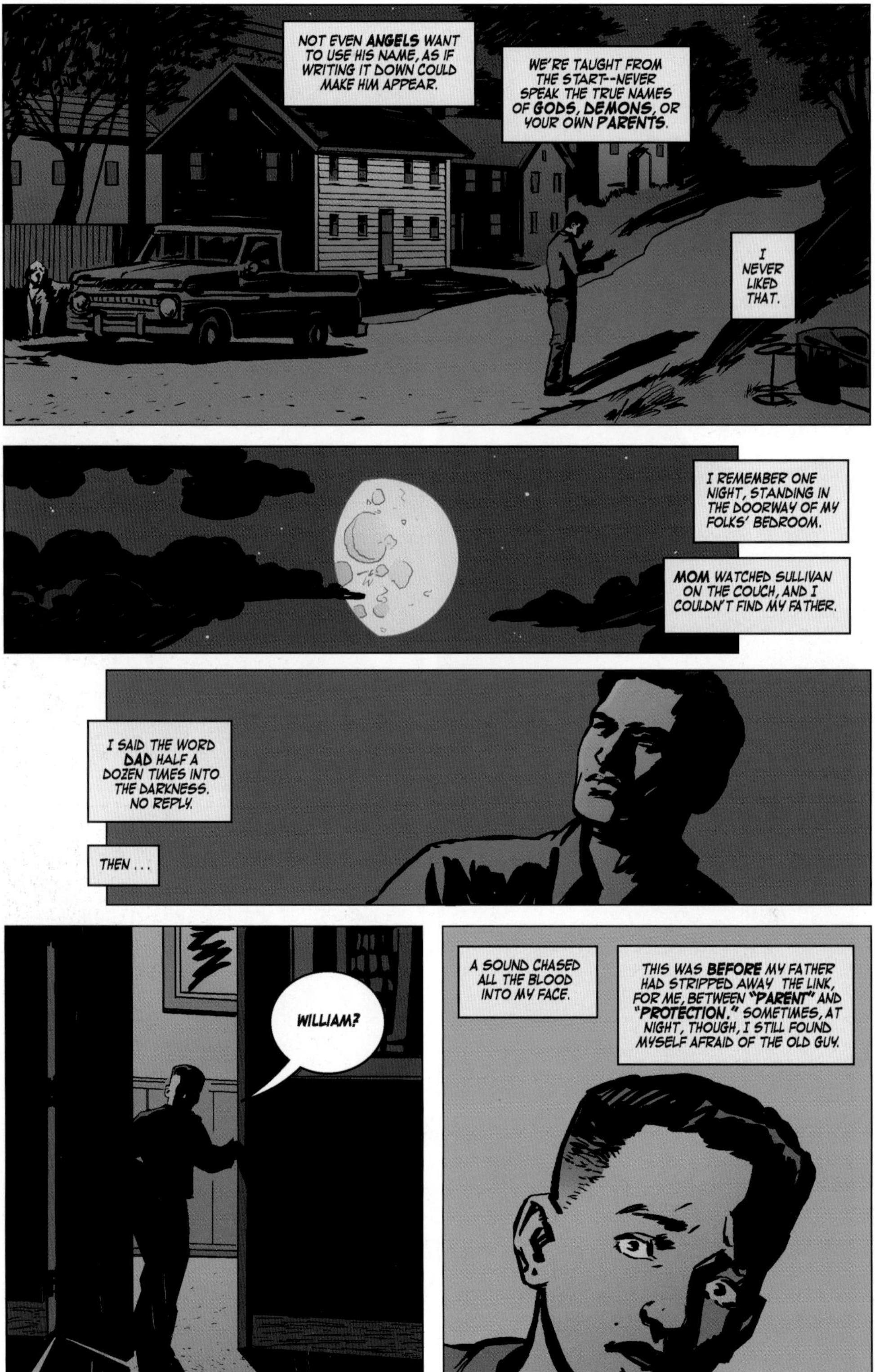

NOT EVEN ANGELS WANT TO USE HIS NAME, AS IF WRITING IT DOWN COULD MAKE HIM APPEAR.
WE'RE TAUGHT FROM THE START--NEVER SPEAK THE TRUE NAMES OF GODS, DEMONS, OR YOUR OWN PARENTS.
I NEVER LIKED THAT.
I REMEMBER ONE NIGHT, STANDING IN THE DOORWAY OF MY FOLKS' BEDROOM.
MOM WATCHED SULLIVAN ON THE COUCH, AND I COULDN'T FIND MY FATHER.
I SAID THE WORD DAD HALF A DOZEN TIMES INTO THE DARKNESS. NO REPLY.
THEN . . .
WILLIAM?
A SOUND CHASED ALL THE BLOOD INTO MY FACE.
THIS WAS BEFORE MY FATHER HAD STRIPPED AWAY THE LINK, FOR ME, BETWEEN "PARENT" AND "PROTECTION." SOMETIMES, AT NIGHT, THOUGH, I STILL FOUND MYSELF AFRAID OF THE OLD GUY.

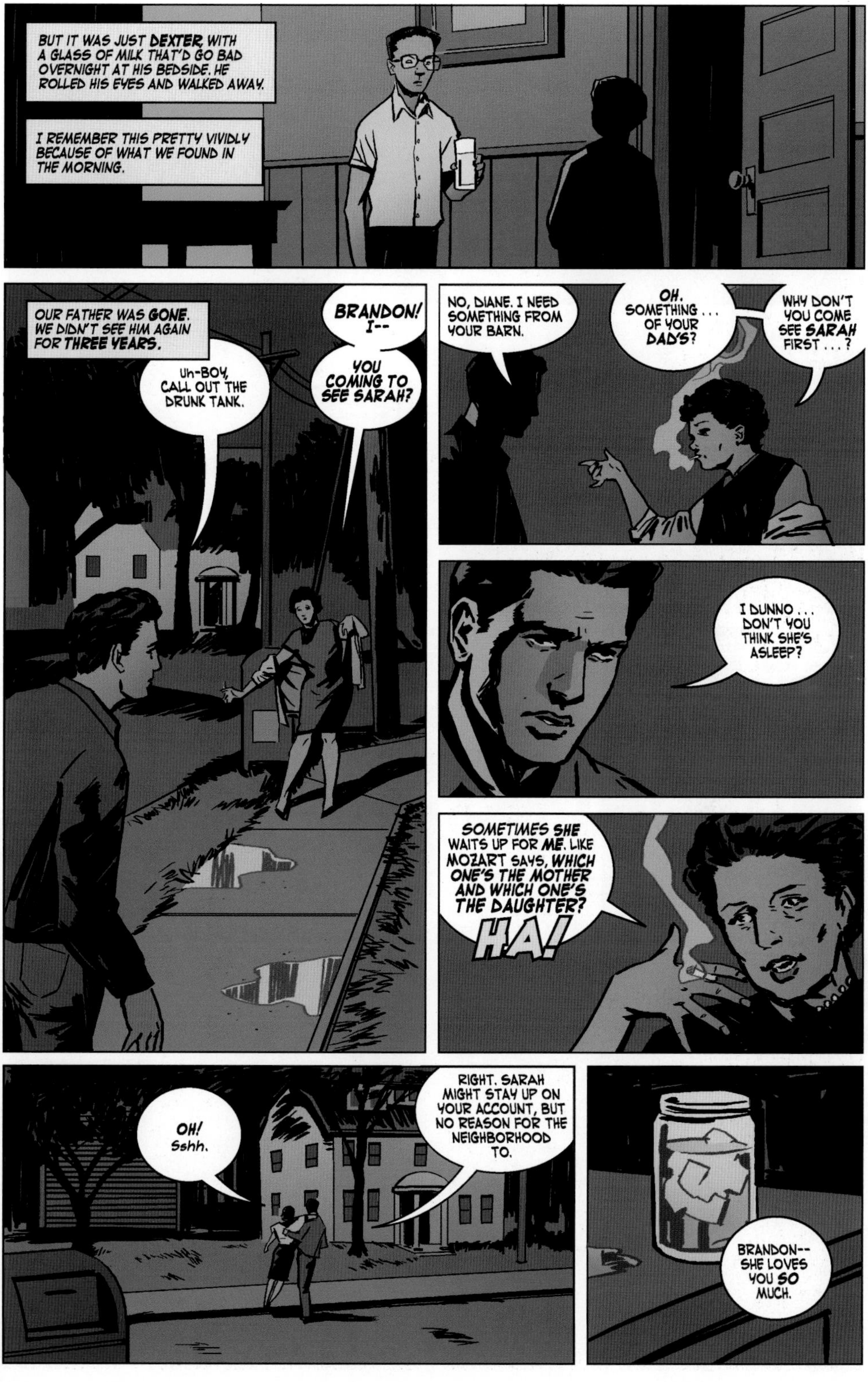
BUT IT WAS JUST DEXTER, WITH A GLASS OF MILK THAT'D GO BAD OVERNIGHT AT HIS BEDSIDE. HE ROLLED HIS EYES AND WALKED AWAY.
I REMEMBER THIS PRETTY VIVIDLY BECAUSE OF WHAT WE FOUND IN THE MORNING.
OUR FATHER WAS GONE. WE DIDN'T SEE HIM AGAIN FOR THREE YEARS.
BRANDON! I--
Uh-BOY, CALL OUT THE DRUNK TANK.
YOU COMING TO SEE SARAH?
NO, DIANE. I NEED SOMETHING FROM YOUR BARN.
OH. SOMETHING . . . OF YOUR DAD'S?
WHY DON'T YOU COME SEE SARAH FIRST . . . ?
I DUNNO . . . DON'T YOU THINK SHE'S ASLEEP?
SOMETIMES SHE WAITS UP FOR ME. LIKE MOZART SAYS, WHICH ONE'S THE MOTHER AND WHICH ONE'S THE DAUGHTER?
HA!
OH! Sshh.
RIGHT. SARAH MIGHT STAY UP ON YOUR ACCOUNT, BUT NO REASON FOR THE NEIGHBORHOOD TO.
BRANDON-- SHE LOVES YOU SO MUCH.

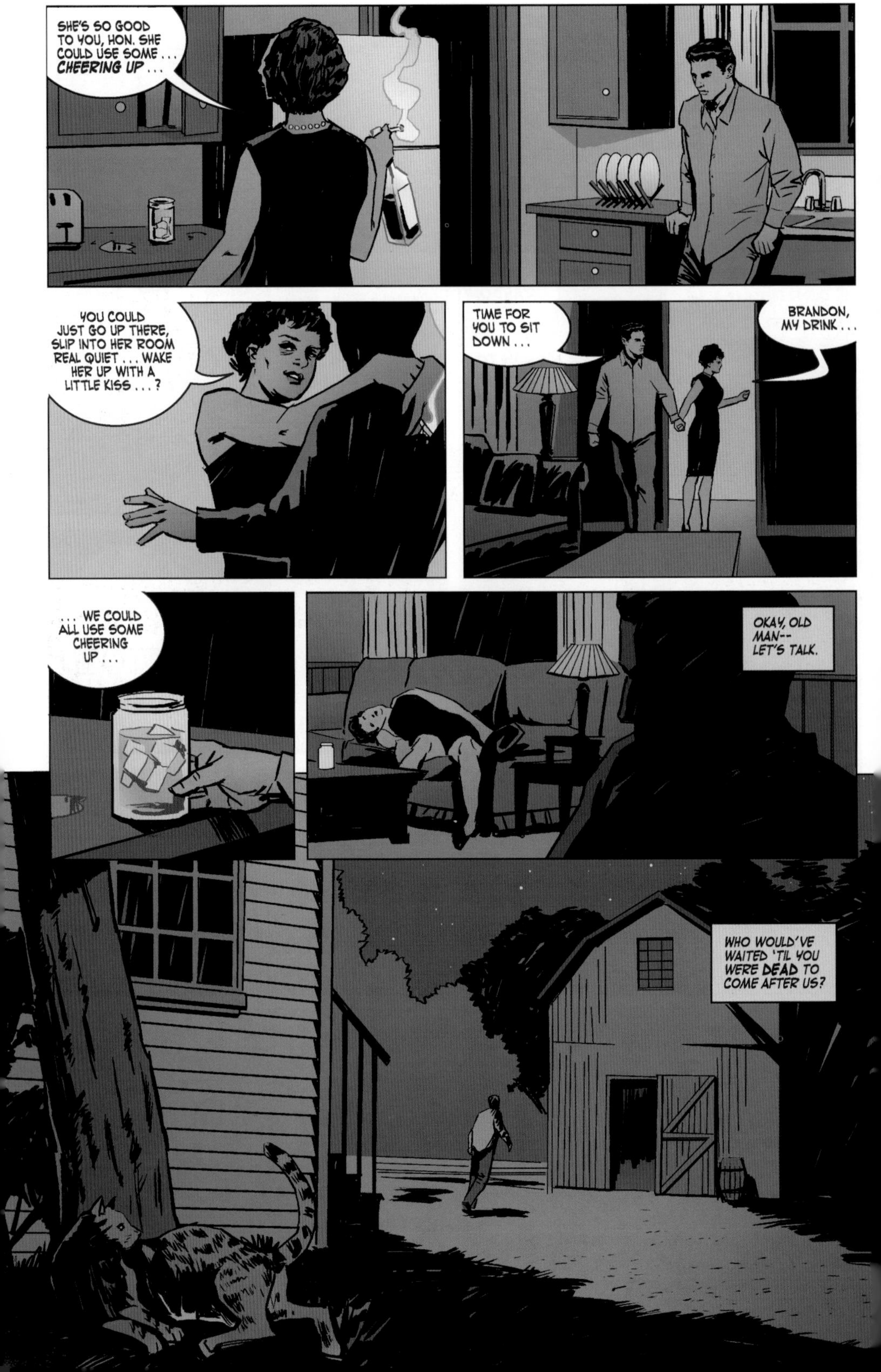
SHE'S SO GOOD TO YOU, HON. SHE COULD USE SOME . . . CHEERING UP . . .
YOU COULD JUST GO UP THERE, SLIP INTO HER ROOM REAL QUIET . . . WAKE HER UP WITH A LITTLE KISS . . . ?
TIME FOR YOU TO SIT DOWN . . .
BRANDON, MY DRINK . . .
. . . WE COULD ALL USE SOME CHEERING UP . . .
OKAY, OLD MAN-- LET'S TALK.
WHO WOULD'VE WAITED 'TIL YOU WERE DEAD TO COME AFTER US?

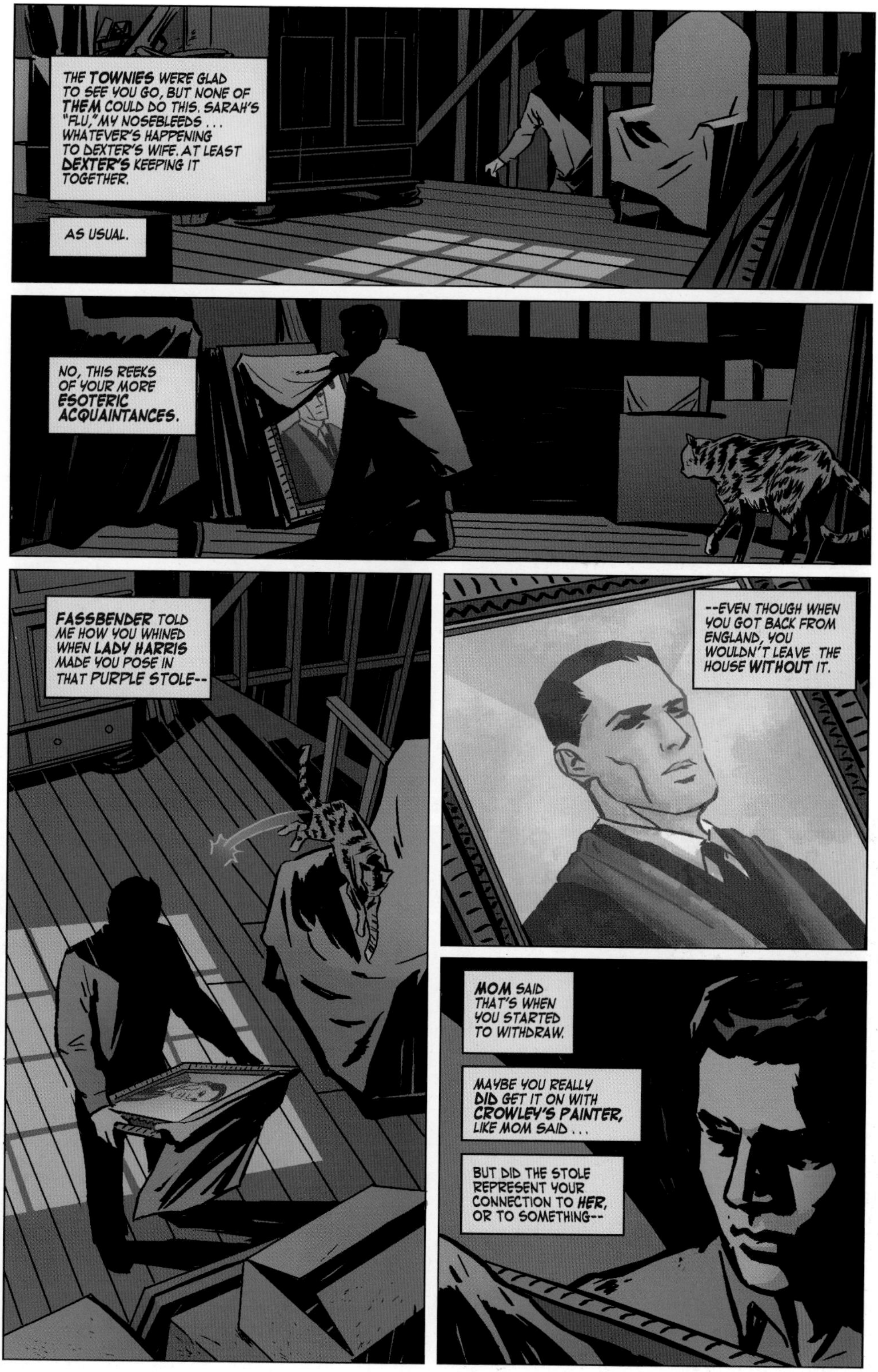
THE TOWNIES WERE GLAD TO SEE YOU GO, BUT NONE OF THEM COULD DO THIS. SARAH'S "FLU," MY NOSEBLEEDS . . . WHATEVER'S HAPPENING TO DEXTER'S WIFE. AT LEAST DEXTER'S KEEPING IT TOGETHER.
AS USUAL.
NO, THIS REEKS OF YOUR MORE ESOTERIC ACQUAINTANCES.
FASSBENDER TOLD ME HOW YOU WHINED WHEN LADY HARRIS MADE YOU POSE IN THAT PURPLE STOLE--
--EVEN THOUGH WHEN YOU GOT BACK FROM ENGLAND, YOU WOULDN'T LEAVE THE HOUSE WITHOUT IT.
MOM SAID THAT'S WHEN YOU STARTED TO WITHDRAW.
MAYBE YOU REALLY DID GET IT ON WITH CROWLEY'S PAINTER, LIKE MOM SAID . . .
BUT DID THE STOLE REPRESENT YOUR CONNECTION TO HER, OR TO SOMETHING--

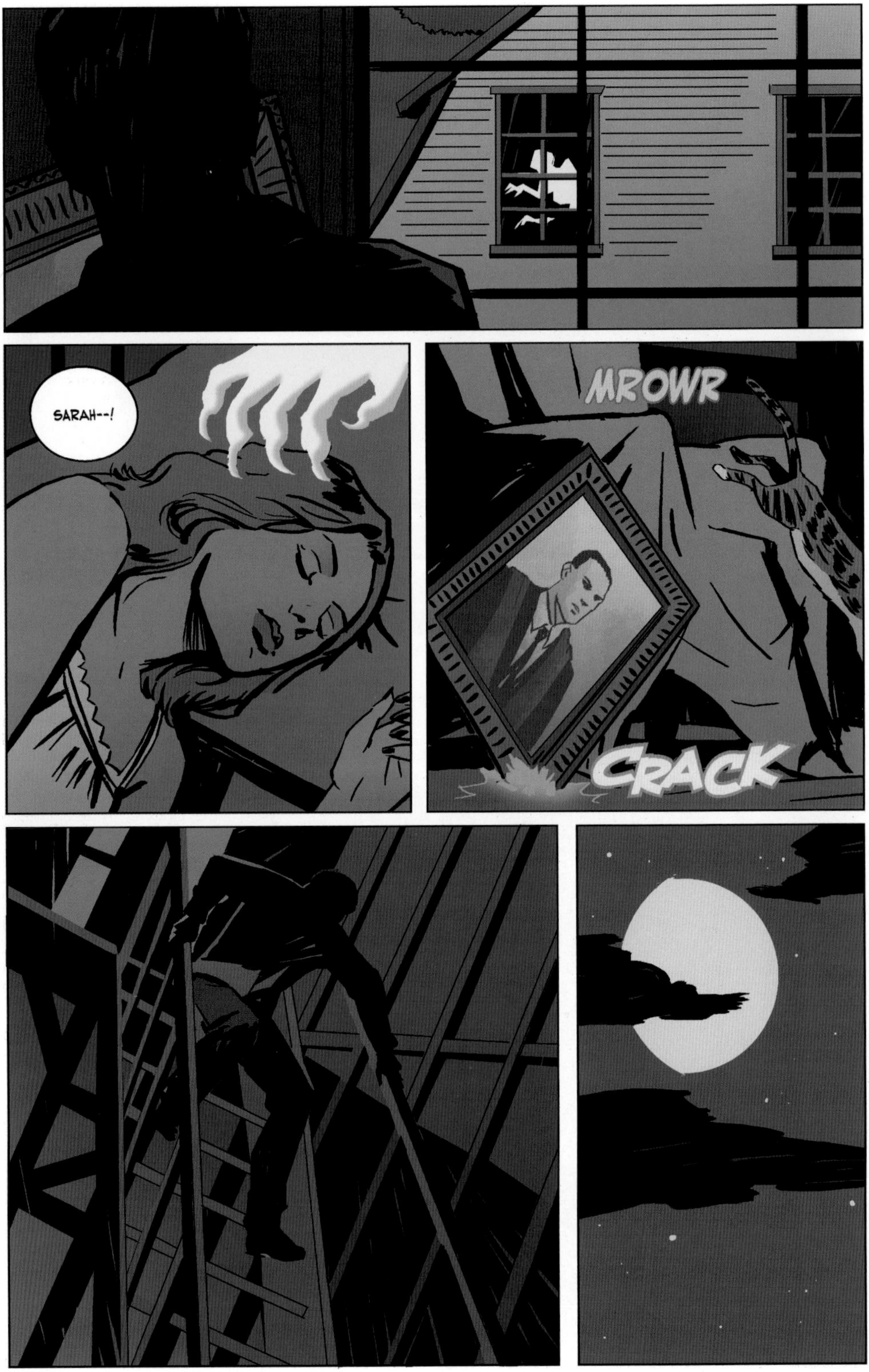
SARAH--!
MROWR
CRACK

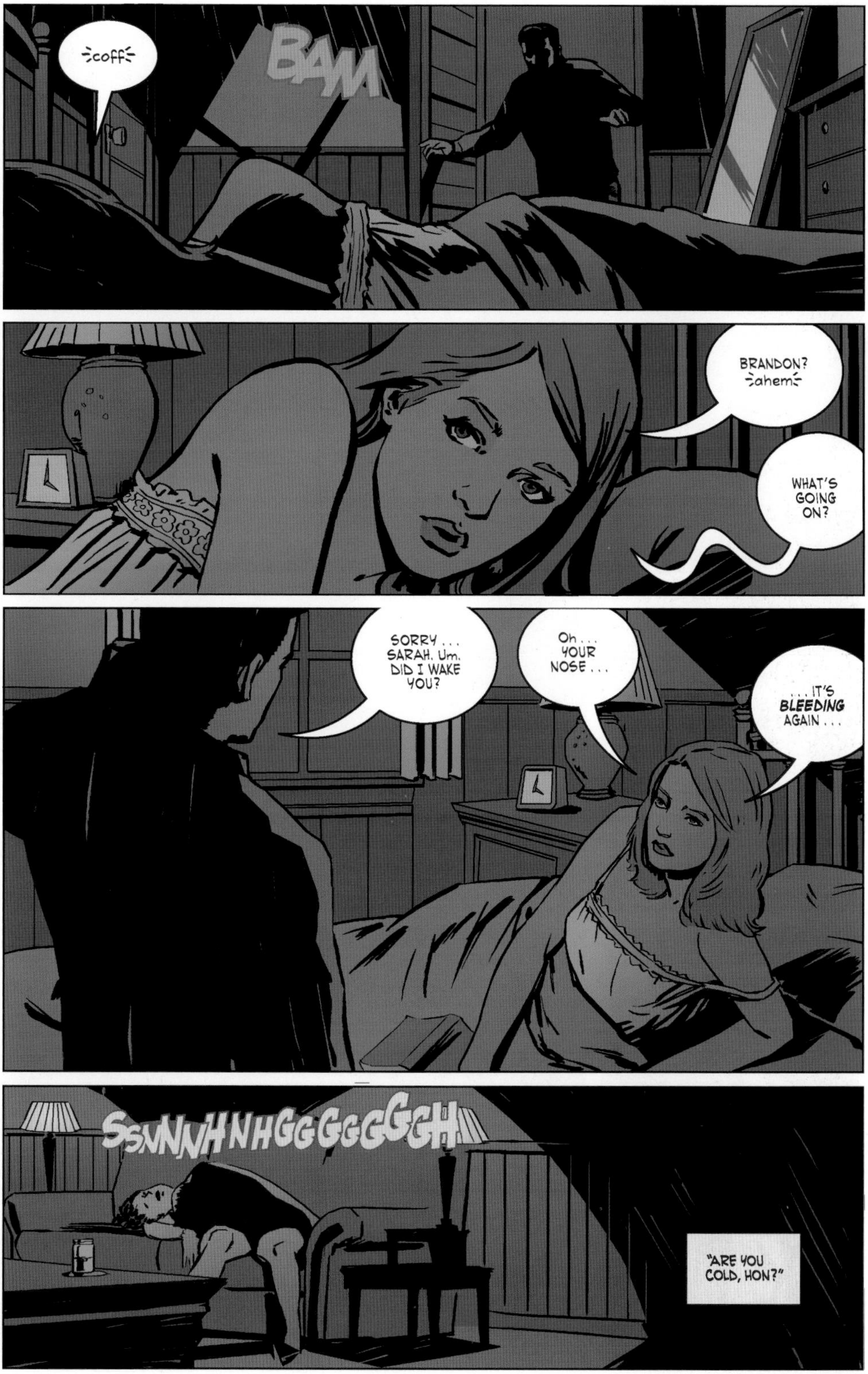

coff
BAM
BRANDON? ahem
WHAT'S GOING ON?
SORRY . . . SARAH. Um. DID I WAKE YOU?
Oh . . . YOUR NOSE . . .
. . . IT'S BLEEDING AGAIN . . .
SSNNNHNHGGGGGGH
"ARE YOU COLD, HON?"

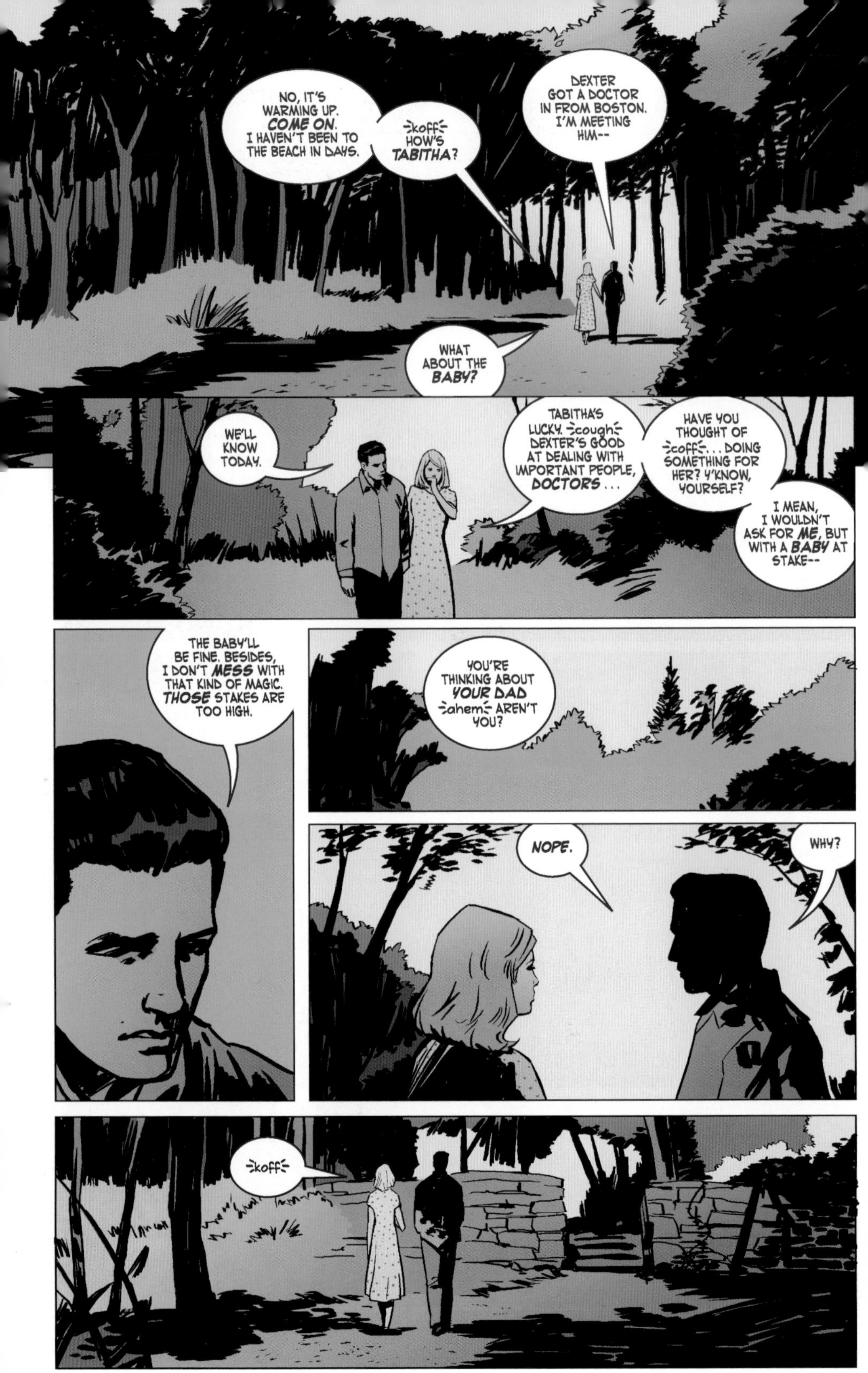
NO, IT'S WARMING UP. COME ON. I HAVEN'T BEEN TO THE BEACH IN DAYS.
-koff- HOW'S TABITHA?
DEXTER GOT A DOCTOR IN FROM BOSTON. I'M MEETING HIM--
WHAT ABOUT THE BABY?
WE'LL KNOW TODAY.
TABITHA'S LUCKY. -cough- DEXTER'S GOOD AT DEALING WITH IMPORTANT PEOPLE, DOCTORS . . .
HAVE YOU THOUGHT OF -coff- . . . DOING SOMETHING FOR HER? Y'KNOW, YOURSELF?
I MEAN, I WOULDN'T ASK FOR ME, BUT WITH A BABY AT STAKE--
THE BABY'LL BE FINE. BESIDES, I DON'T MESS WITH THAT KIND OF MAGIC. THOSE STAKES ARE TOO HIGH.
YOU'RE THINKING ABOUT YOUR DAD -ahem- AREN'T YOU?
NOPE.
WHY?
-koff-

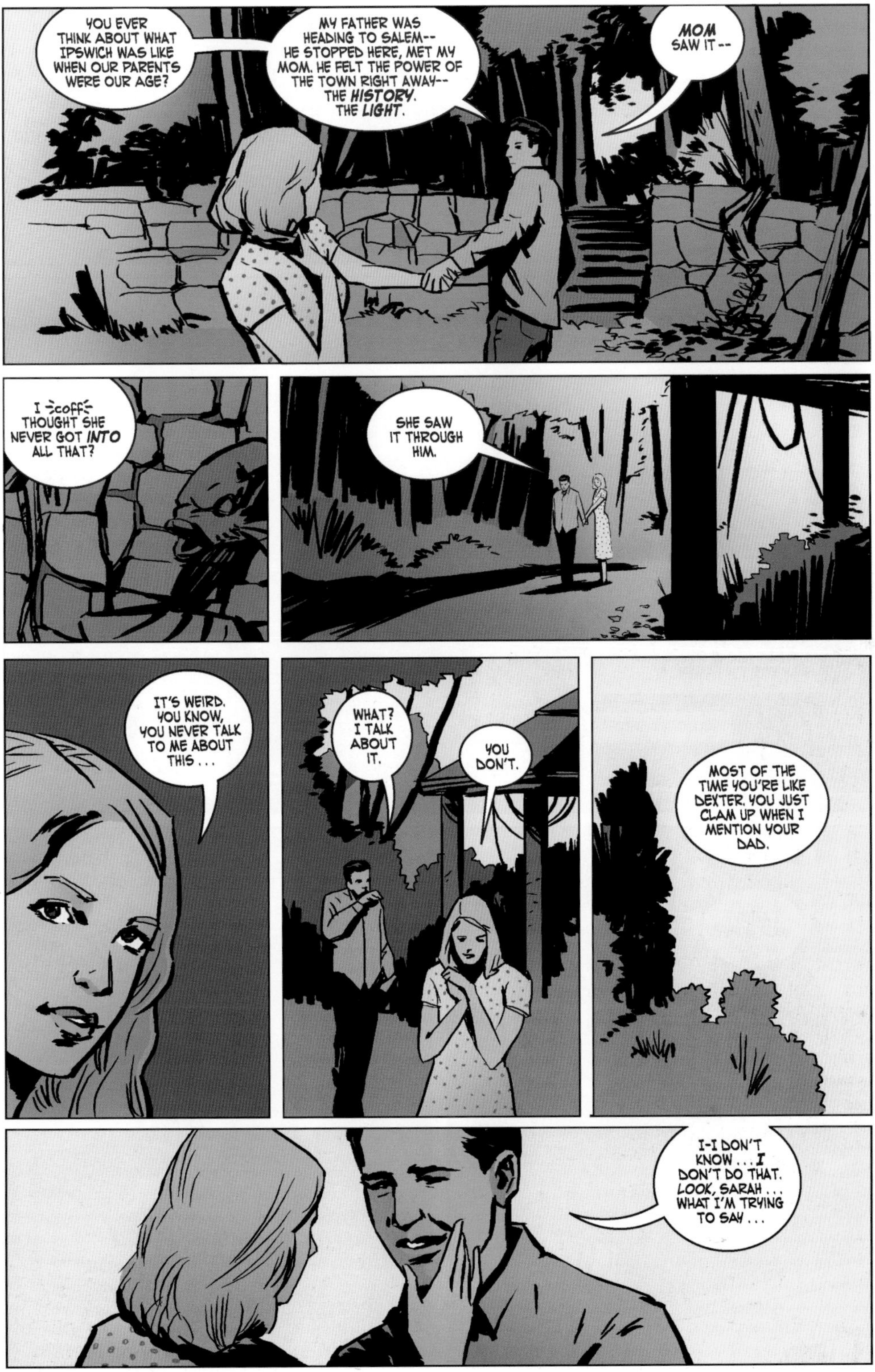

YOU EVER THINK ABOUT WHAT IPSWICH WAS LIKE WHEN OUR PARENTS WERE OUR AGE?
MY FATHER WAS HEADING TO SALEM-- HE STOPPED HERE, MET MY MOM. HE FELT THE POWER OF THE TOWN RIGHT AWAY-- THE HISTORY. THE LIGHT.
MOM SAW IT --
I -coff- THOUGHT SHE NEVER GOT INTO ALL THAT?
SHE SAW IT THROUGH HIM.
IT'S WEIRD. YOU KNOW, YOU NEVER TALK TO ME ABOUT THIS . . .
WHAT? I TALK ABOUT IT.
YOU DON'T.
MOST OF THE TIME YOU'RE LIKE DEXTER. YOU JUST CLAM UP WHEN I MENTION YOUR DAD.
I-I DON'T KNOW . . . I DON'T DO THAT. LOOK, SARAH . . . WHAT I'M TRYING TO SAY . . .

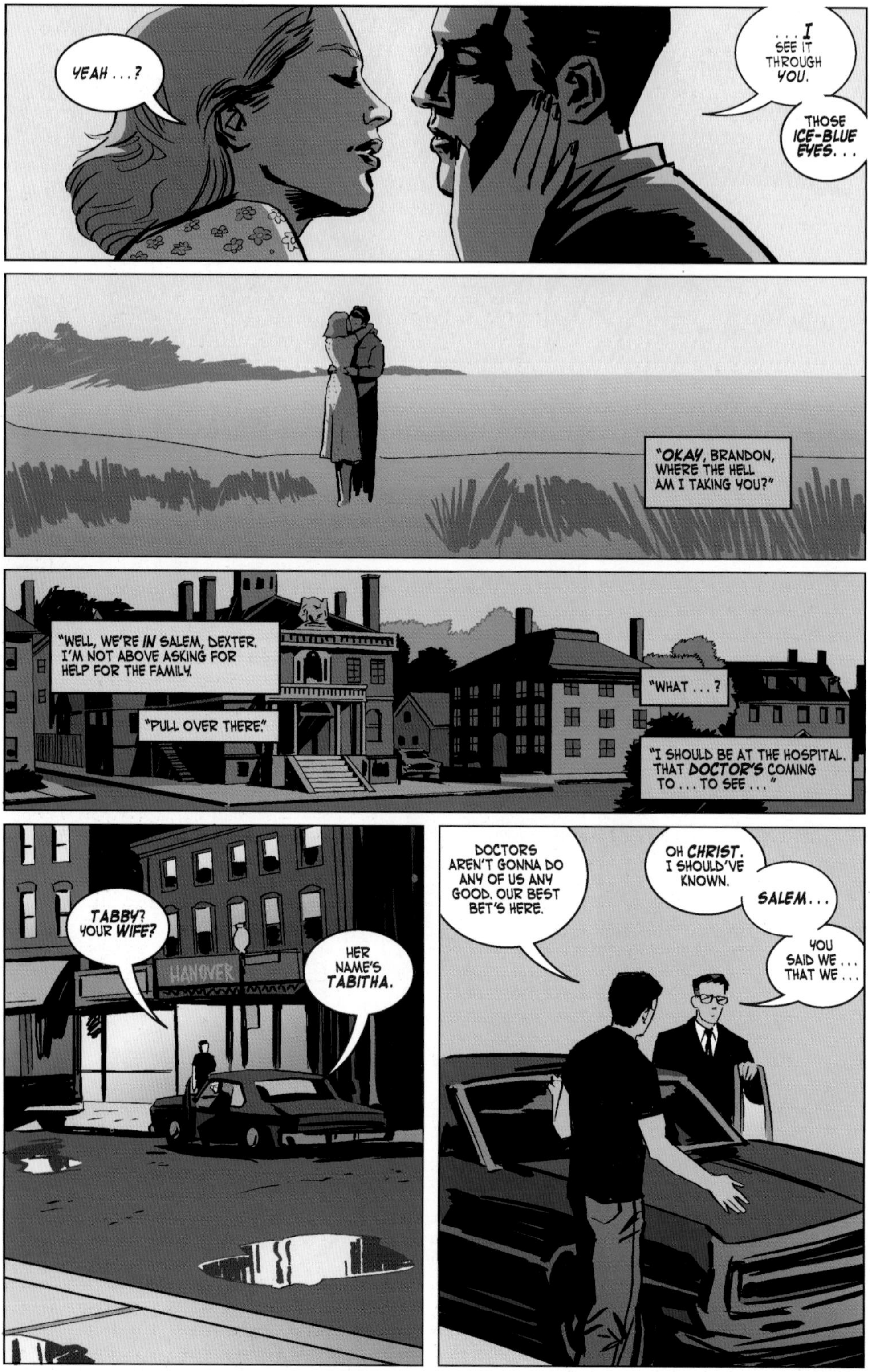
YEAH . . .?
. . . I SEE IT THROUGH YOU.
THOSE ICE-BLUE EYES . . .
"OKAY, BRANDON, WHERE THE HELL AM I TAKING YOU?"
"WELL, WE'RE IN SALEM, DEXTER. I'M NOT ABOVE ASKING FOR HELP FOR THE FAMILY.
"PULL OVER THERE."
"WHAT . . .?
"I SHOULD BE AT THE HOSPITAL. THAT DOCTOR'S COMING TO . . . TO SEE . . ."
TABBY? YOUR WIFE?
HANOVER
HER NAME'S TABITHA.
DOCTORS AREN'T GONNA DO ANY OF US ANY GOOD. OUR BEST BET'S HERE.
OH CHRIST. I SHOULD'VE KNOWN.
SALEM . . .
YOU SAID WE . . . THAT WE . . .

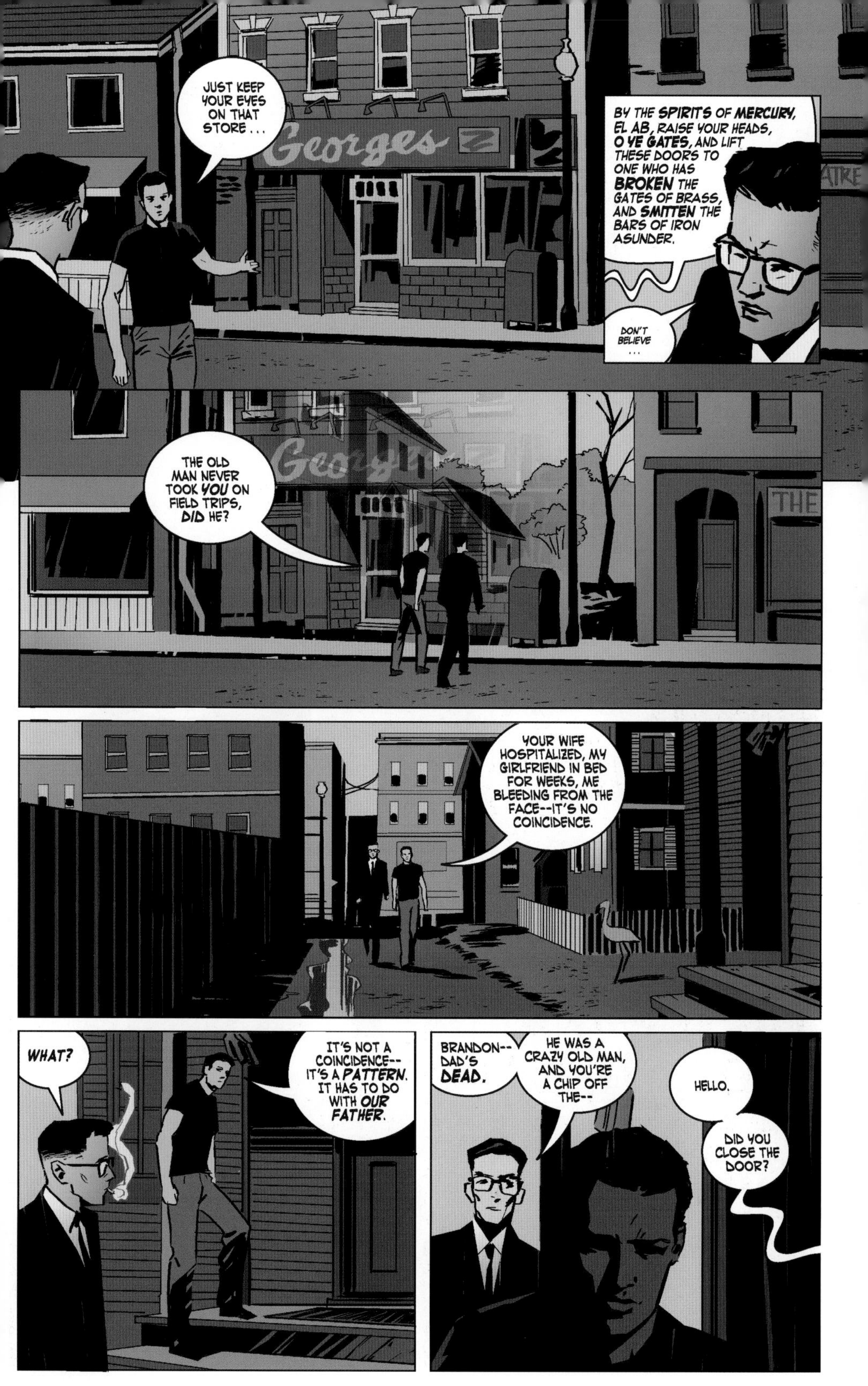
JUST KEEP YOUR EYES ON THAT STORE . . .
Georges
BY THE SPIRITS OF MERCURY, EL AB, RAISE YOUR HEADS, O YE GATES, AND LIFT THESE DOORS TO ONE WHO HAS BROKEN THE GATES OF BRASS, AND SMITTEN THE BARS OF IRON ASUNDER.
DON'T BELIEVE . . .
THE OLD MAN NEVER TOOK YOU ON FIELD TRIPS, DID HE?
THE
YOUR WIFE HOSPITALIZED, MY GIRLFRIEND IN BED FOR WEEKS, ME BLEEDING FROM THE FACE--IT'S NO COINCIDENCE.
WHAT?
IT'S NOT A COINCIDENCE--IT'S A PATTERN. IT HAS TO DO WITH OUR FATHER.
BRANDON--DAD'S DEAD.
HE WAS A CRAZY OLD MAN, AND YOU'RE A CHIP OFF THE--
HELLO.
DID YOU CLOSE THE DOOR?

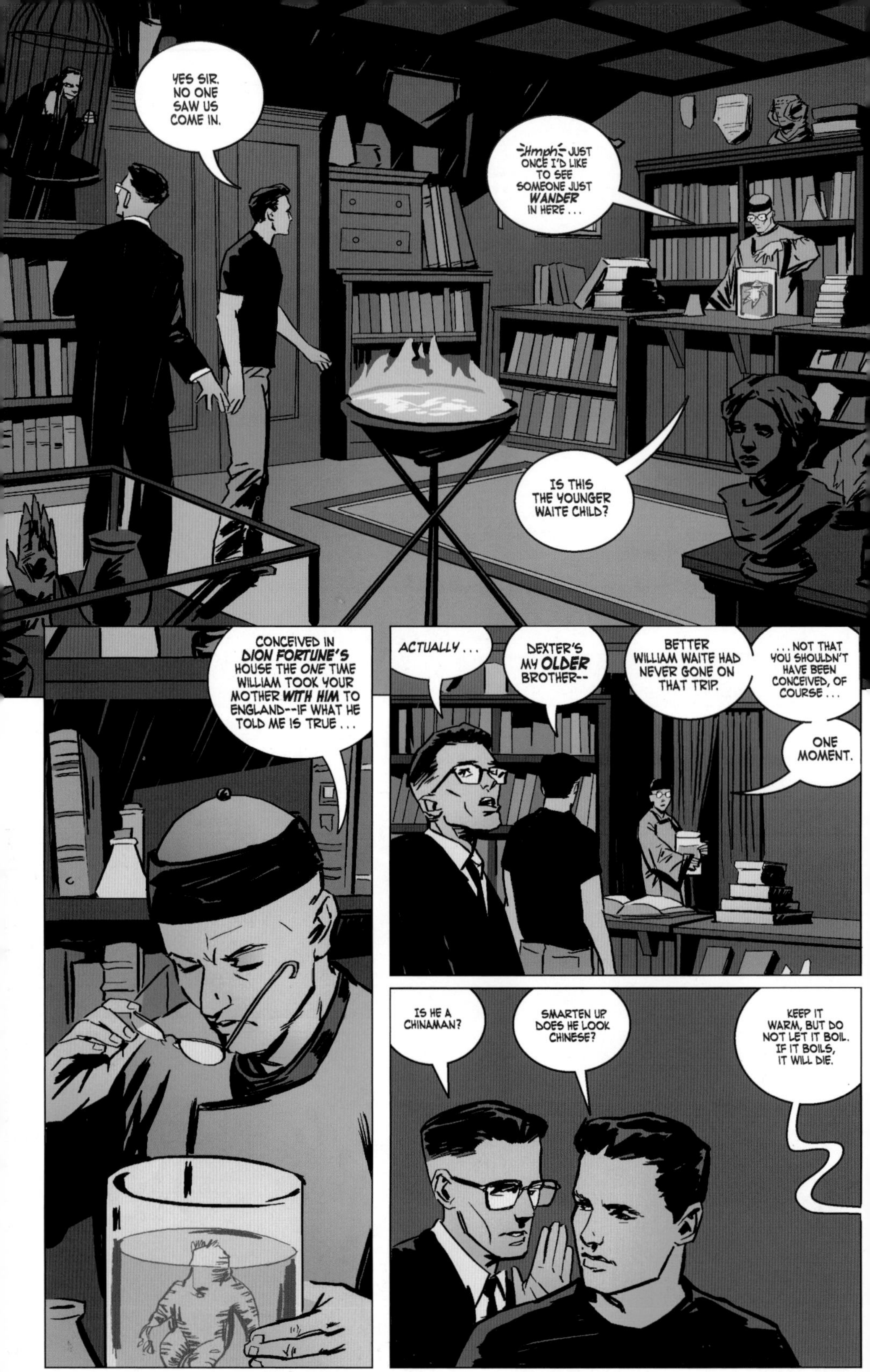
YES SIR. NO ONE SAW US COME IN.
Hmph! JUST ONCE I'D LIKE TO SEE SOMEONE JUST WANDER IN HERE . . .
IS THIS THE YOUNGER WAITE CHILD?
CONCEIVED IN DION FORTUNE'S HOUSE THE ONE TIME WILLIAM TOOK YOUR MOTHER WITH HIM TO ENGLAND--IF WHAT HE TOLD ME IS TRUE . . .
ACTUALLY . . .
DEXTER'S MY OLDER BROTHER--
BETTER WILLIAM WAITE HAD NEVER GONE ON THAT TRIP.
. . . NOT THAT YOU SHOULDN'T HAVE BEEN CONCEIVED, OF COURSE . . .
ONE MOMENT.
IS HE A CHINAMAN?
SMARTEN UP. DOES HE LOOK CHINESE?
KEEP IT WARM, BUT DO NOT LET IT BOIL. IF IT BOILS, IT WILL DIE.

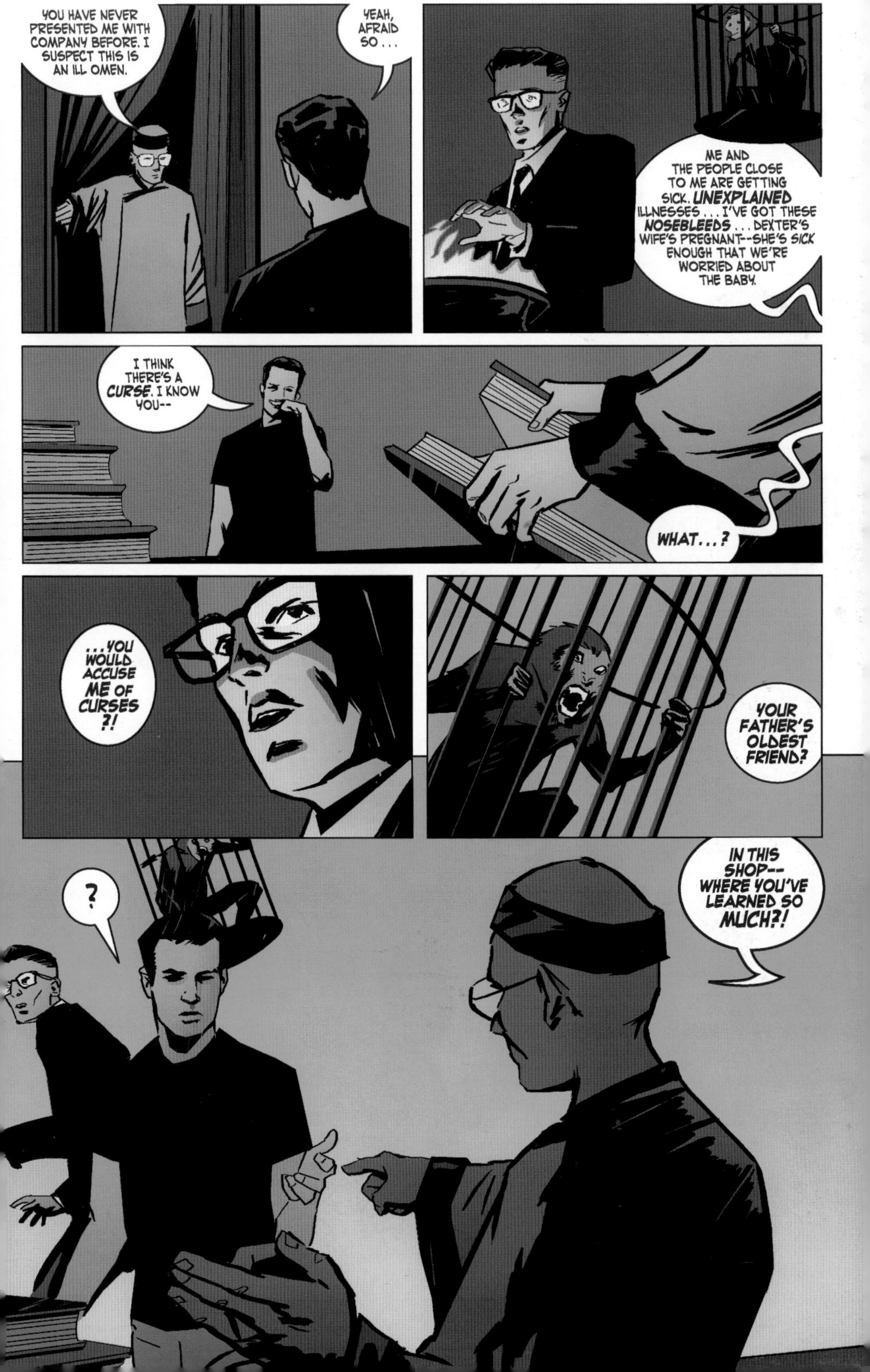
YOU HAVE NEVER PRESENTED ME WITH COMPANY BEFORE. I SUSPECT THIS IS AN ILL OMEN.
YEAH, AFRAID SO . . .
ME AND THE PEOPLE CLOSE TO ME ARE GETTING SICK. UNEXPLAINED ILLNESSES . . . I'VE GOT THESE NOSEBLEEDS . . . DEXTER'S WIFE'S PREGNANT--SHE'S SICK ENOUGH THAT WE'RE WORRIED ABOUT THE BABY.
I THINK THERE'S A CURSE. I KNOW YOU--
WHAT. . . ?
. . . YOU WOULD ACCUSE ME OF CURSES ?!
YOUR FATHER'S OLDEST FRIEND?
?
IN THIS SHOP-- WHERE YOU'VE LEARNED SO MUCH?!

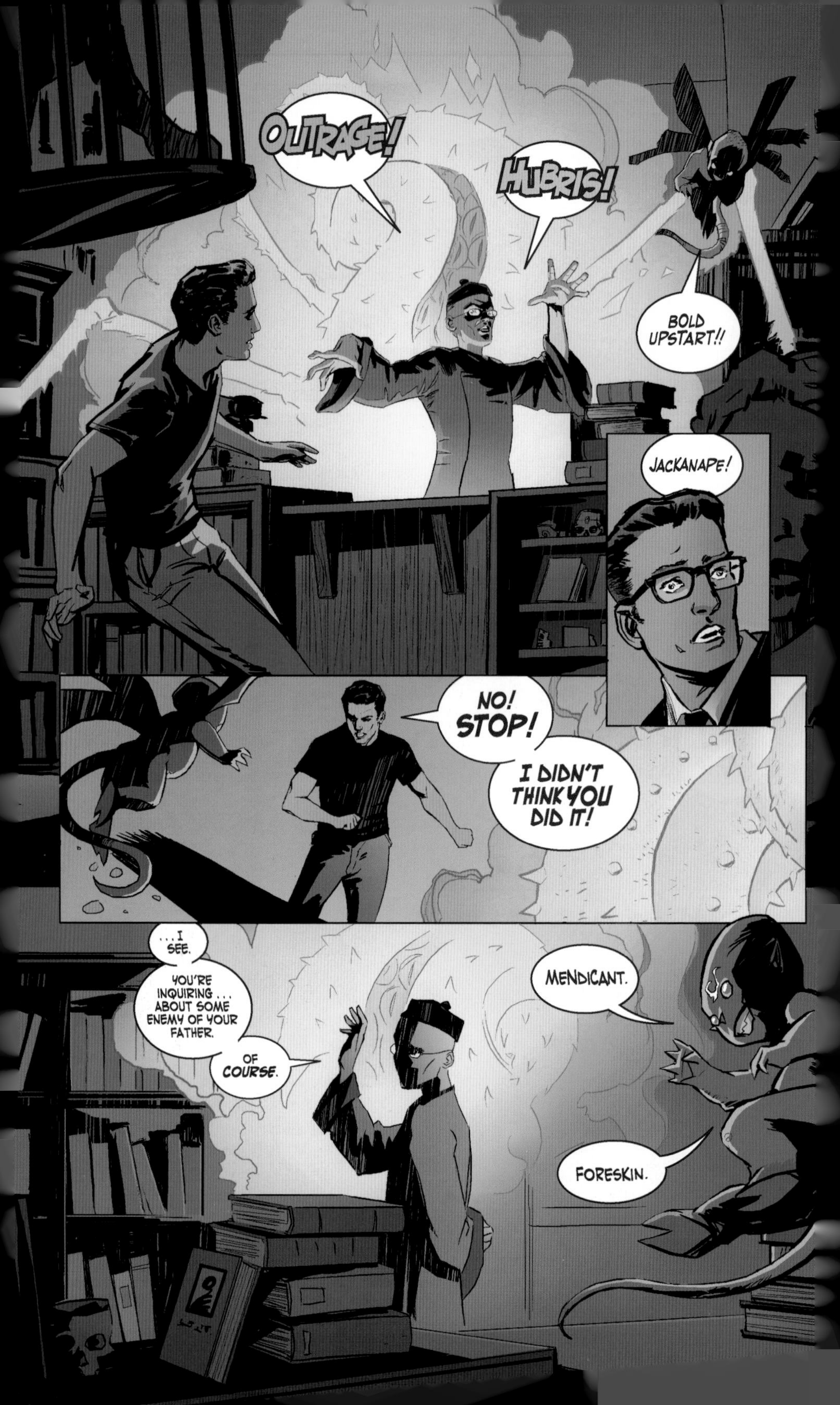
OUTRAGE!
HUBRIS!
BOLD UPSTART!!
JACKANAPE!
NO! STOP!
I DIDN'T THINK YOU DID IT!
...I SEE.
YOU'RE INQUIRING... ABOUT SOME ENEMY OF YOUR FATHER.
OF COURSE.
MENDICANT.
FORESKIN.

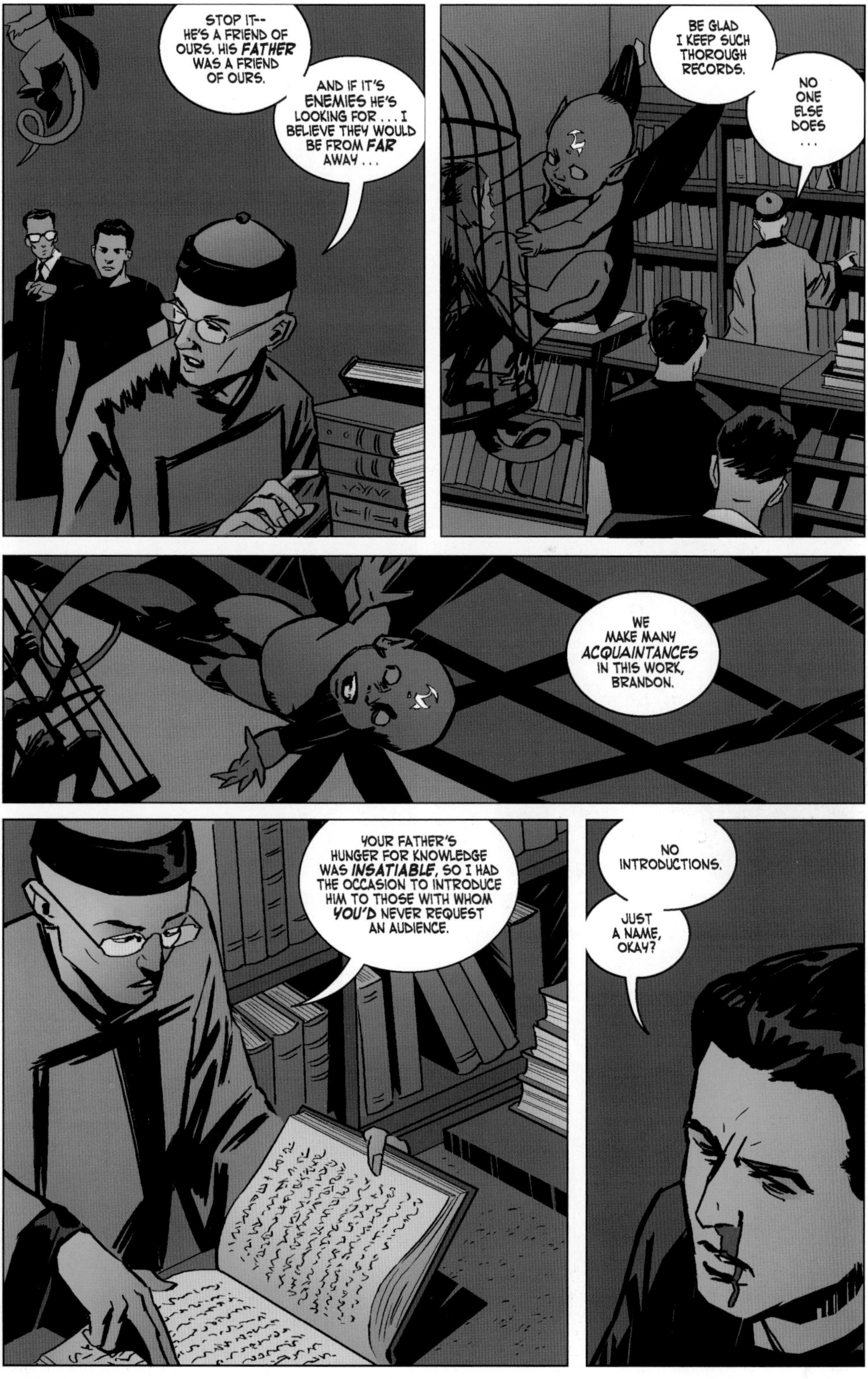

STOP IT-- HE'S A FRIEND OF OURS. HIS FATHER WAS A FRIEND OF OURS.
AND IF IT'S ENEMIES HE'S LOOKING FOR . . . I BELIEVE THEY WOULD BE FROM FAR AWAY . . .
BE GLAD I KEEP SUCH THOROUGH RECORDS.
NO ONE ELSE DOES . . .
WE MAKE MANY ACQUAINTANCES IN THIS WORK, BRANDON.
YOUR FATHER'S HUNGER FOR KNOWLEDGE WAS INSATIABLE, SO I HAD THE OCCASION TO INTRODUCE HIM TO THOSE WITH WHOM YOU'D NEVER REQUEST AN AUDIENCE.
NO INTRODUCTIONS.
JUST A NAME, OKAY?

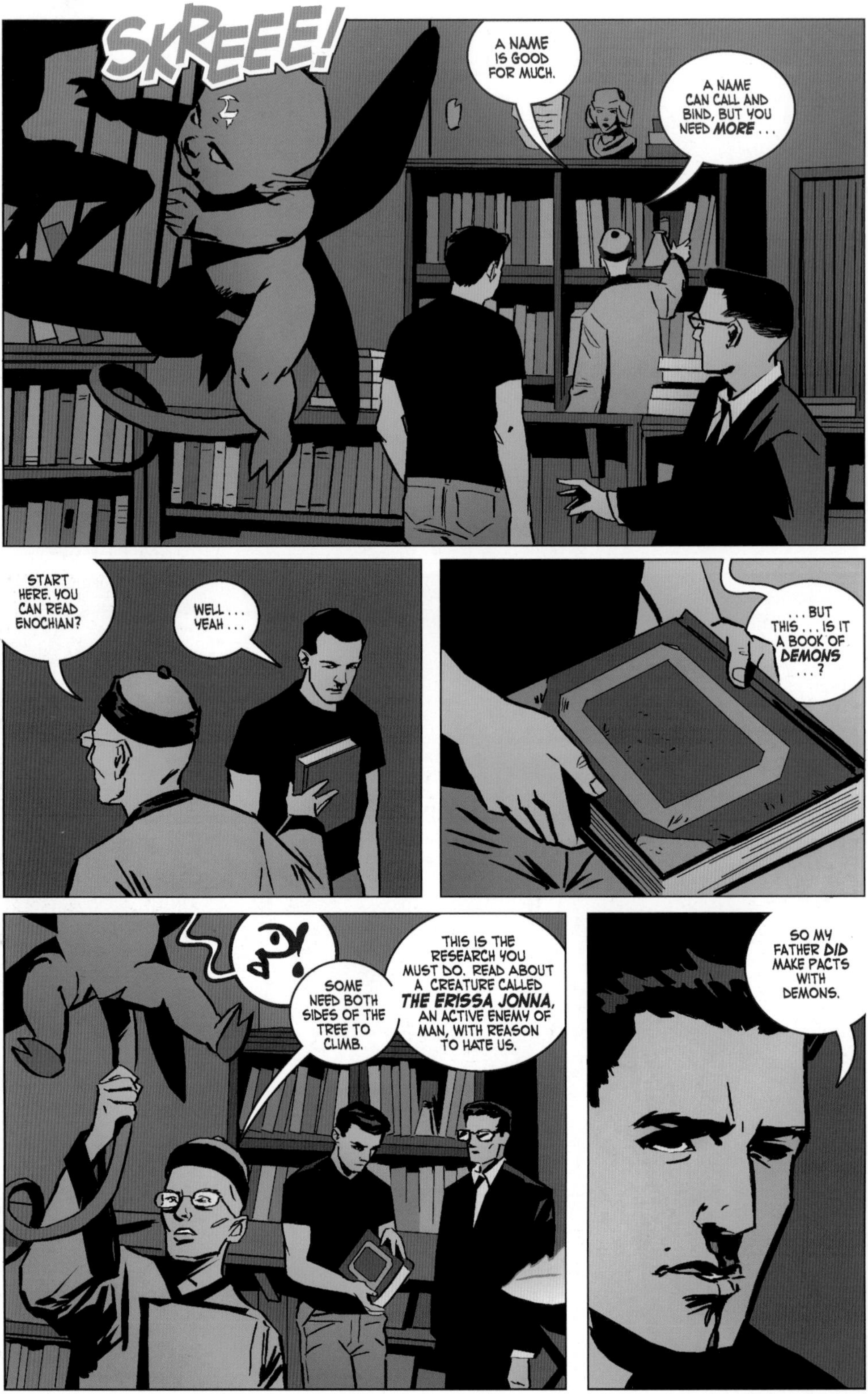

SKREEE!
A NAME IS GOOD FOR MUCH.
A NAME CAN CALL AND BIND, BUT YOU NEED *MORE* . . .
START HERE. YOU CAN READ ENOCHIAN?
WELL . . . YEAH . . .
. . . BUT THIS . . . IS IT A BOOK OF *DEMONS* . . . ?
SOME NEED BOTH SIDES OF THE TREE TO CLIMB.
THIS IS THE RESEARCH YOU MUST DO. READ ABOUT A CREATURE CALLED *THE ERISSA JONNA,* AN ACTIVE ENEMY OF MAN, WITH REASON TO HATE US.
SO MY FATHER *DID* MAKE PACTS WITH DEMONS.

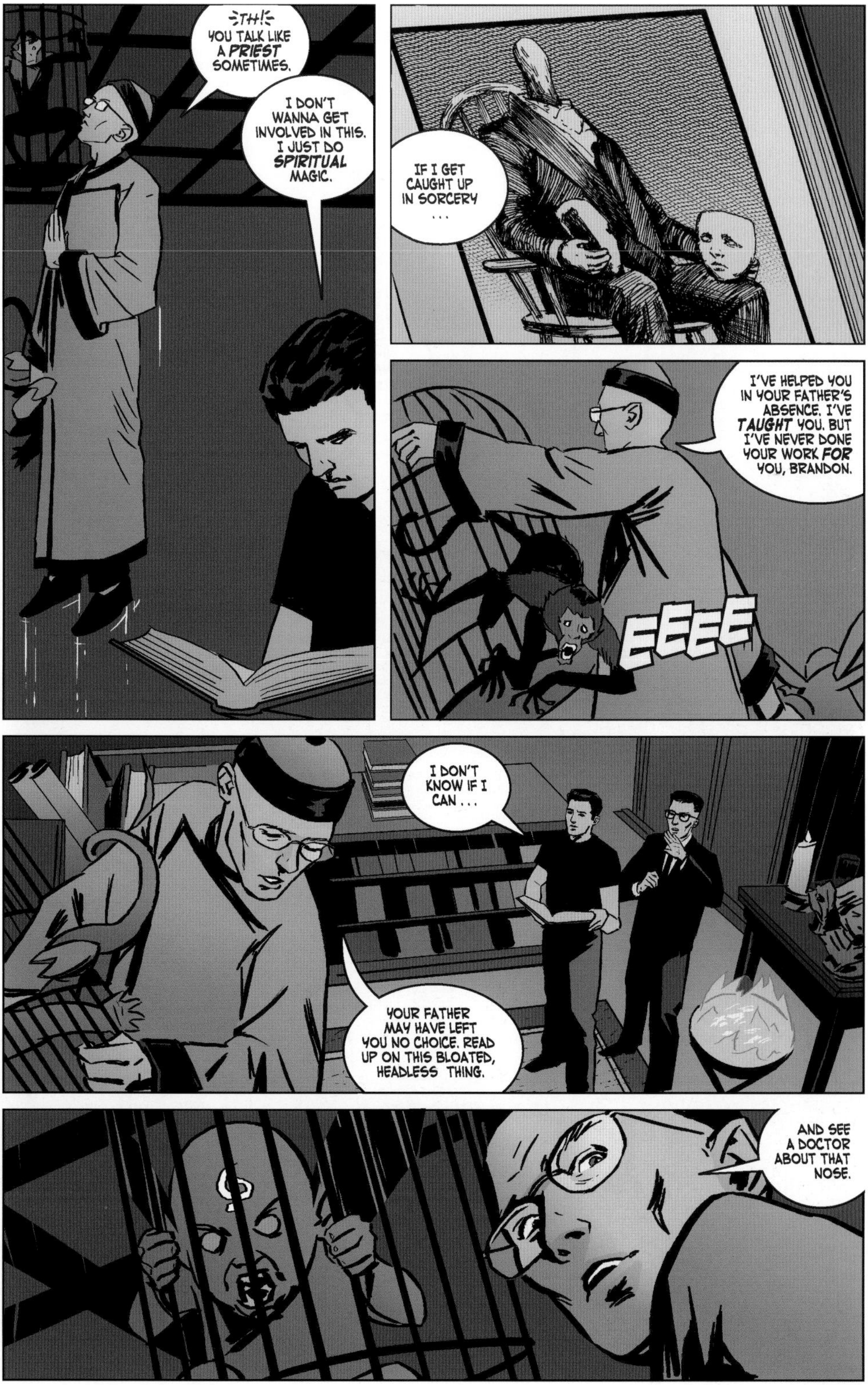

TH!
YOU TALK LIKE A PRIEST SOMETIMES.
I DON'T WANNA GET INVOLVED IN THIS. I JUST DO SPIRITUAL MAGIC.
IF I GET CAUGHT UP IN SORCERY . . .
I'VE HELPED YOU IN YOUR FATHER'S ABSENCE. I'VE TAUGHT YOU. BUT I'VE NEVER DONE YOUR WORK FOR YOU, BRANDON.
EEEE
I DON'T KNOW IF I CAN . . .
YOUR FATHER MAY HAVE LEFT YOU NO CHOICE. READ UP ON THIS BLOATED, HEADLESS THING.
AND SEE A DOCTOR ABOUT THAT NOSE.

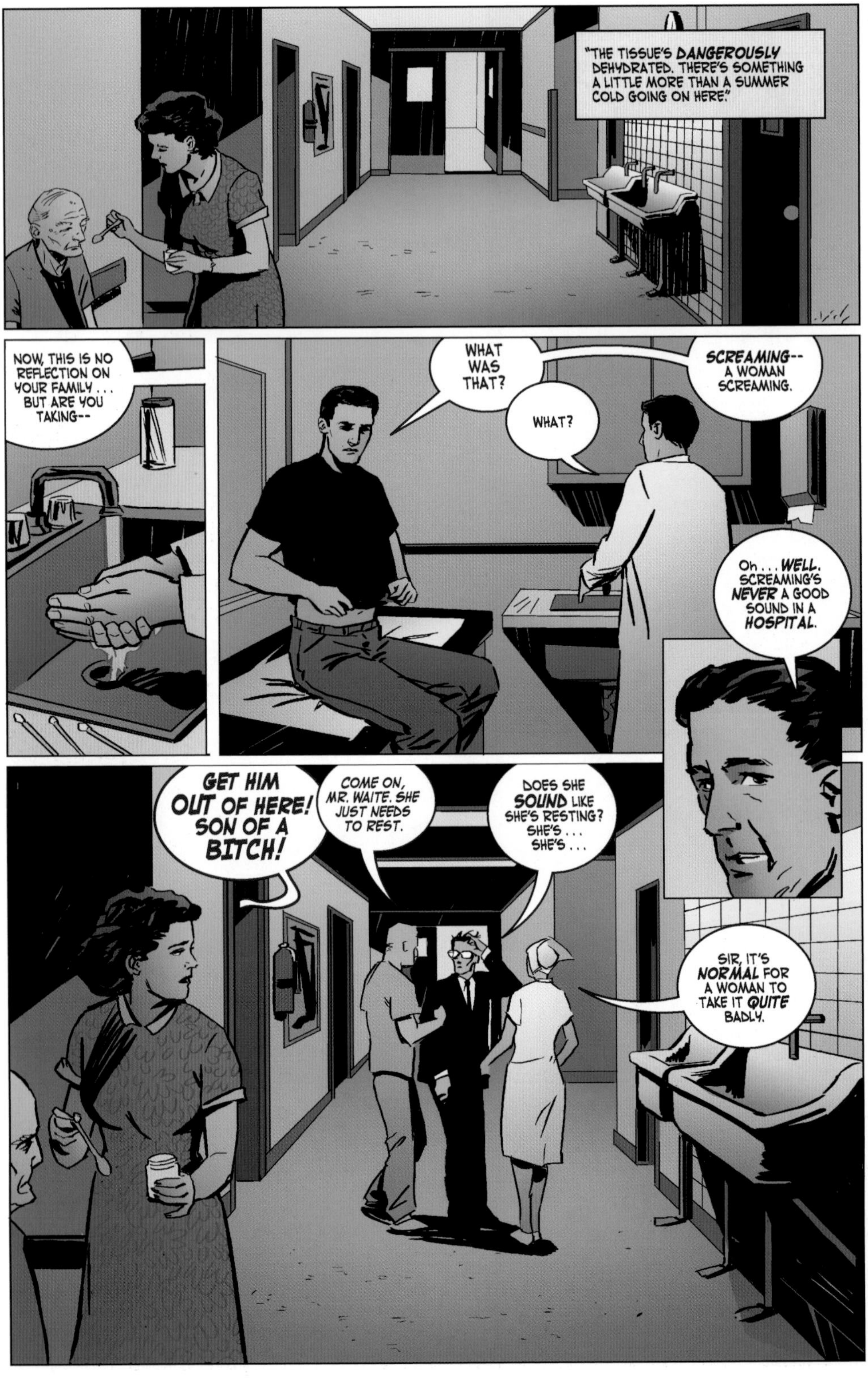
"THE TISSUE'S DANGEROUSLY DEHYDRATED. THERE'S SOMETHING A LITTLE MORE THAN A SUMMER COLD GOING ON HERE."
NOW, THIS IS NO REFLECTION ON YOUR FAMILY . . . BUT ARE YOU TAKING--
WHAT WAS THAT?
WHAT?
SCREAMING-- A WOMAN SCREAMING.
Oh . . . WELL. SCREAMING'S NEVER A GOOD SOUND IN A HOSPITAL.
GET HIM OUT OF HERE! SON OF A BITCH!
COME ON, MR. WAITE. SHE JUST NEEDS TO REST.
DOES SHE SOUND LIKE SHE'S RESTING? SHE'S . . . SHE'S . . .
SIR, IT'S NORMAL FOR A WOMAN TO TAKE IT QUITE BADLY.

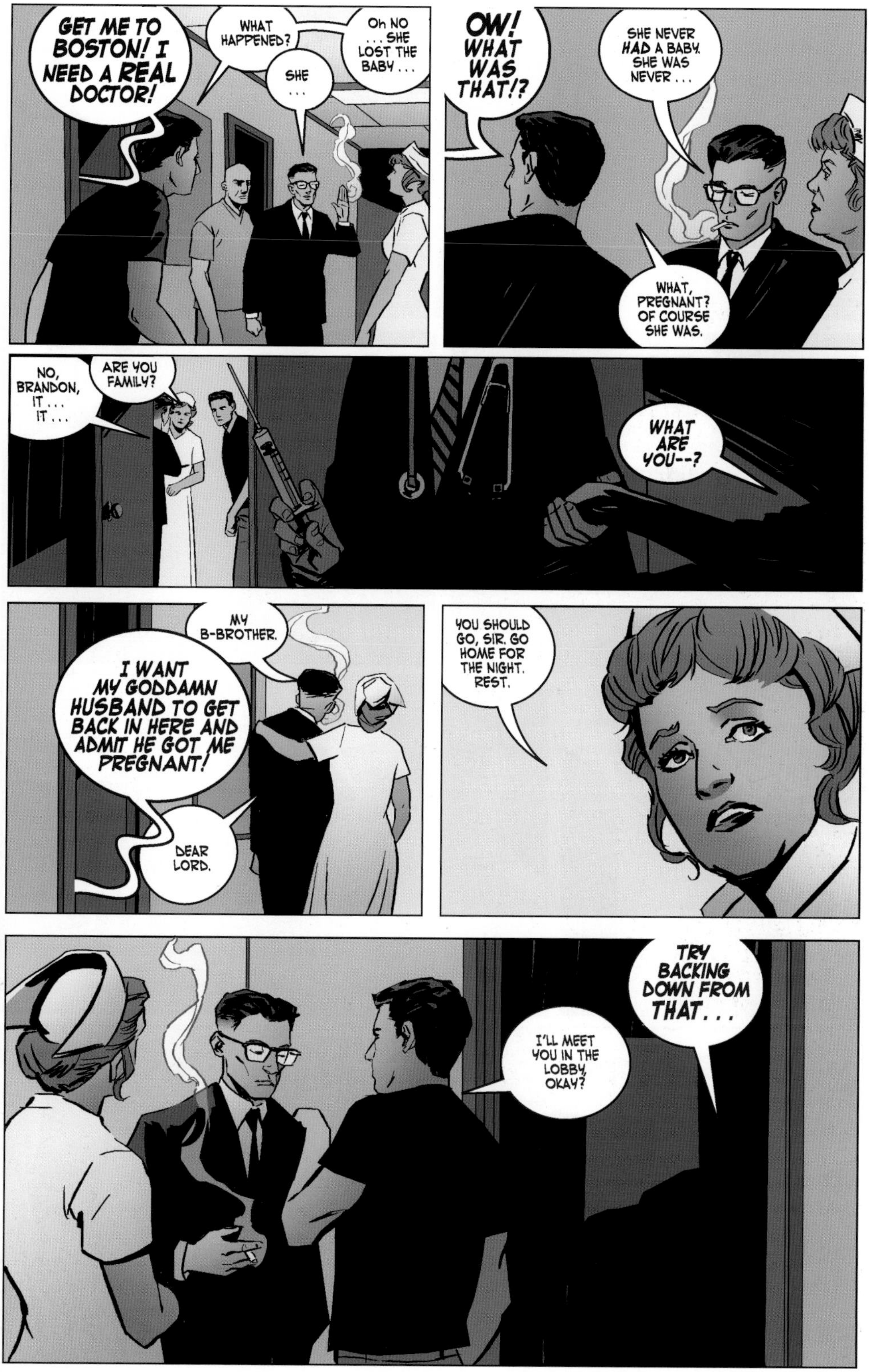
GET ME TO BOSTON! I NEED A REAL DOCTOR!
WHAT HAPPENED?
SHE . . .
Oh NO . . . SHE LOST THE BABY . . .
OW! WHAT WAS THAT!?
SHE NEVER HAD A BABY. SHE WAS NEVER . . .
WHAT, PREGNANT? OF COURSE SHE WAS.
NO, BRANDON, IT . . . IT . . .
ARE YOU FAMILY?
WHAT ARE YOU--?
MY B-BROTHER.
I WANT MY GODDAMN HUSBAND TO GET BACK IN HERE AND ADMIT HE GOT ME PREGNANT!
DEAR LORD.
YOU SHOULD GO, SIR. GO HOME FOR THE NIGHT. REST.
TRY BACKING DOWN FROM THAT . . .
I'LL MEET YOU IN THE LOBBY, OKAY?

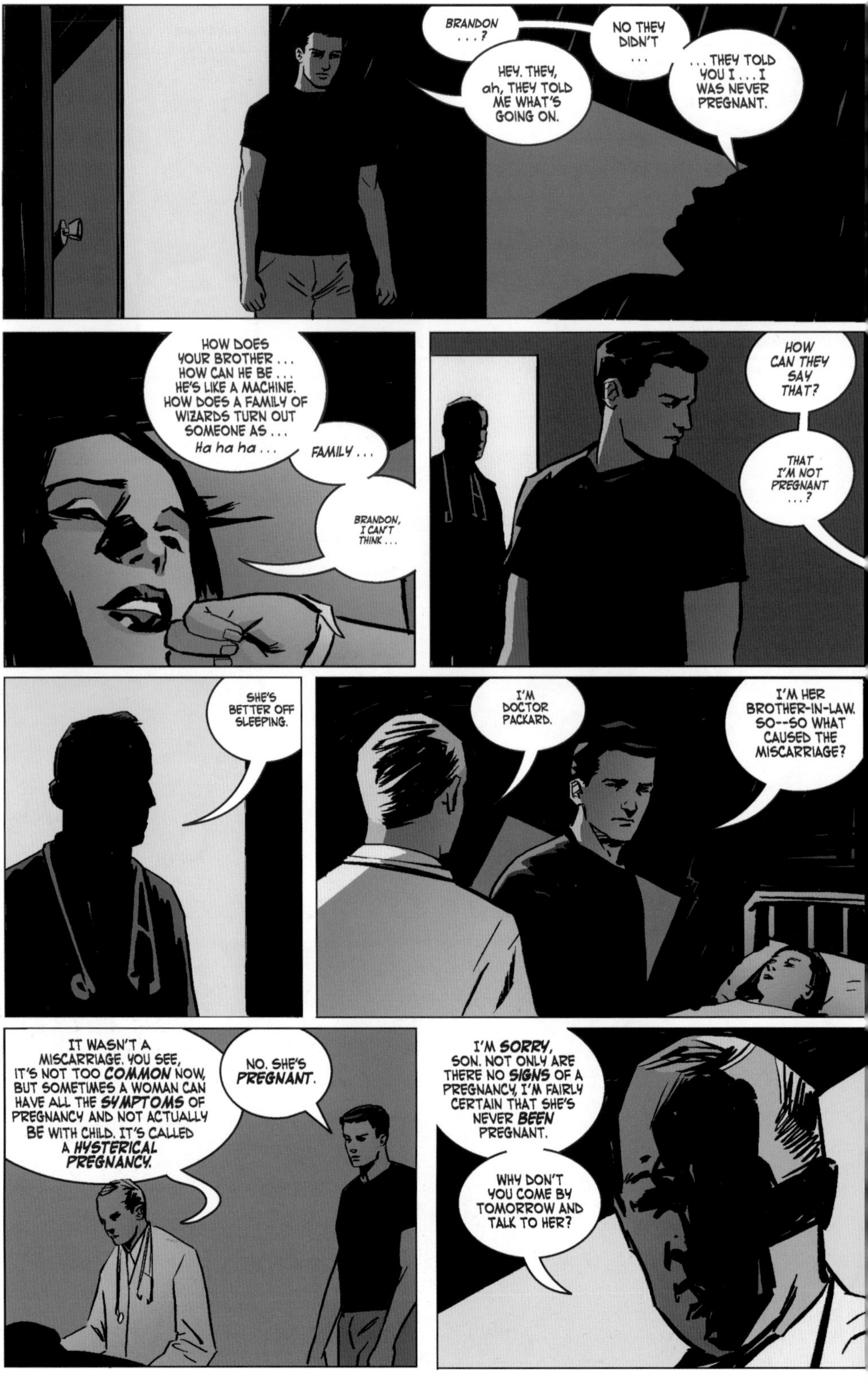

BRANDON . . . ?
HEY. THEY, ah, THEY TOLD ME WHAT'S GOING ON.
NO THEY DIDN'T . . .
. . . THEY TOLD YOU I . . . I WAS NEVER PREGNANT.
HOW DOES YOUR BROTHER . . . HOW CAN HE BE . . . HE'S LIKE A MACHINE. HOW DOES A FAMILY OF WIZARDS TURN OUT SOMEONE AS . . . Ha ha ha . . .
FAMILY . . .
BRANDON, I CAN'T THINK . . .
HOW CAN THEY SAY THAT?
THAT I'M NOT PREGNANT . . . ?
SHE'S BETTER OFF SLEEPING.
I'M DOCTOR PACKARD.
I'M HER BROTHER-IN-LAW. SO--SO WHAT CAUSED THE MISCARRIAGE?
IT WASN'T A MISCARRIAGE. YOU SEE, IT'S NOT TOO COMMON NOW, BUT SOMETIMES A WOMAN CAN HAVE ALL THE SYMPTOMS OF PREGNANCY AND NOT ACTUALLY BE WITH CHILD. IT'S CALLED A HYSTERICAL PREGNANCY.
NO. SHE'S PREGNANT.
I'M SORRY, SON. NOT ONLY ARE THERE NO SIGNS OF A PREGNANCY, I'M FAIRLY CERTAIN THAT SHE'S NEVER BEEN PREGNANT.
WHY DON'T YOU COME BY TOMORROW AND TALK TO HER?

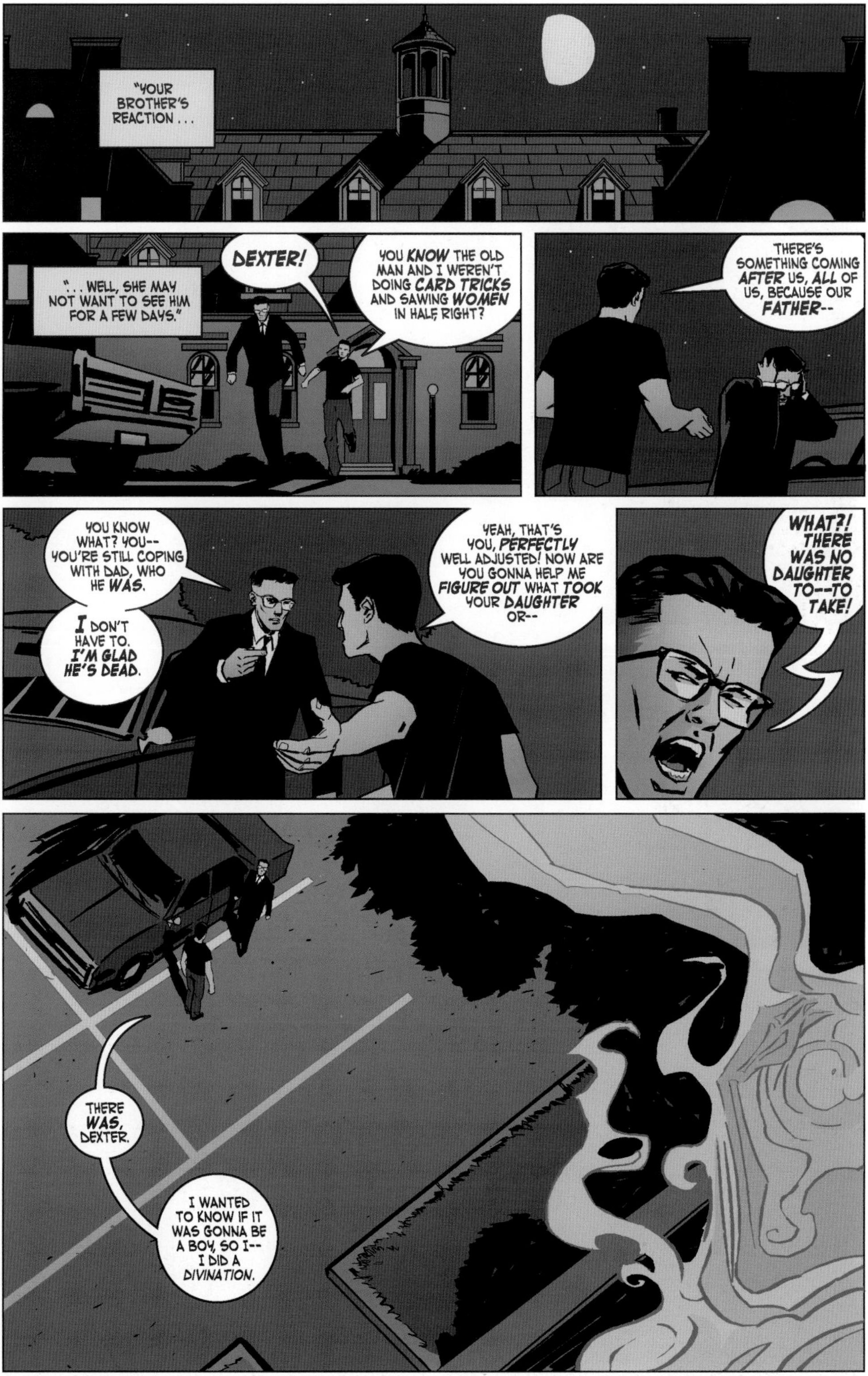
"YOUR BROTHER'S REACTION . . .
". . . WELL, SHE MAY NOT WANT TO SEE HIM FOR A FEW DAYS."
DEXTER!
YOU KNOW THE OLD MAN AND I WEREN'T DOING CARD TRICKS AND SAWING WOMEN IN HALF, RIGHT?
THERE'S SOMETHING COMING AFTER US, ALL OF US, BECAUSE OUR FATHER--
YOU KNOW WHAT? YOU-- YOU'RE STILL COPING WITH DAD, WHO HE WAS.
I DON'T HAVE TO. I'M GLAD HE'S DEAD.
YEAH, THAT'S YOU, PERFECTLY WELL ADJUSTED! NOW ARE YOU GONNA HELP ME FIGURE OUT WHAT TOOK YOUR DAUGHTER OR--
WHAT?! THERE WAS NO DAUGHTER TO--TO TAKE!
THERE WAS, DEXTER.
I WANTED TO KNOW IF IT WAS GONNA BE A BOY, SO I-- I DID A DIVINATION.

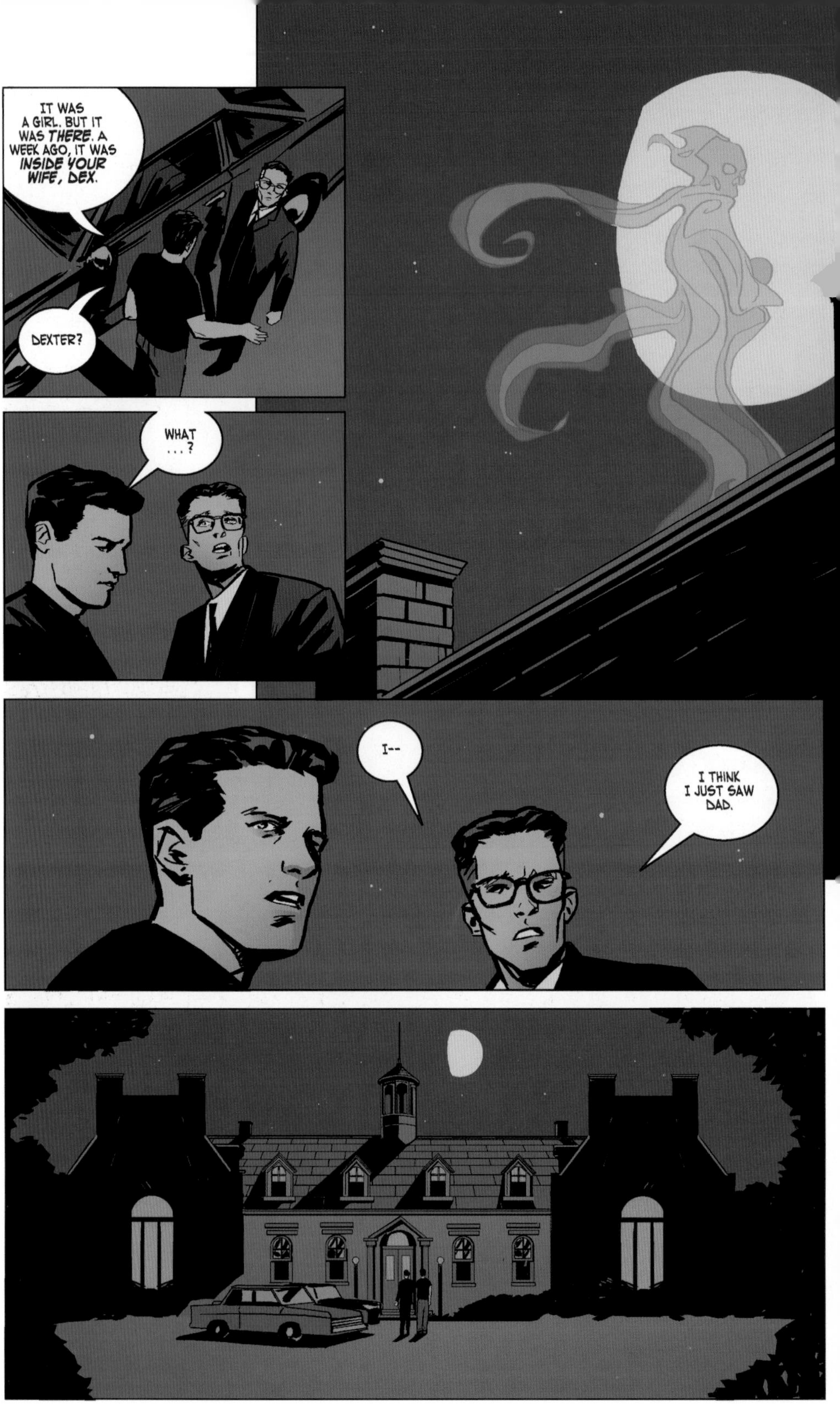
IT WAS A GIRL. BUT IT WAS THERE. A WEEK AGO, IT WAS INSIDE YOUR WIFE, DEX.
DEXTER?
WHAT . . . ?
I--
I THINK I JUST SAW DAD.

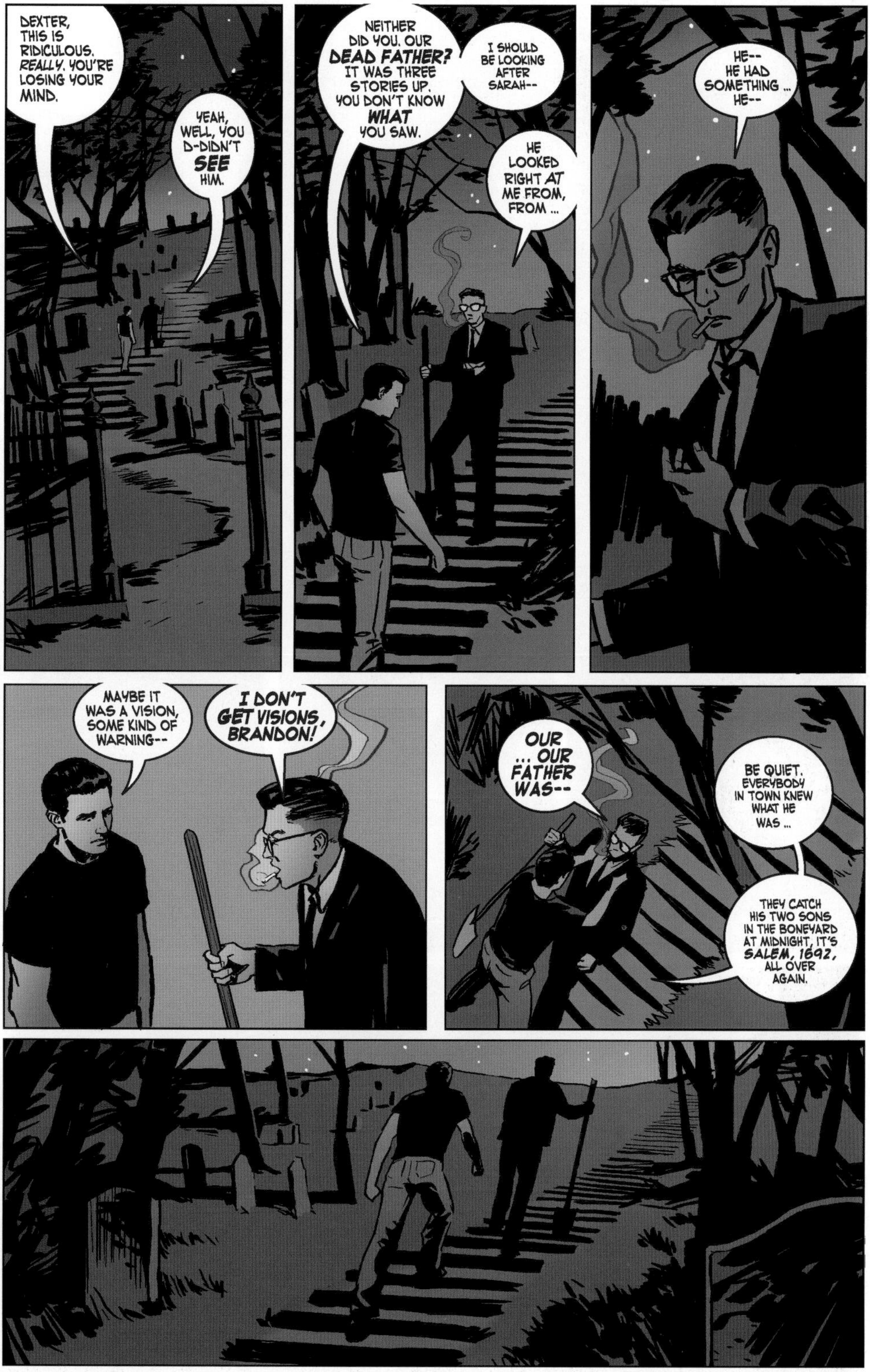
DEXTER, THIS IS RIDICULOUS. *REALLY.* YOU'RE LOSING YOUR MIND.
YEAH, WELL, YOU D-DIDN'T **SEE** HIM.
NEITHER DID YOU. OUR **DEAD FATHER?** IT WAS THREE STORIES UP. YOU DON'T KNOW **WHAT** YOU SAW.
I SHOULD BE LOOKING AFTER SARAH--
HE LOOKED RIGHT AT ME FROM, FROM ...
HE-- HE HAD SOMETHING ... HE--
MAYBE IT WAS A VISION, SOME KIND OF WARNING--
I DON'T GET VISIONS, BRANDON!
OUR ... OUR FATHER WAS--
BE QUIET. EVERYBODY IN TOWN KNEW WHAT HE WAS ...
THEY CATCH HIS TWO SONS IN THE BONEYARD AT MIDNIGHT, IT'S *SALEM, 1692,* ALL OVER AGAIN.

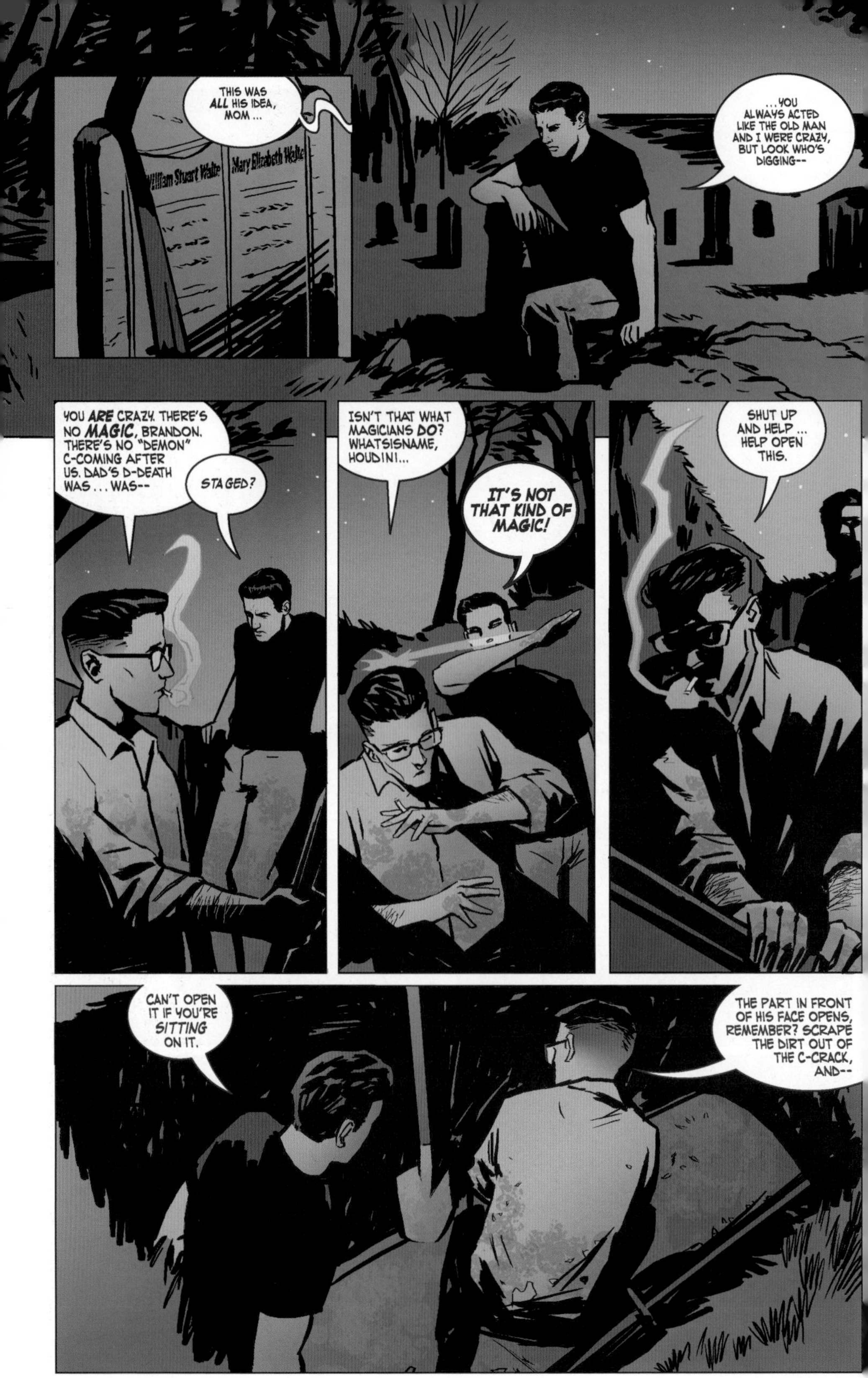
William Stuart Waite
Mary Elizabeth Waite
THIS WAS ALL HIS IDEA, MOM ...
...YOU ALWAYS ACTED LIKE THE OLD MAN AND I WERE CRAZY, BUT LOOK WHO'S DIGGING--
YOU ARE CRAZY. THERE'S NO MAGIC, BRANDON. THERE'S NO "DEMON" C-COMING AFTER US. DAD'S D-DEATH WAS . . . WAS--
STAGED?
ISN'T THAT WHAT MAGICIANS DO? WHATSISNAME, HOUDINI...
IT'S NOT THAT KIND OF MAGIC!
SHUT UP AND HELP ... HELP OPEN THIS.
CAN'T OPEN IT IF YOU'RE SITTING ON IT.
THE PART IN FRONT OF HIS FACE OPENS, REMEMBER? SCRAPE THE DIRT OUT OF THE C-CRACK, AND--

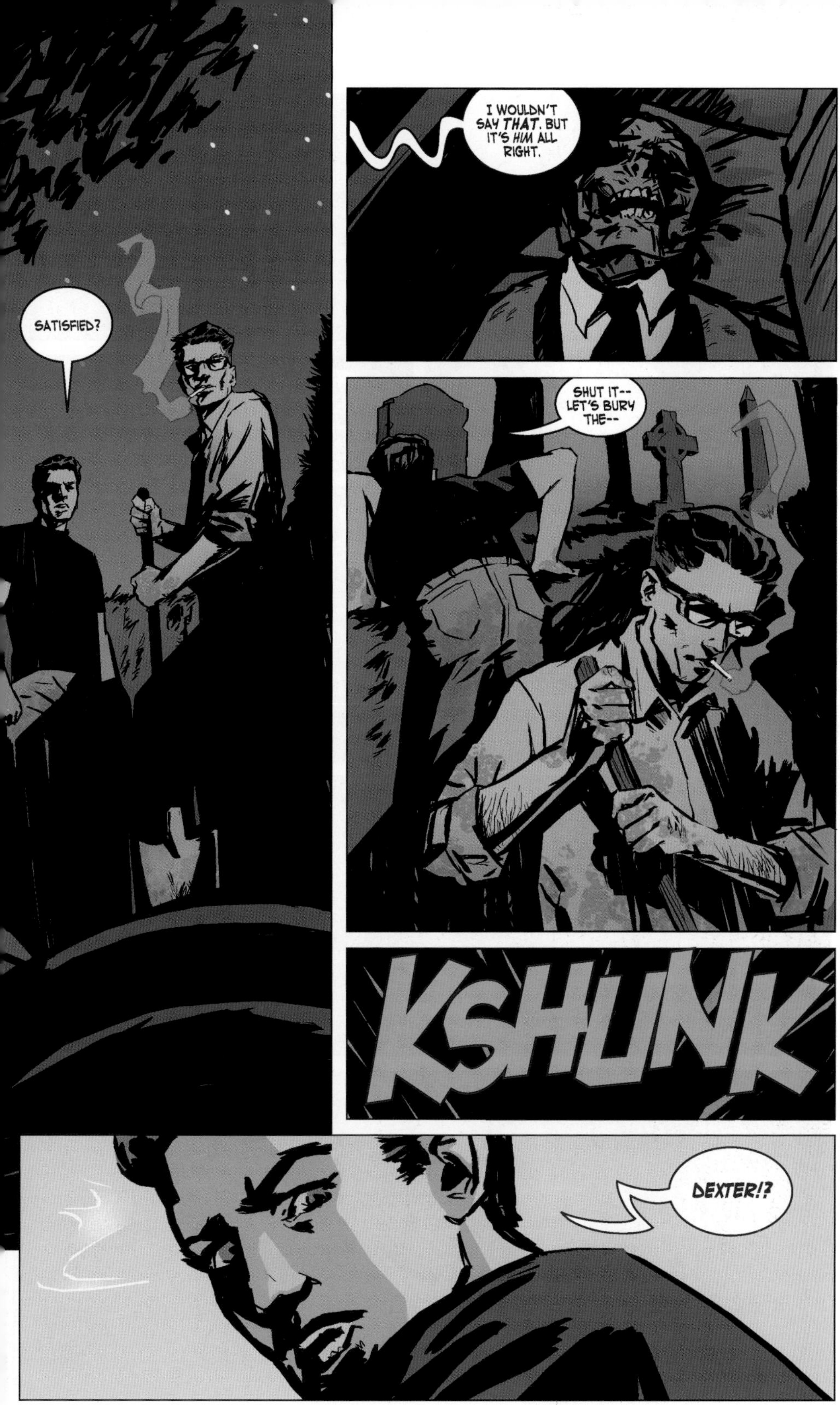
SATISFIED?
I WOULDN'T SAY THAT. BUT IT'S HIM ALL RIGHT.
SHUT IT-- LET'S BURY THE--
KSHUNK
DEXTER!?

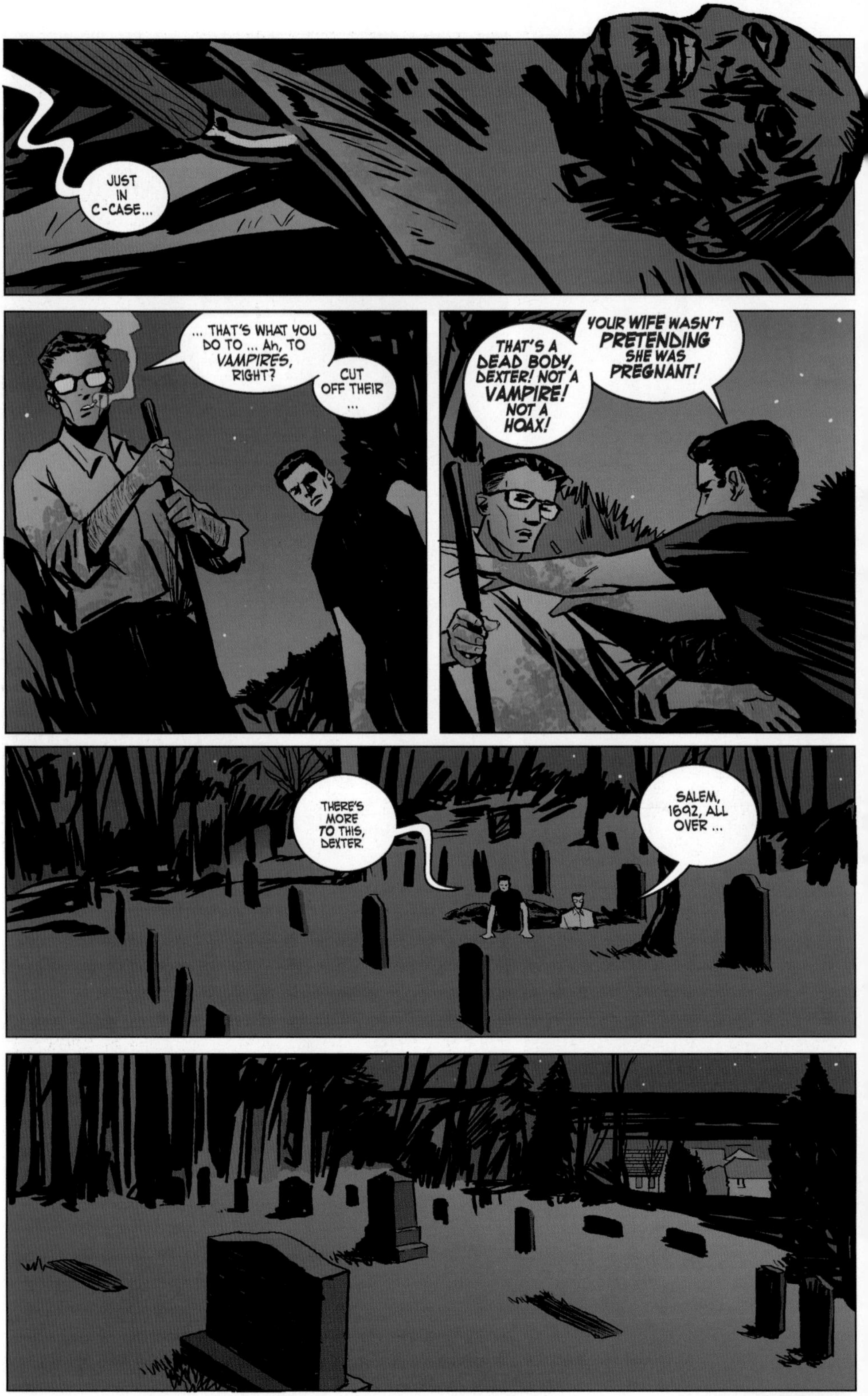
JUST IN C-CASE...
... THAT'S WHAT YOU DO TO ... Ah, TO VAMPIRES, RIGHT?
CUT OFF THEIR ...
YOUR WIFE WASN'T PRETENDING SHE WAS PREGNANT!
THAT'S A DEAD BODY, DEXTER! NOT A VAMPIRE! NOT A HOAX!
THERE'S MORE TO THIS, DEXTER.
SALEM, 1692, ALL OVER ...

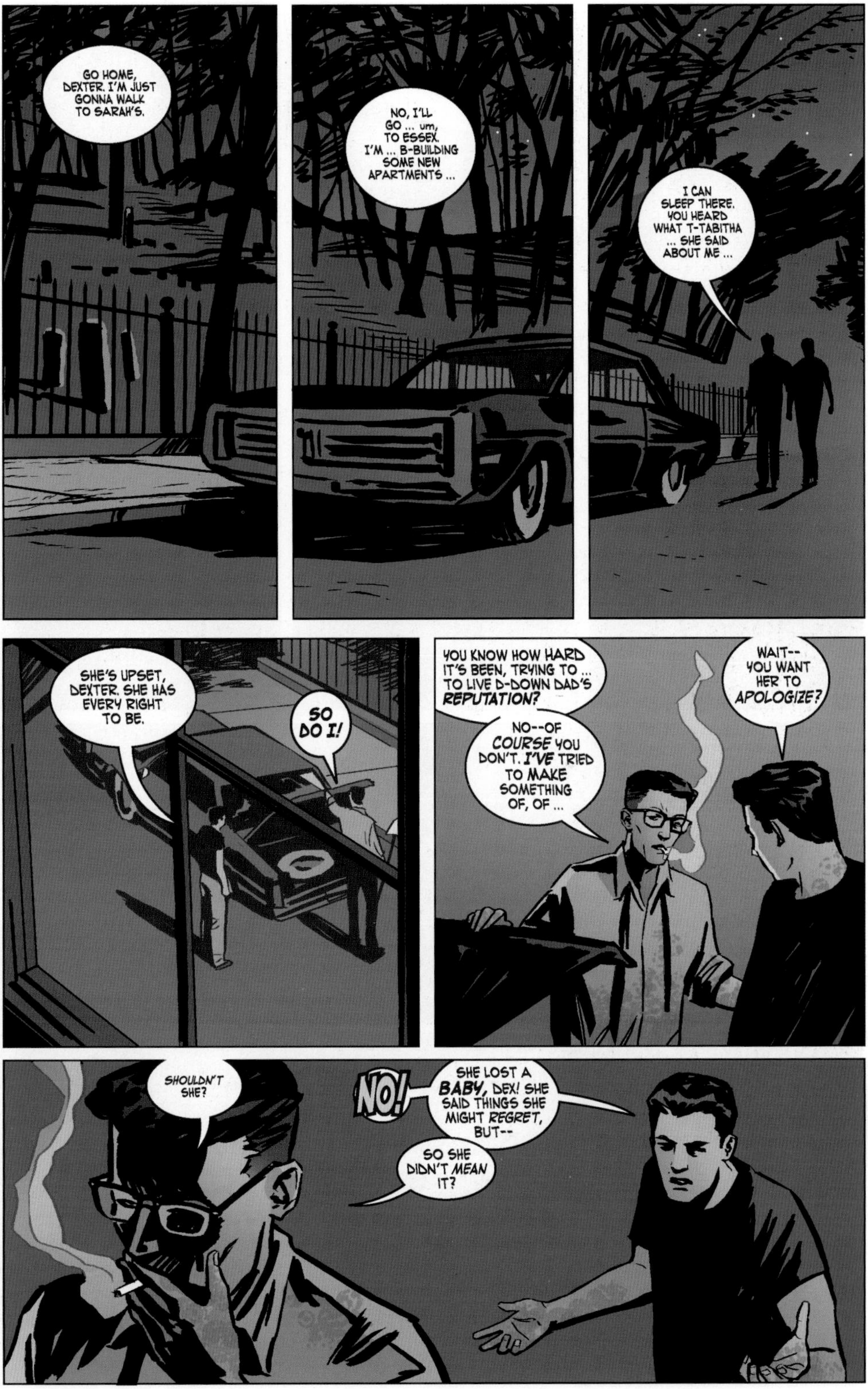
GO HOME, DEXTER. I'M JUST GONNA WALK TO SARAH'S.
NO, I'LL GO ... um, TO ESSEX. I'M ... B-BUILDING SOME NEW APARTMENTS ...
I CAN SLEEP THERE. YOU HEARD WHAT T-TABITHA ... SHE SAID ABOUT ME ...
SHE'S UPSET, DEXTER. SHE HAS EVERY RIGHT TO BE.
SO DO I!
YOU KNOW HOW HARD IT'S BEEN, TRYING TO ... TO LIVE D-DOWN DAD'S REPUTATION?
NO--OF COURSE YOU DON'T. I'VE TRIED TO MAKE SOMETHING OF, OF ...
WAIT-- YOU WANT HER TO APOLOGIZE?
SHOULDN'T SHE?
NO!
SHE LOST A BABY, DEX! SHE SAID THINGS SHE MIGHT REGRET, BUT--
SO SHE DIDN'T MEAN IT?

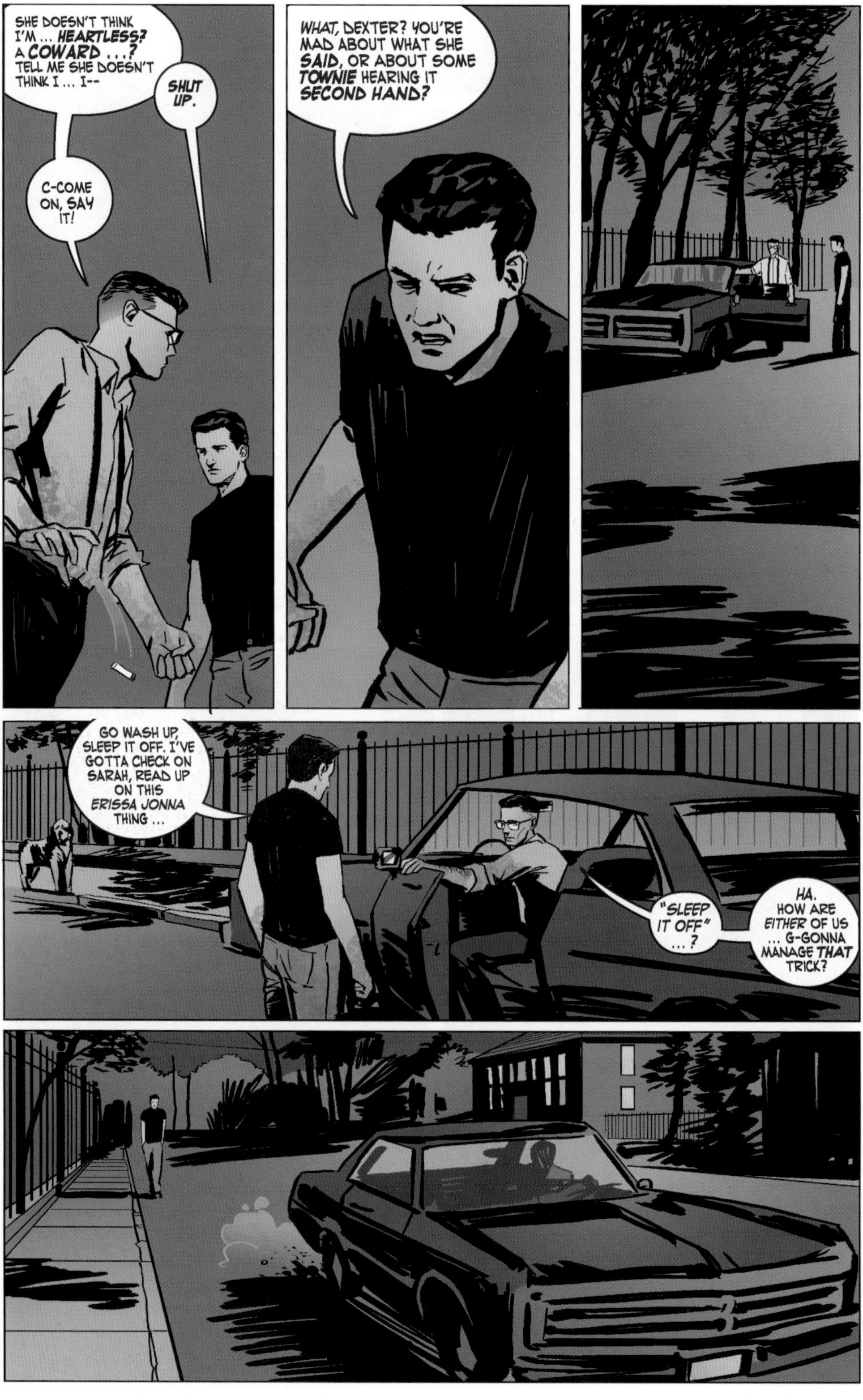

SHE DOESN'T THINK I'M ... HEARTLESS? A COWARD ...? TELL ME SHE DOESN'T THINK I ... I--
SHUT UP.
C-COME ON, SAY IT!
WHAT, DEXTER? YOU'RE MAD ABOUT WHAT SHE SAID, OR ABOUT SOME TOWNIE HEARING IT SECOND HAND?
GO WASH UP, SLEEP IT OFF. I'VE GOTTA CHECK ON SARAH, READ UP ON THIS ERISSA JONNA THING ...
"SLEEP IT OFF" ...?
HA. HOW ARE EITHER OF US ... G-GONNA MANAGE THAT TRICK?

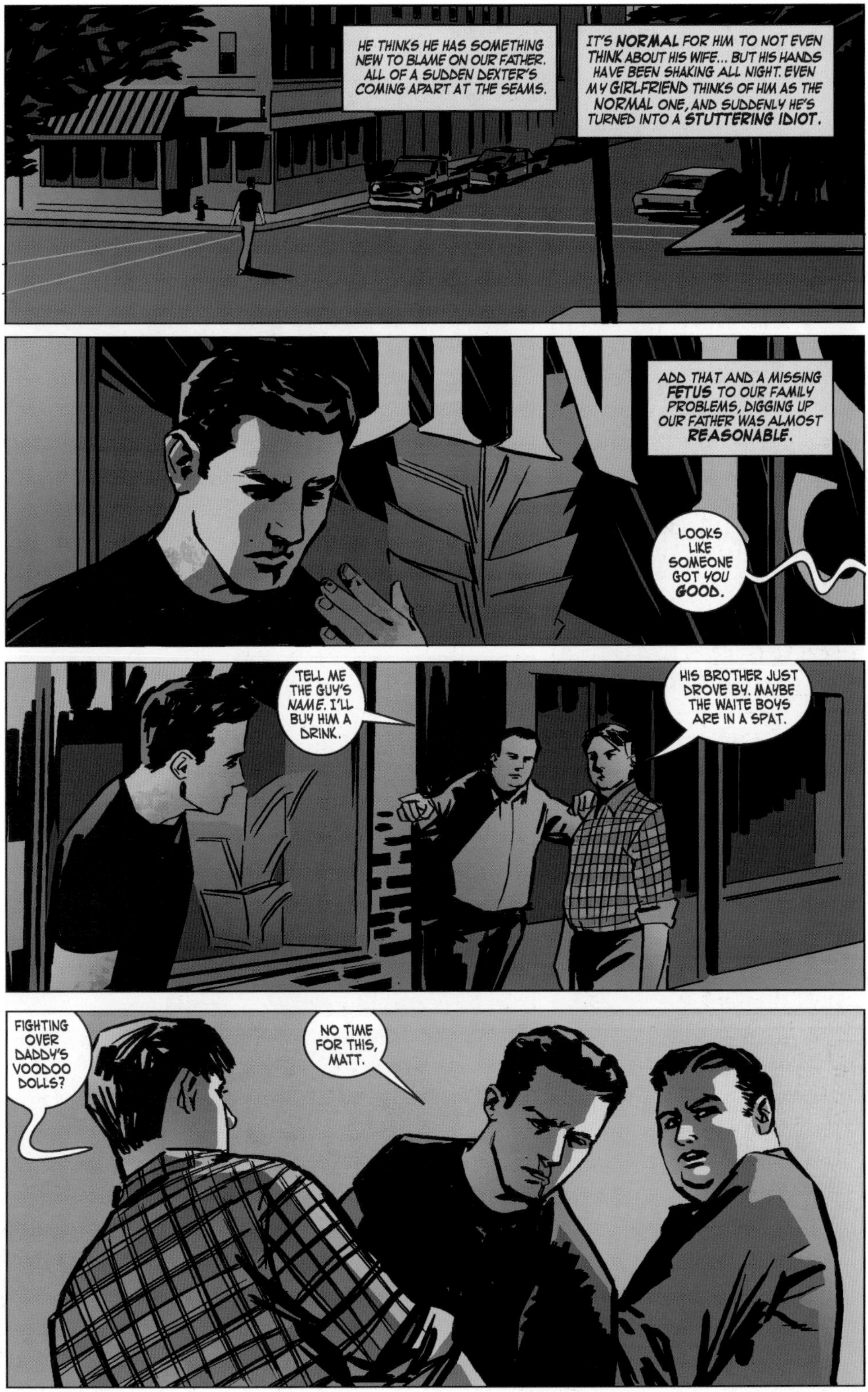
HE THINKS HE HAS SOMETHING NEW TO BLAME ON OUR FATHER. ALL OF A SUDDEN DEXTER'S COMING APART AT THE SEAMS.
IT'S NORMAL FOR HIM TO NOT EVEN THINK ABOUT HIS WIFE... BUT HIS HANDS HAVE BEEN SHAKING ALL NIGHT. EVEN MY GIRLFRIEND THINKS OF HIM AS THE NORMAL ONE, AND SUDDENLY HE'S TURNED INTO A STUTTERING IDIOT.
ADD THAT AND A MISSING FETUS TO OUR FAMILY PROBLEMS, DIGGING UP OUR FATHER WAS ALMOST REASONABLE.
LOOKS LIKE SOMEONE GOT YOU GOOD.
TELL ME THE GUY'S NAME. I'LL BUY HIM A DRINK.
HIS BROTHER JUST DROVE BY. MAYBE THE WAITE BOYS ARE IN A SPAT.
FIGHTING OVER DADDY'S VOODOO DOLLS?
NO TIME FOR THIS, MATT.

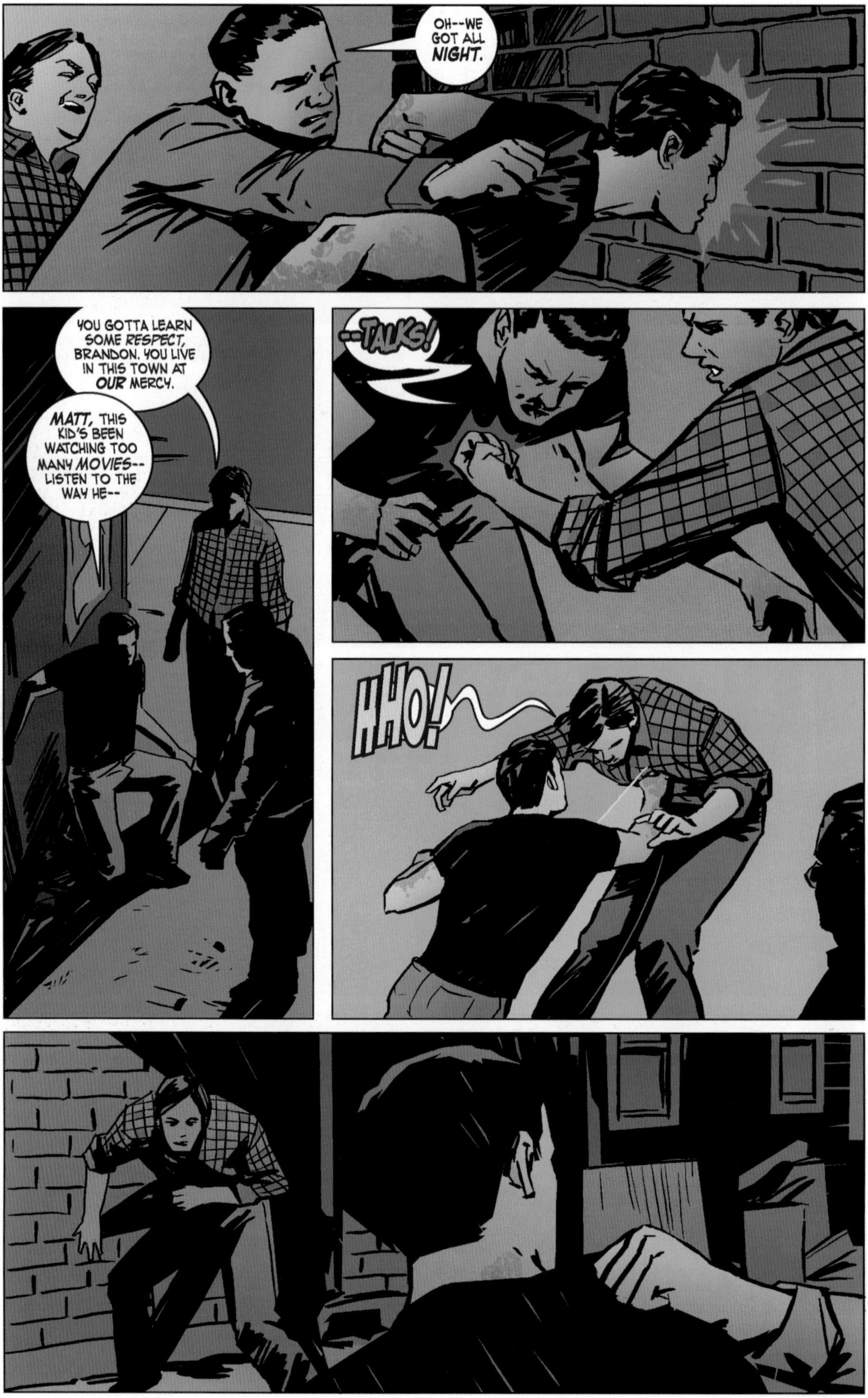
OH--WE GOT ALL NIGHT.
YOU GOTTA LEARN SOME RESPECT, BRANDON. YOU LIVE IN THIS TOWN AT OUR MERCY.
MATT, THIS KID'S BEEN WATCHING TOO MANY MOVIES-- LISTEN TO THE WAY HE--
--TALKS!
HHO!

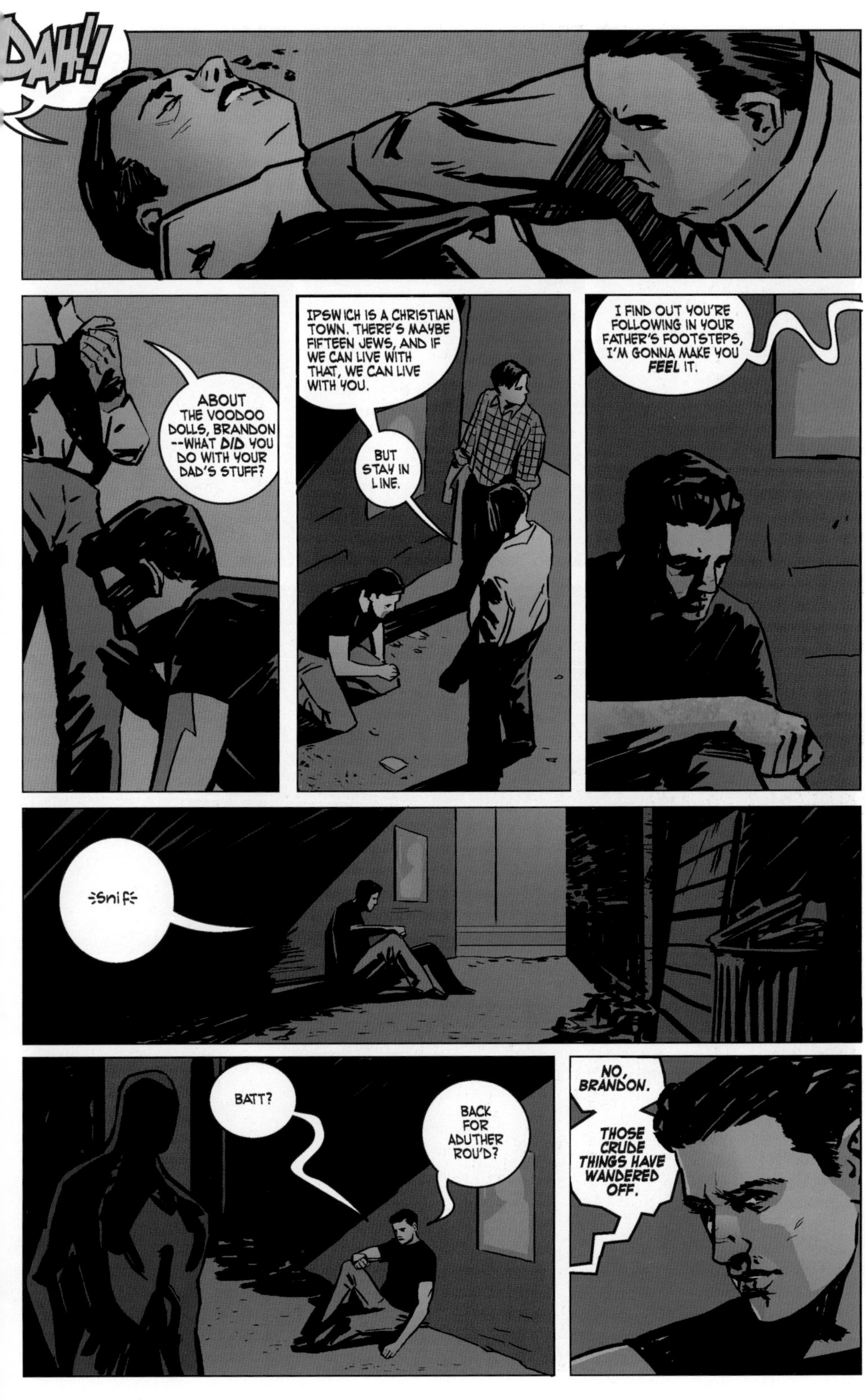
DAH!!
ABOUT THE VOODOO DOLLS, BRANDON --WHAT DID YOU DO WITH YOUR DAD'S STUFF?
IPSWICH IS A CHRISTIAN TOWN. THERE'S MAYBE FIFTEEN JEWS, AND IF WE CAN LIVE WITH THAT, WE CAN LIVE WITH YOU.
BUT STAY IN LINE.
I FIND OUT YOU'RE FOLLOWING IN YOUR FATHER'S FOOTSTEPS, I'M GONNA MAKE YOU FEEL IT.
=Snif=
BATT?
BACK FOR ADUTHER ROU'D?
NO, BRANDON.
THOSE CRUDE THINGS HAVE WANDERED OFF.

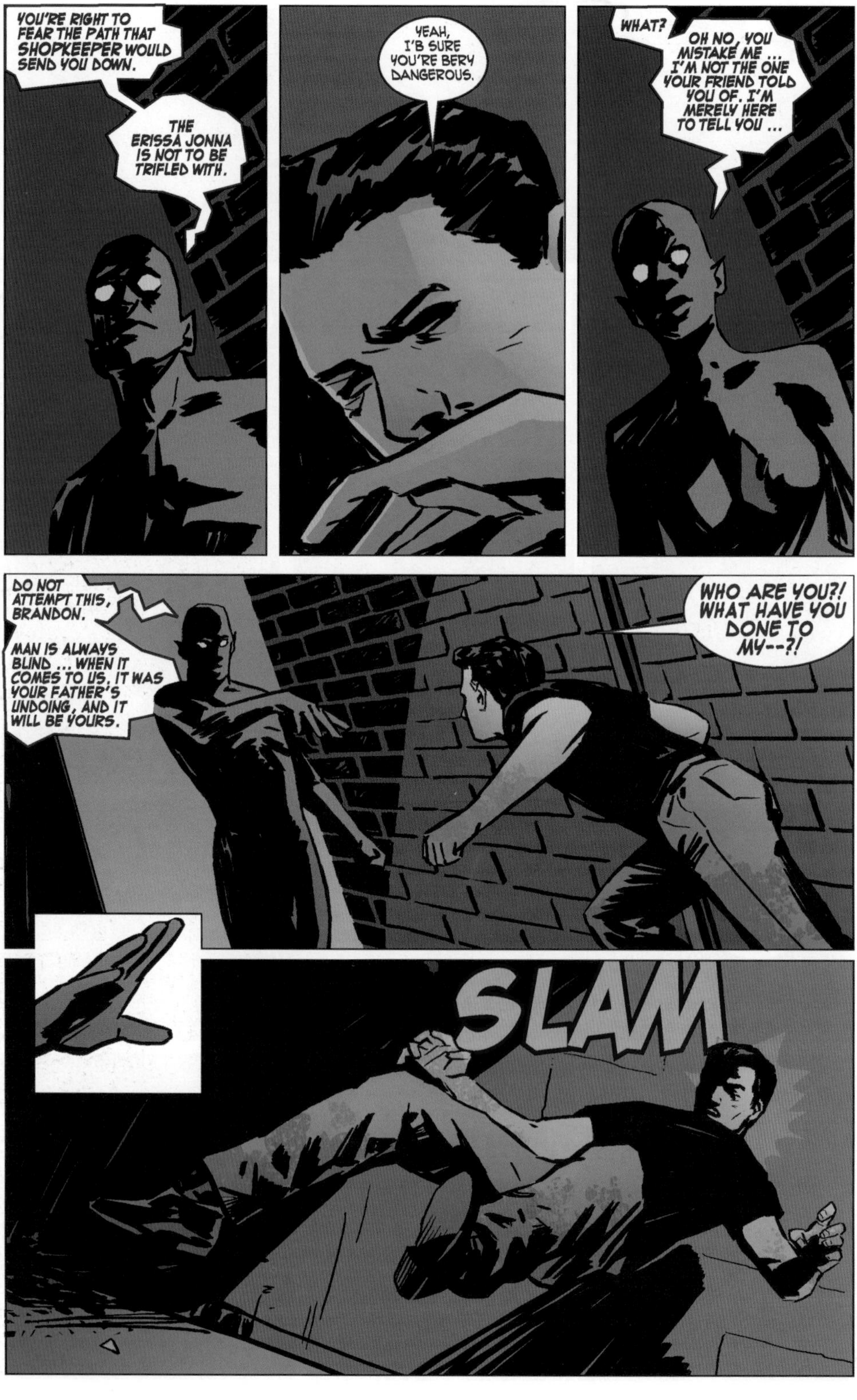
YOU'RE RIGHT TO FEAR THE PATH THAT SHOPKEEPER WOULD SEND YOU DOWN.
THE ERISSA JONNA IS NOT TO BE TRIFLED WITH.
YEAH, I'B SURE YOU'RE BERY DANGEROUS.
WHAT?
OH NO, YOU MISTAKE ME ... I'M NOT THE ONE YOUR FRIEND TOLD YOU OF. I'M MERELY HERE TO TELL YOU ...
DO NOT ATTEMPT THIS, BRANDON.
MAN IS ALWAYS BLIND ... WHEN IT COMES TO US. IT WAS YOUR FATHER'S UNDOING, AND IT WILL BE YOURS.
WHO ARE YOU?! WHAT HAVE YOU DONE TO MY--?!
SLAM

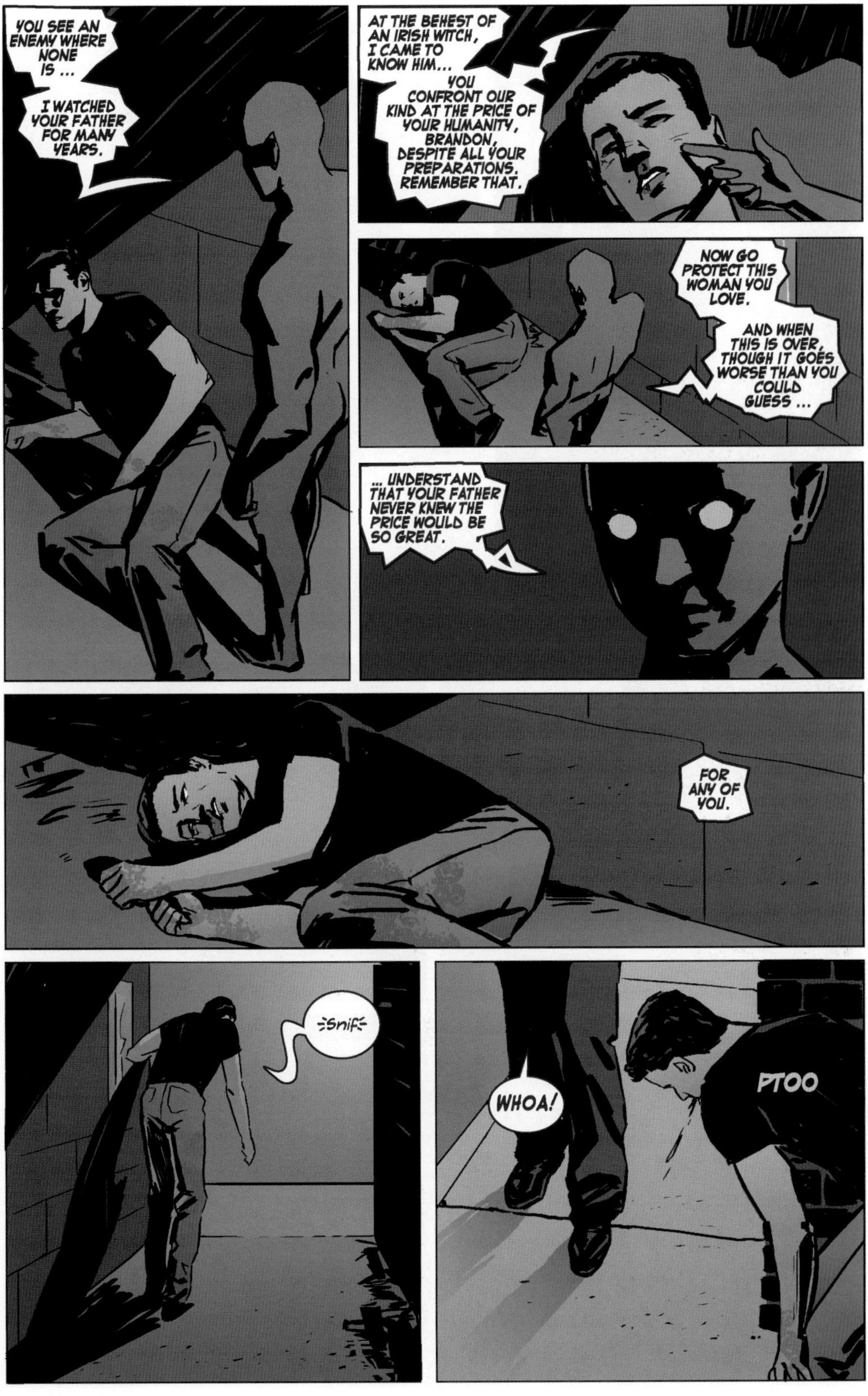
YOU SEE AN ENEMY WHERE NONE IS ...
I WATCHED YOUR FATHER FOR MANY YEARS.
AT THE BEHEST OF AN IRISH WITCH, I CAME TO KNOW HIM...
YOU CONFRONT OUR KIND AT THE PRICE OF YOUR HUMANITY, BRANDON, DESPITE ALL YOUR PREPARATIONS. REMEMBER THAT.
NOW GO PROTECT THIS WOMAN YOU LOVE.
AND WHEN THIS IS OVER, THOUGH IT GOES WORSE THAN YOU COULD GUESS ...
... UNDERSTAND THAT YOUR FATHER NEVER KNEW THE PRICE WOULD BE SO GREAT.
FOR ANY OF YOU.
Snif
WHOA!
PTOO

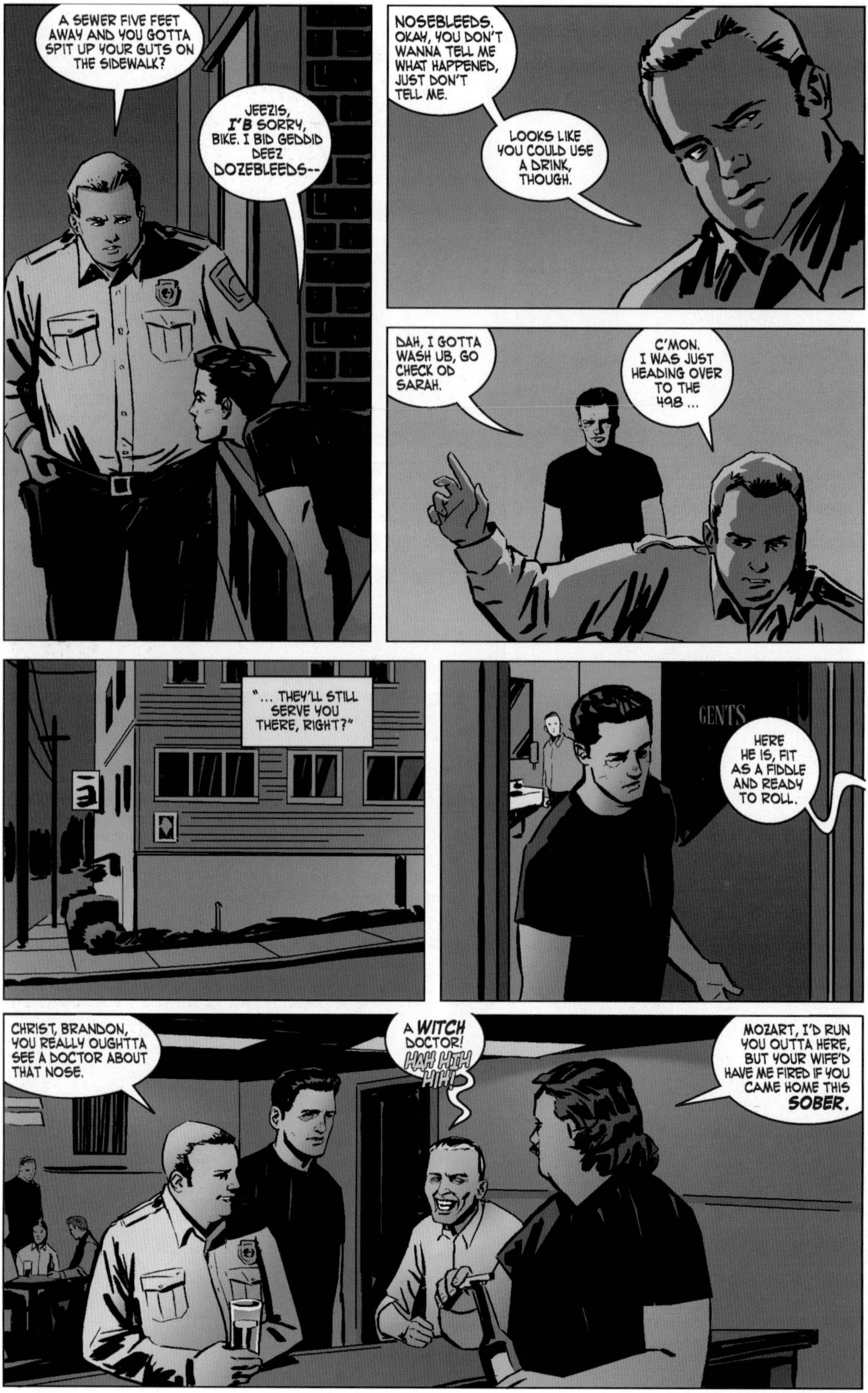
A SEWER FIVE FEET AWAY AND YOU GOTTA SPIT UP YOUR GUTS ON THE SIDEWALK?
JEEZIS, I'B SORRY, BIKE. I BID GEDDID DEEZ DOZEBLEEDS--
NOSEBLEEDS. OKAY, YOU DON'T WANNA TELL ME WHAT HAPPENED, JUST DON'T TELL ME.
LOOKS LIKE YOU COULD USE A DRINK, THOUGH.
DAH, I GOTTA WASH UB, GO CHECK OD SARAH.
C'MON. I WAS JUST HEADING OVER TO THE 498 ...
"... THEY'LL STILL SERVE YOU THERE, RIGHT?"
GENTS
HERE HE IS, FIT AS A FIDDLE AND READY TO ROLL.
CHRIST, BRANDON, YOU REALLY OUGHTTA SEE A DOCTOR ABOUT THAT NOSE.
A WITCH DOCTOR! HAH HEH HEH!
MOZART, I'D RUN YOU OUTTA HERE, BUT YOUR WIFE'D HAVE ME FIRED IF YOU CAME HOME THIS SOBER.

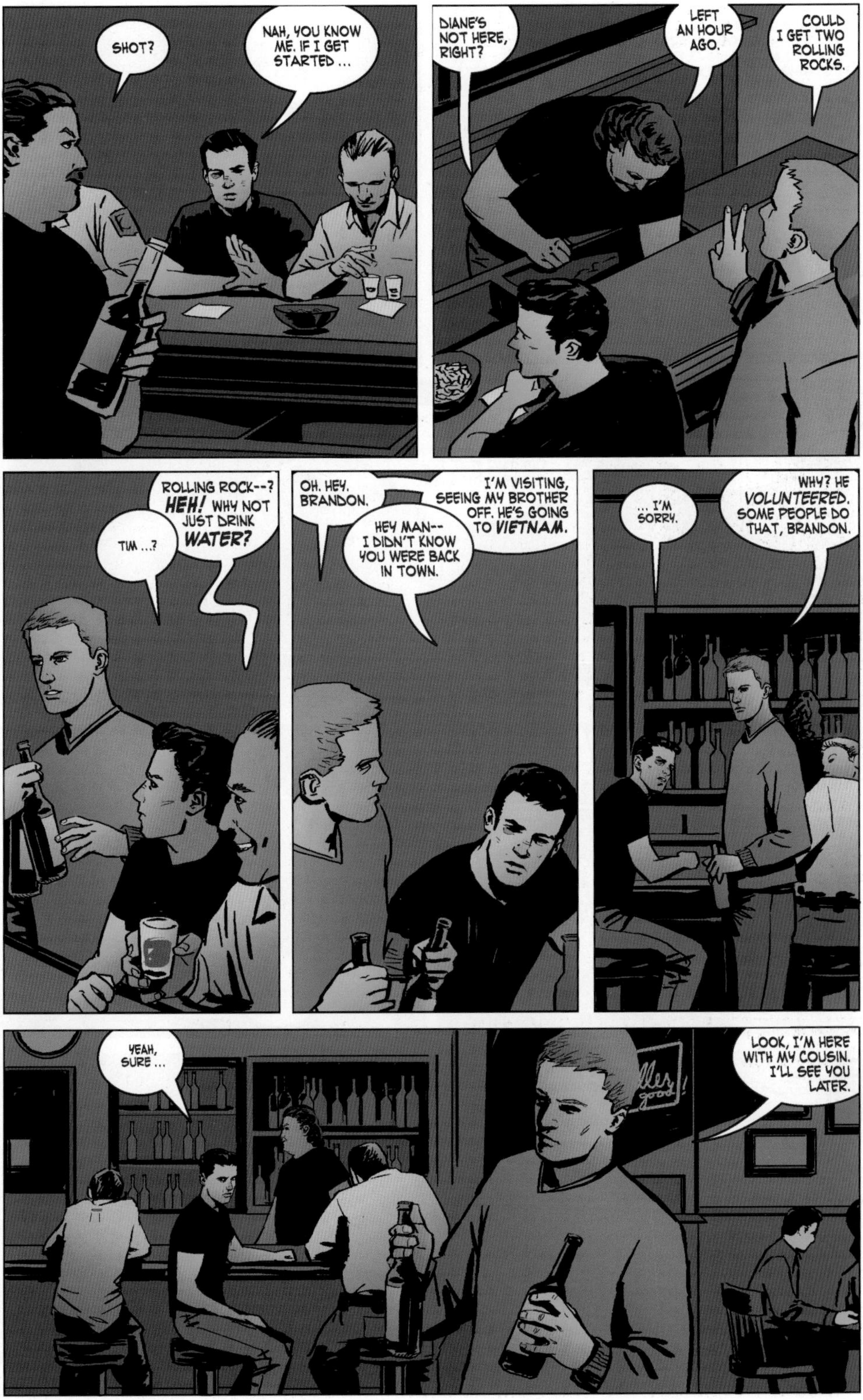
SHOT?
NAH, YOU KNOW ME. IF I GET STARTED ...
DIANE'S NOT HERE, RIGHT?
LEFT AN HOUR AGO.
COULD I GET TWO ROLLING ROCKS.
ROLLING ROCK--? HEH! WHY NOT JUST DRINK WATER?
TIM ...?
OH. HEY. BRANDON.
I'M VISITING, SEEING MY BROTHER OFF. HE'S GOING TO VIETNAM.
HEY MAN-- I DIDN'T KNOW YOU WERE BACK IN TOWN.
... I'M SORRY.
WHY? HE VOLUNTEERED. SOME PEOPLE DO THAT, BRANDON.
YEAH, SURE ...
LOOK, I'M HERE WITH MY COUSIN. I'LL SEE YOU LATER.

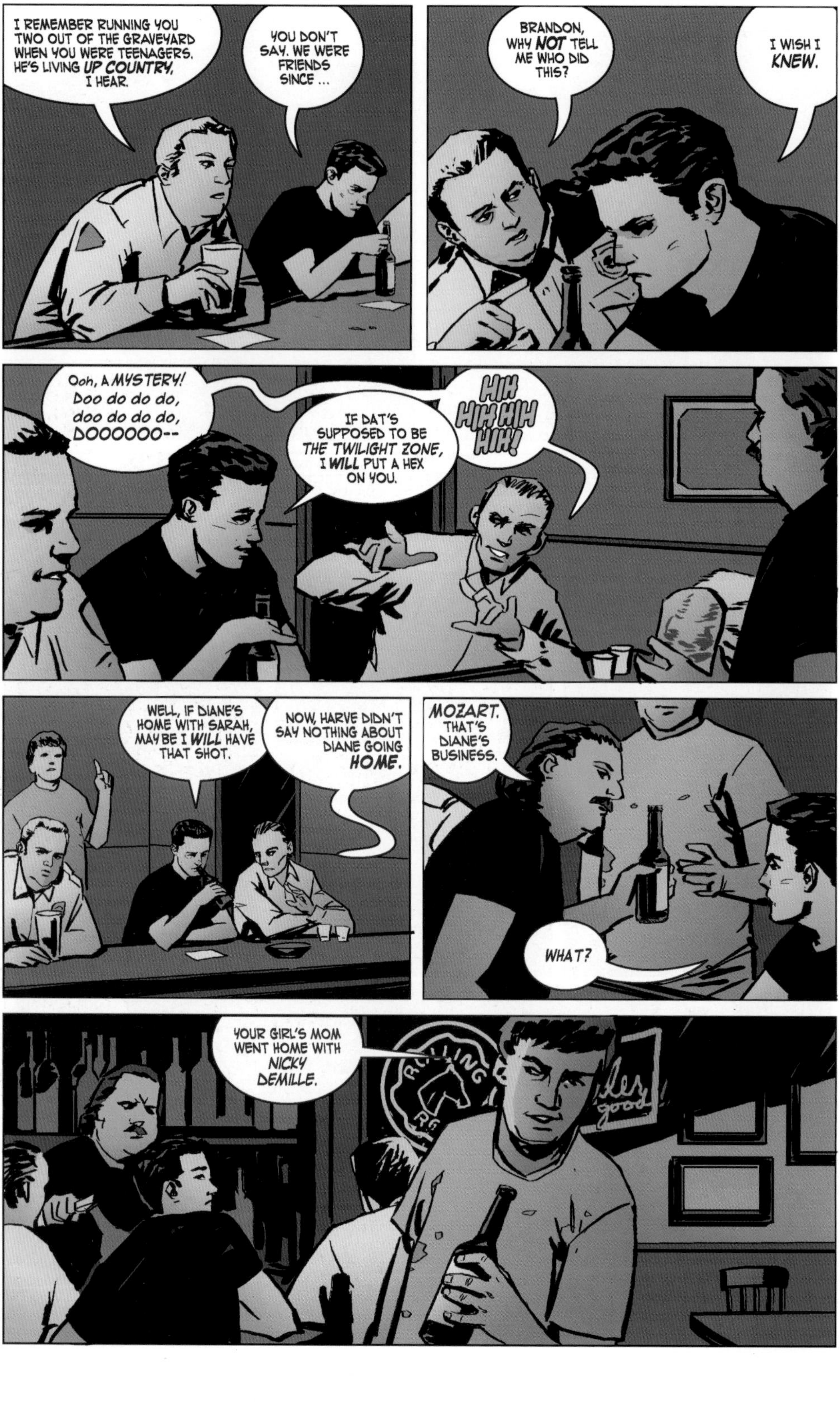
I REMEMBER RUNNING YOU TWO OUT OF THE GRAVEYARD WHEN YOU WERE TEENAGERS. HE'S LIVING UP COUNTRY, I HEAR.
YOU DON'T SAY. WE WERE FRIENDS SINCE ...
BRANDON, WHY NOT TELL ME WHO DID THIS?
I WISH I KNEW.
Ooh, A MYSTERY! Doo do do do, doo do do do, DOOOOOO--
HIH HIH HIH HIH HIH!
IF DAT'S SUPPOSED TO BE THE TWILIGHT ZONE, I WILL PUT A HEX ON YOU.
WELL, IF DIANE'S HOME WITH SARAH, MAYBE I WILL HAVE THAT SHOT.
NOW, HARVE DIDN'T SAY NOTHING ABOUT DIANE GOING HOME.
MOZART. THAT'S DIANE'S BUSINESS.
WHAT?
YOUR GIRL'S MOM WENT HOME WITH NICKY DEMILLE.

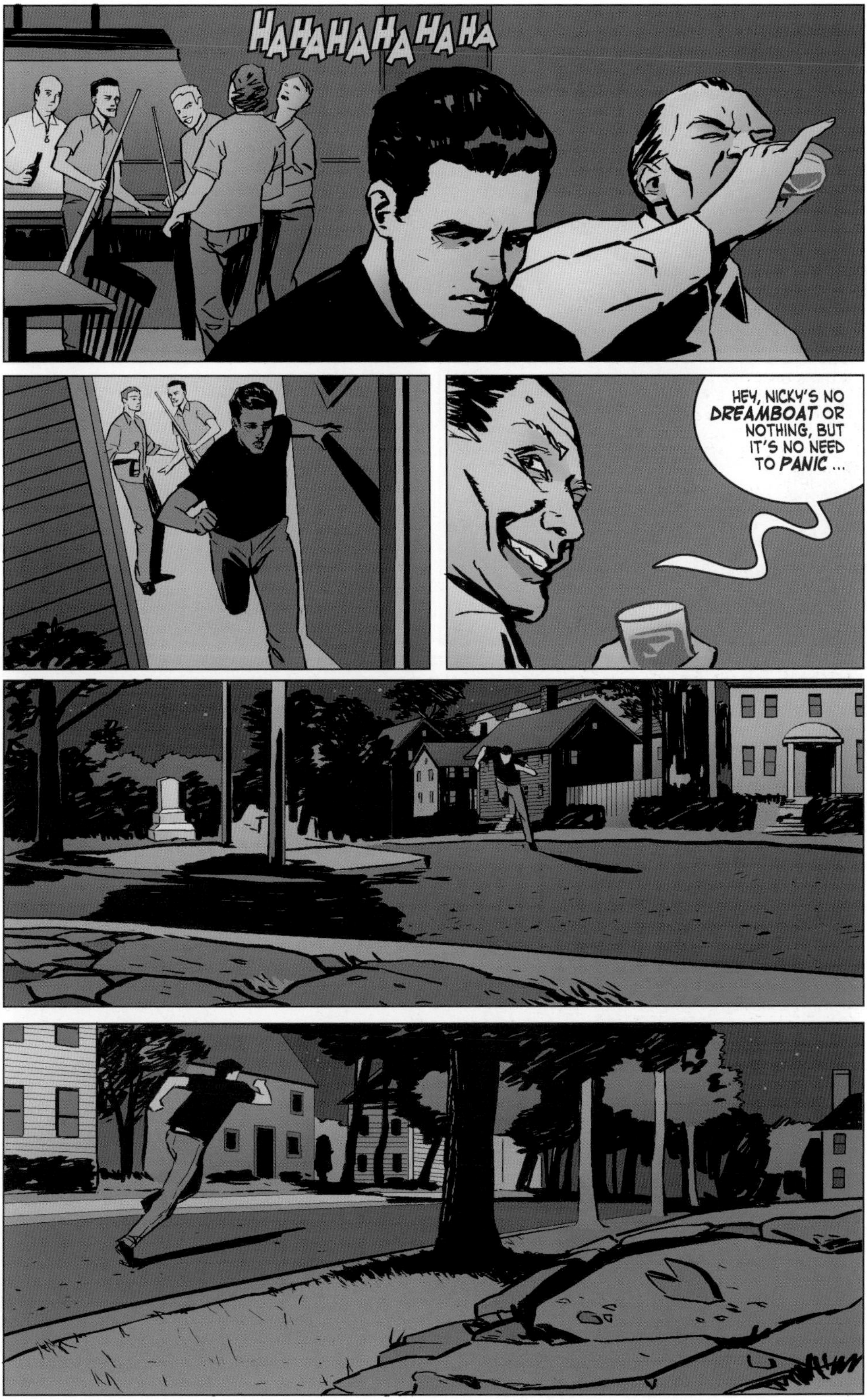
HAHAHAHAHAHAHA
HEY, NICKY'S NO DREAMBOAT OR NOTHING, BUT IT'S NO NEED TO PANIC ...

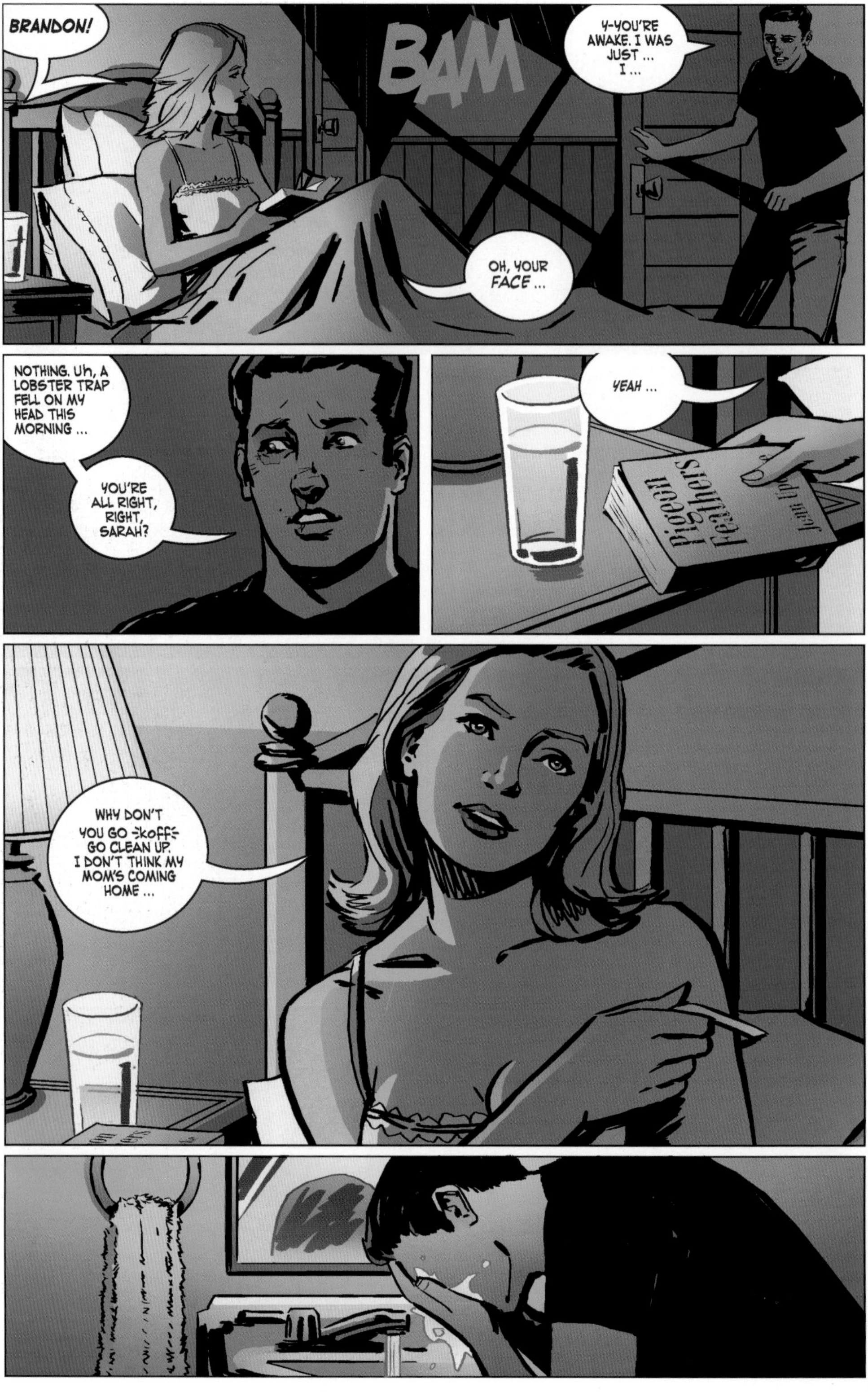
BRANDON!
BAM
Y-YOU'RE AWAKE. I WAS JUST ... I ...
OH, YOUR FACE ...
NOTHING. Uh, A LOBSTER TRAP FELL ON MY HEAD THIS MORNING ...
YOU'RE ALL RIGHT, RIGHT, SARAH?
YEAH ...
Pigeon Feathers
WHY DON'T YOU GO =koff= GO CLEAN UP. I DON'T THINK MY MOM'S COMING HOME ...

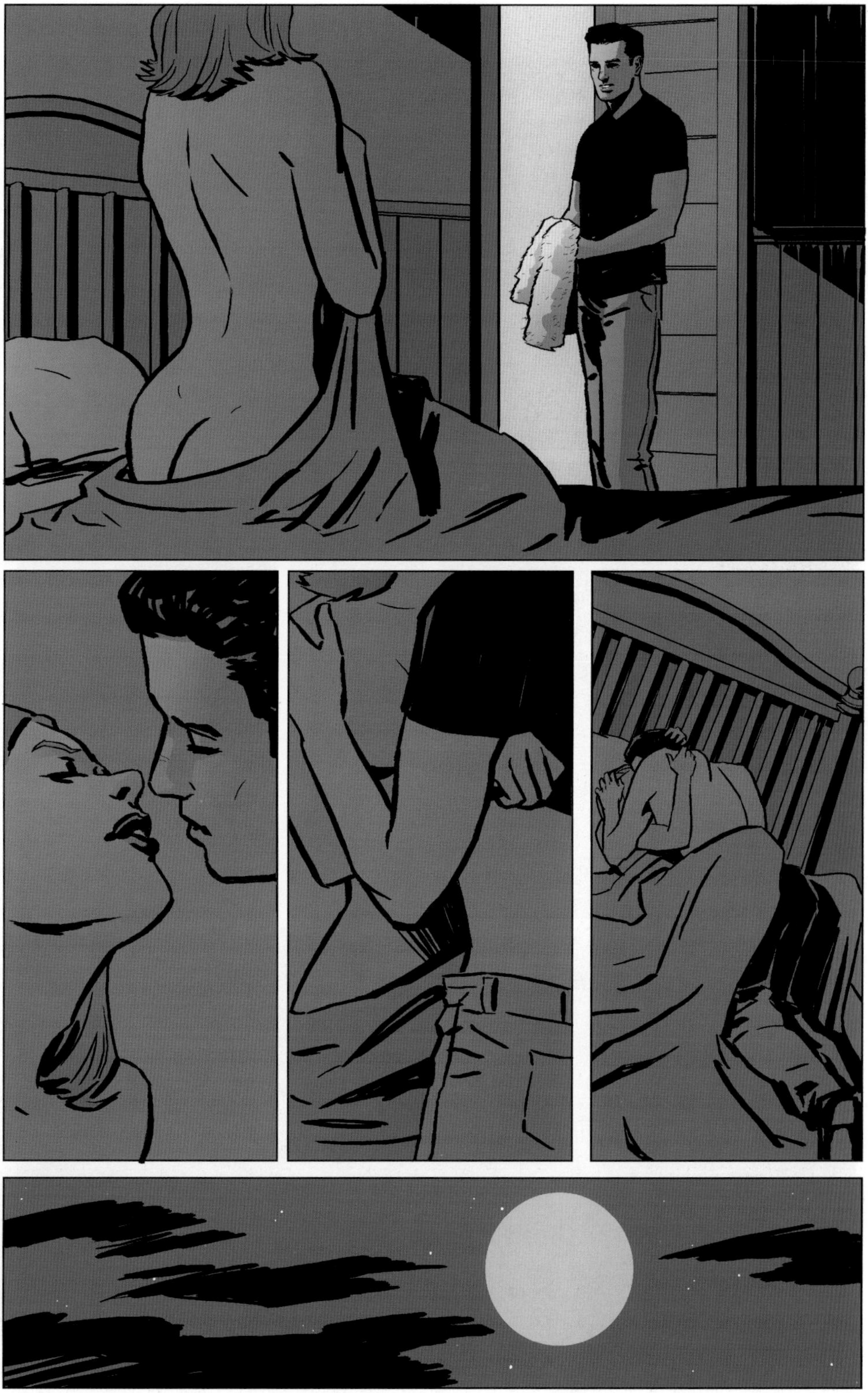

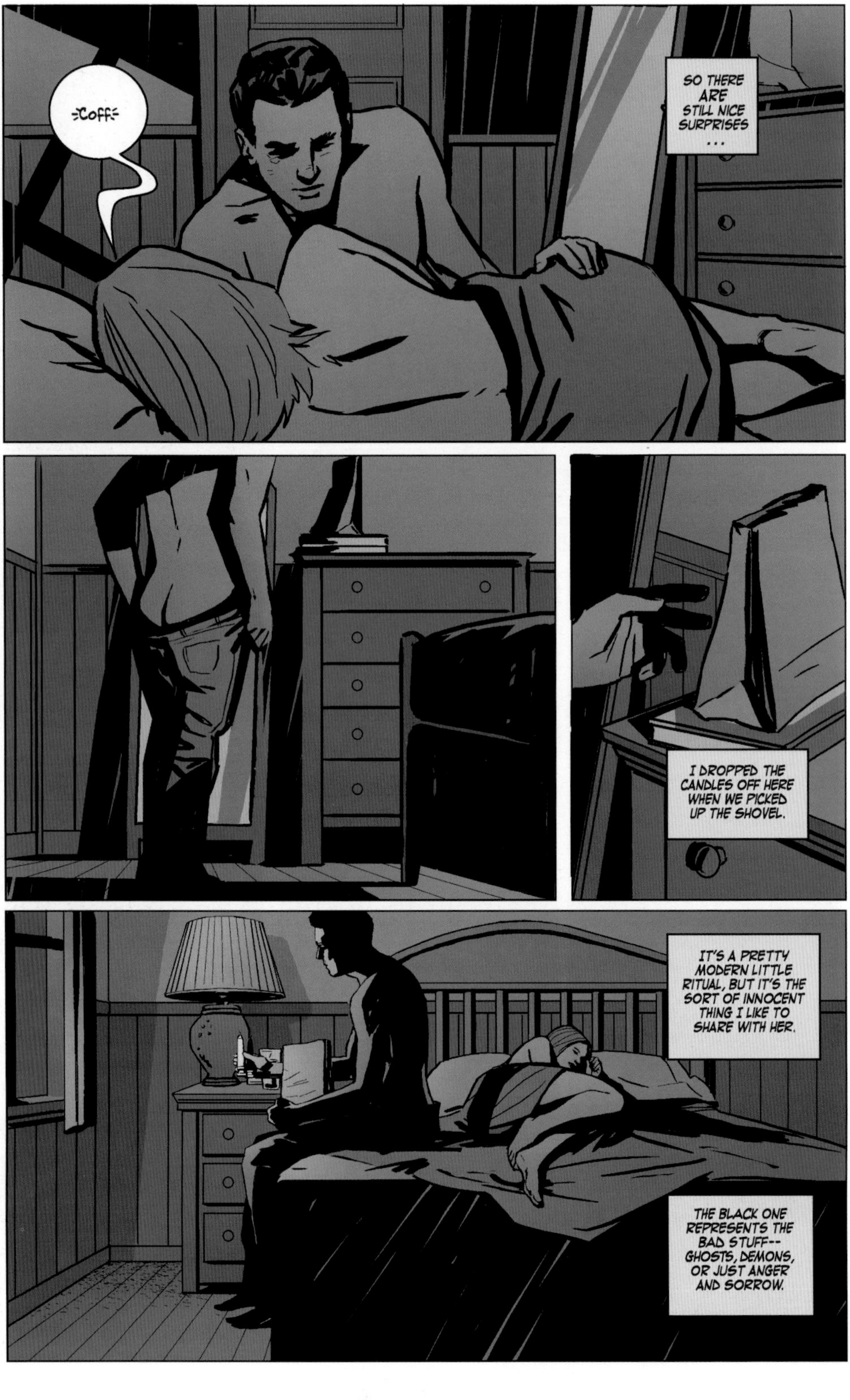
=COFF=
SO THERE ARE STILL NICE SURPRISES . . .
I DROPPED THE CANDLES OFF HERE WHEN WE PICKED UP THE SHOVEL.
IT'S A PRETTY MODERN LITTLE RITUAL, BUT IT'S THE SORT OF INNOCENT THING I LIKE TO SHARE WITH HER.
THE BLACK ONE REPRESENTS THE BAD STUFF-- GHOSTS, DEMONS, OR JUST ANGER AND SORROW.

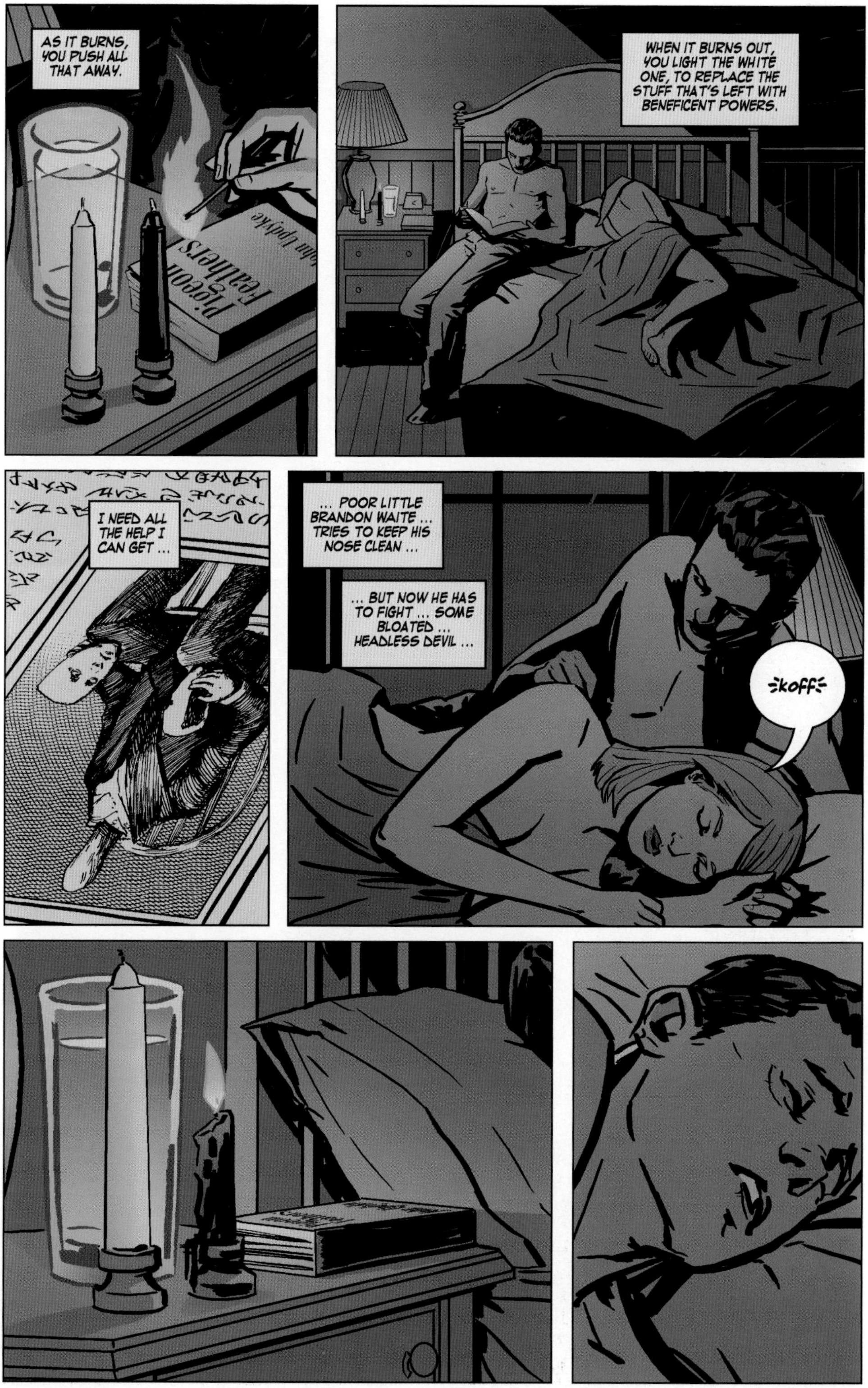
AS IT BURNS, YOU PUSH ALL THAT AWAY.
Pigeon Feathers
John Updike
WHEN IT BURNS OUT, YOU LIGHT THE WHITE ONE, TO REPLACE THE STUFF THAT'S LEFT WITH BENEFICENT POWERS.
I NEED ALL THE HELP I CAN GET ...
... POOR LITTLE BRANDON WAITE ... TRIES TO KEEP HIS NOSE CLEAN ...
... BUT NOW HE HAS TO FIGHT ... SOME BLOATED ... HEADLESS DEVIL ...
koff

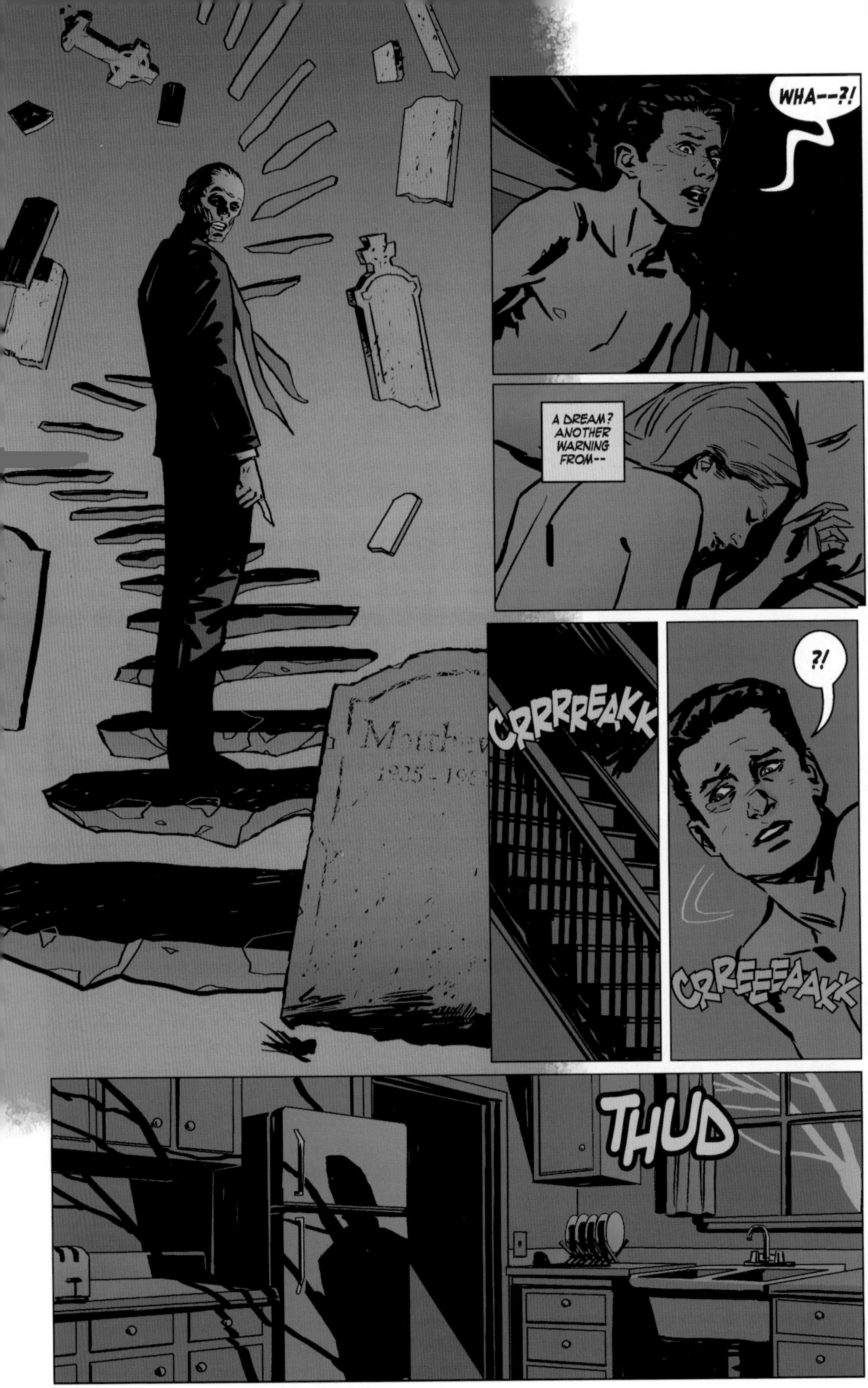
WHA--?!
A DREAM? ANOTHER WARNING FROM--
CRRRREAKK
?!
CREEEEAAKK
THUD

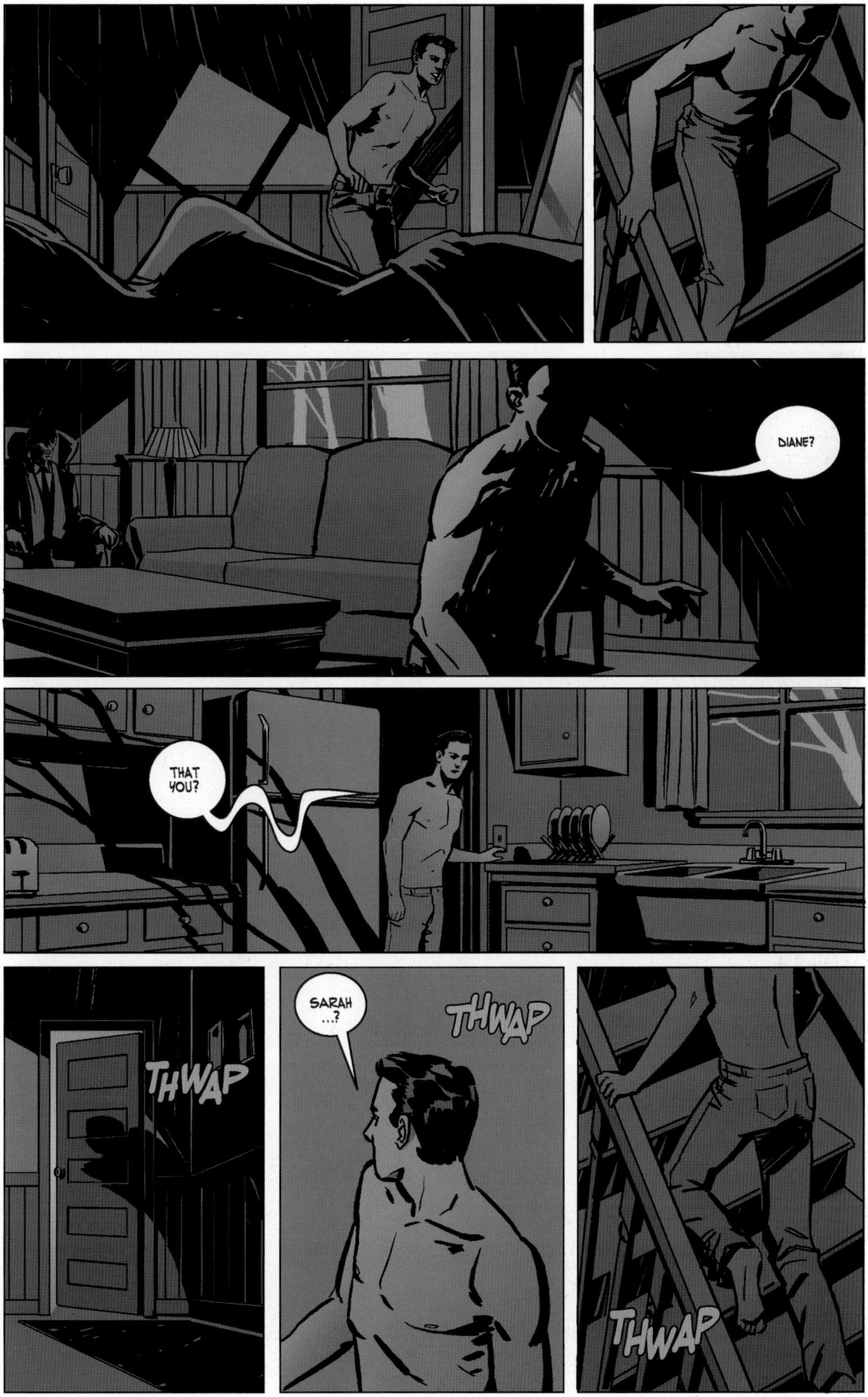
DIANE?
THAT YOU?
THWAP
SARAH ...?
THWAP
THWAP

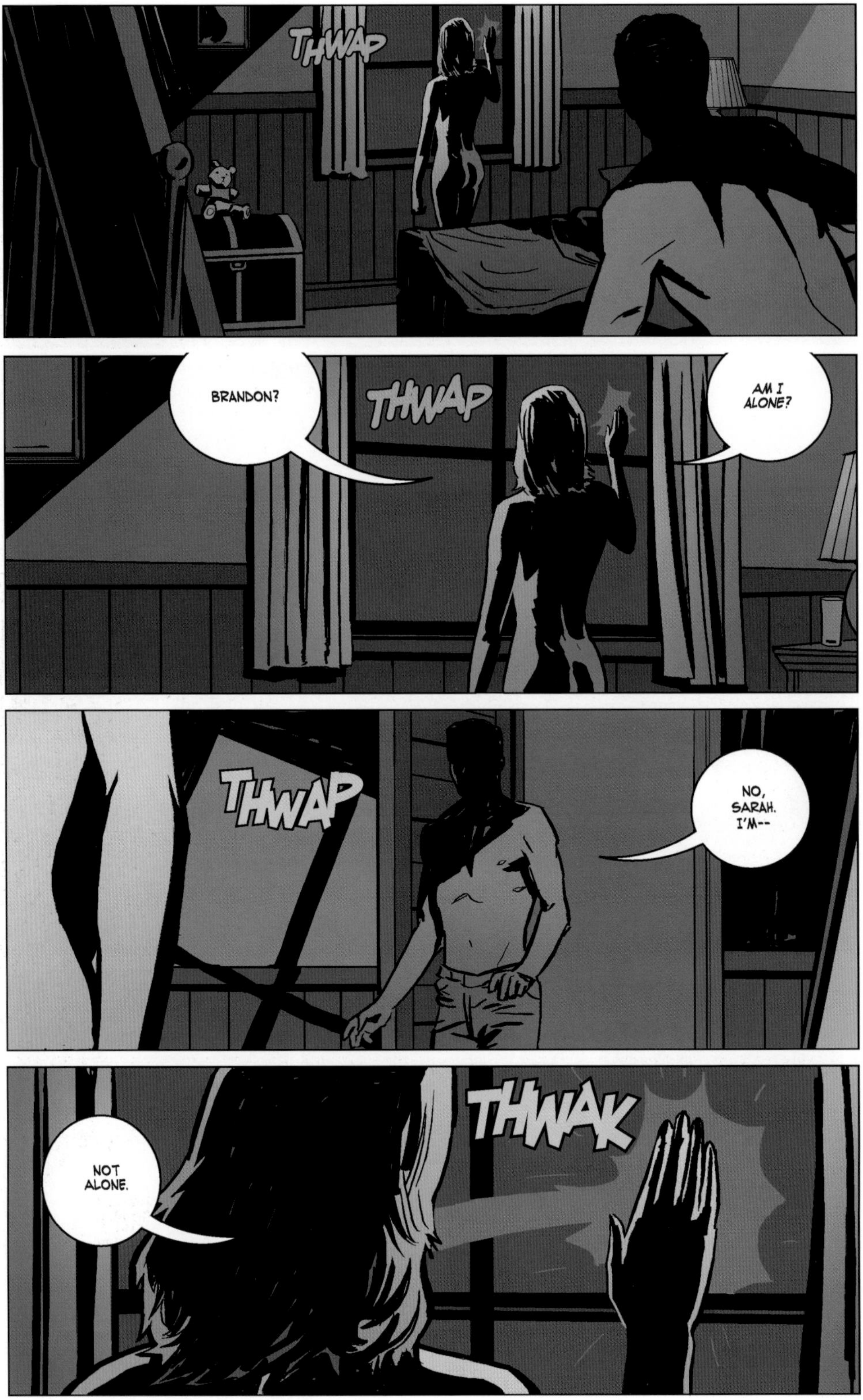
THWAP
BRANDON?
THWAP
AM I ALONE?
THWAP
NO, SARAH. I'M--
THWAK
NOT ALONE.

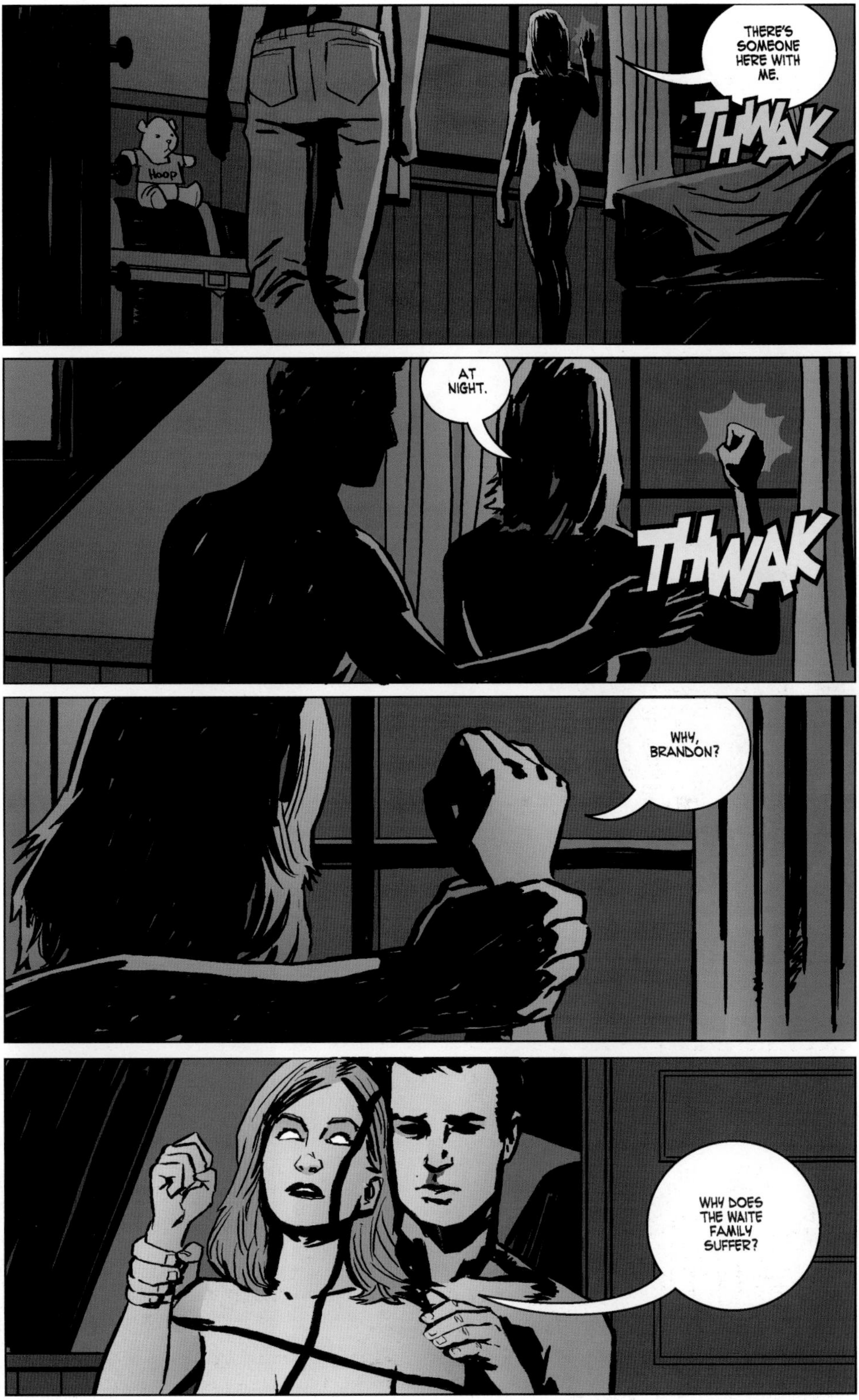
THERE'S SOMEONE HERE WITH ME.
THWAK
AT NIGHT.
THWAK
WHY, BRANDON?
WHY DOES THE WAITE FAMILY SUFFER?

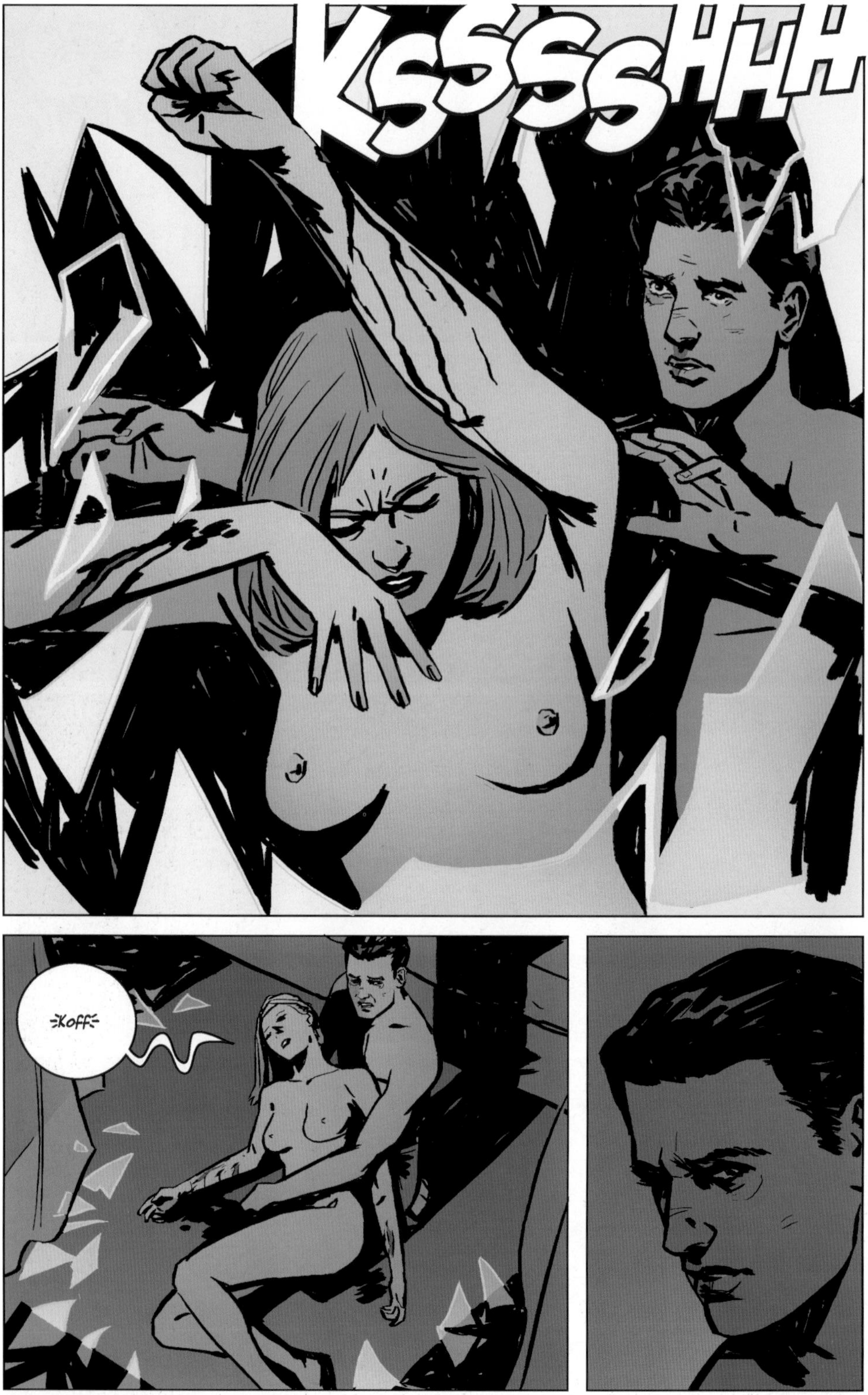
KSSSSHHH
=KOFF=

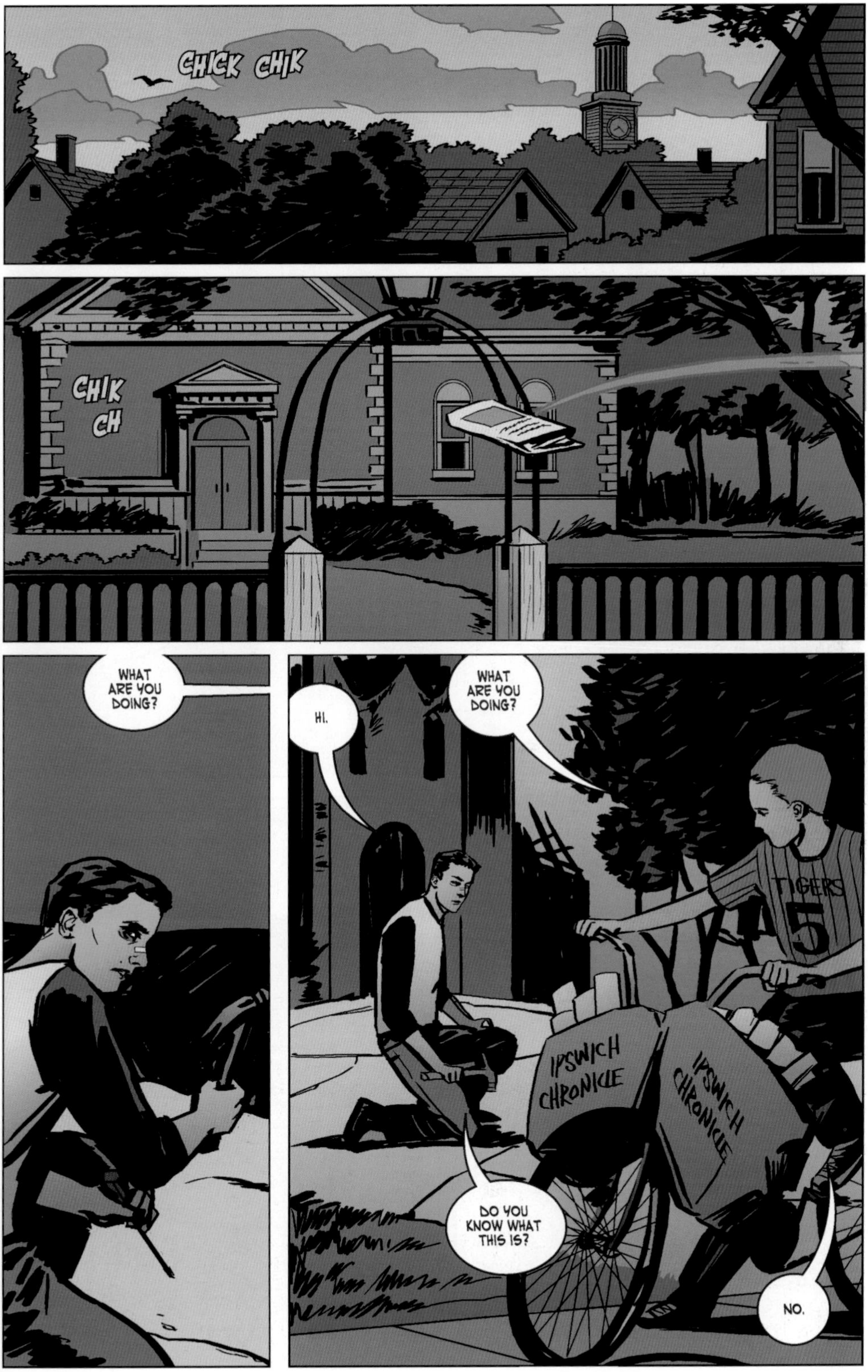
CHICK CHIK
CHIK CH
WHAT ARE YOU DOING?
HI.
WHAT ARE YOU DOING?
TIGERS 5
IPSWICH CHRONICLE
IPSWICH CHRONICLE
DO YOU KNOW WHAT THIS IS?
NO.

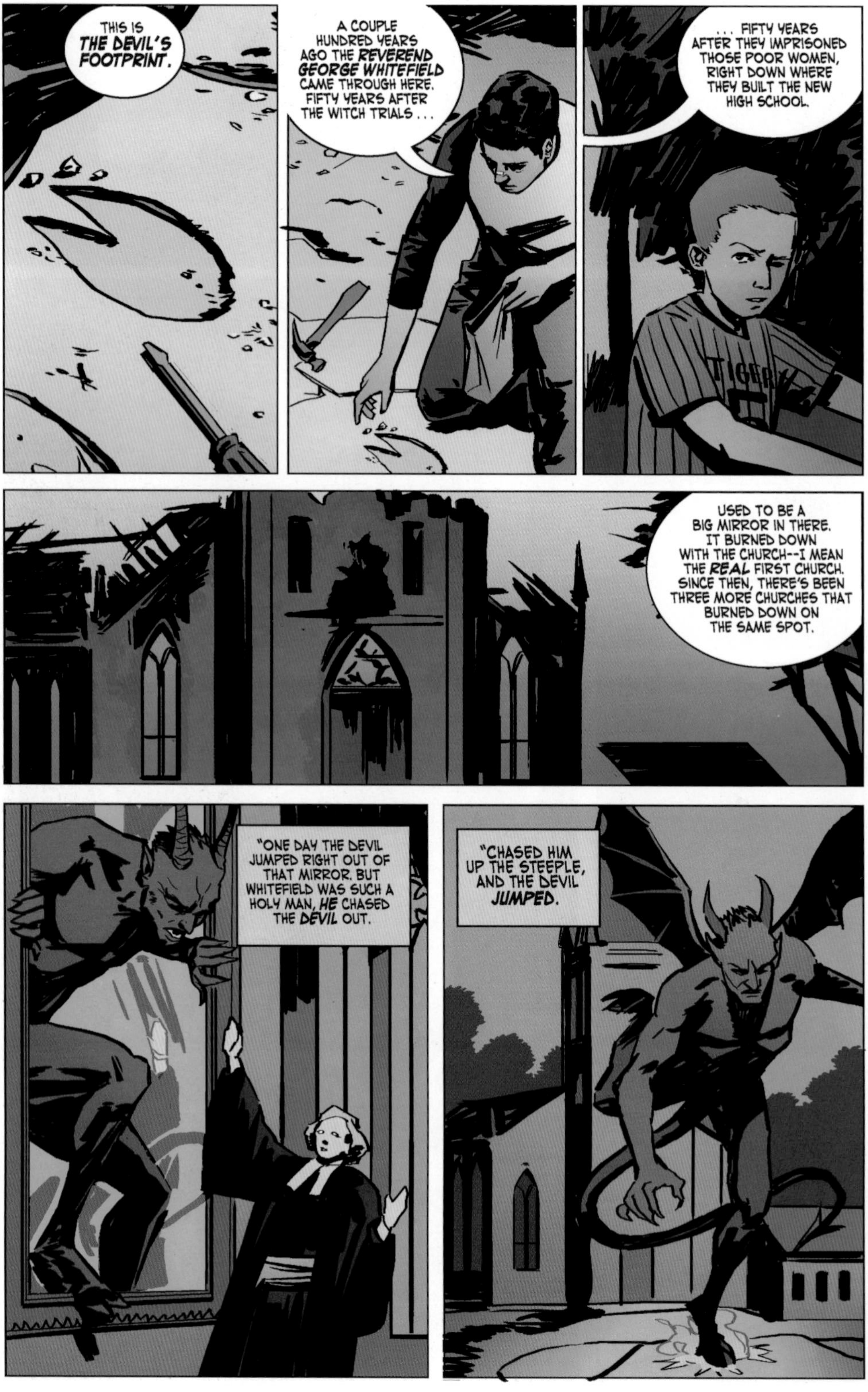
THIS IS THE DEVIL'S FOOTPRINT.
A COUPLE HUNDRED YEARS AGO THE REVEREND GEORGE WHITEFIELD CAME THROUGH HERE. FIFTY YEARS AFTER THE WITCH TRIALS . . .
. . . FIFTY YEARS AFTER THEY IMPRISONED THOSE POOR WOMEN, RIGHT DOWN WHERE THEY BUILT THE NEW HIGH SCHOOL.
TIGER
USED TO BE A BIG MIRROR IN THERE. IT BURNED DOWN WITH THE CHURCH--I MEAN THE REAL FIRST CHURCH. SINCE THEN, THERE'S BEEN THREE MORE CHURCHES THAT BURNED DOWN ON THE SAME SPOT.
"ONE DAY THE DEVIL JUMPED RIGHT OUT OF THAT MIRROR. BUT WHITEFIELD WAS SUCH A HOLY MAN, HE CHASED THE DEVIL OUT.
"CHASED HIM UP THE STEEPLE, AND THE DEVIL JUMPED.

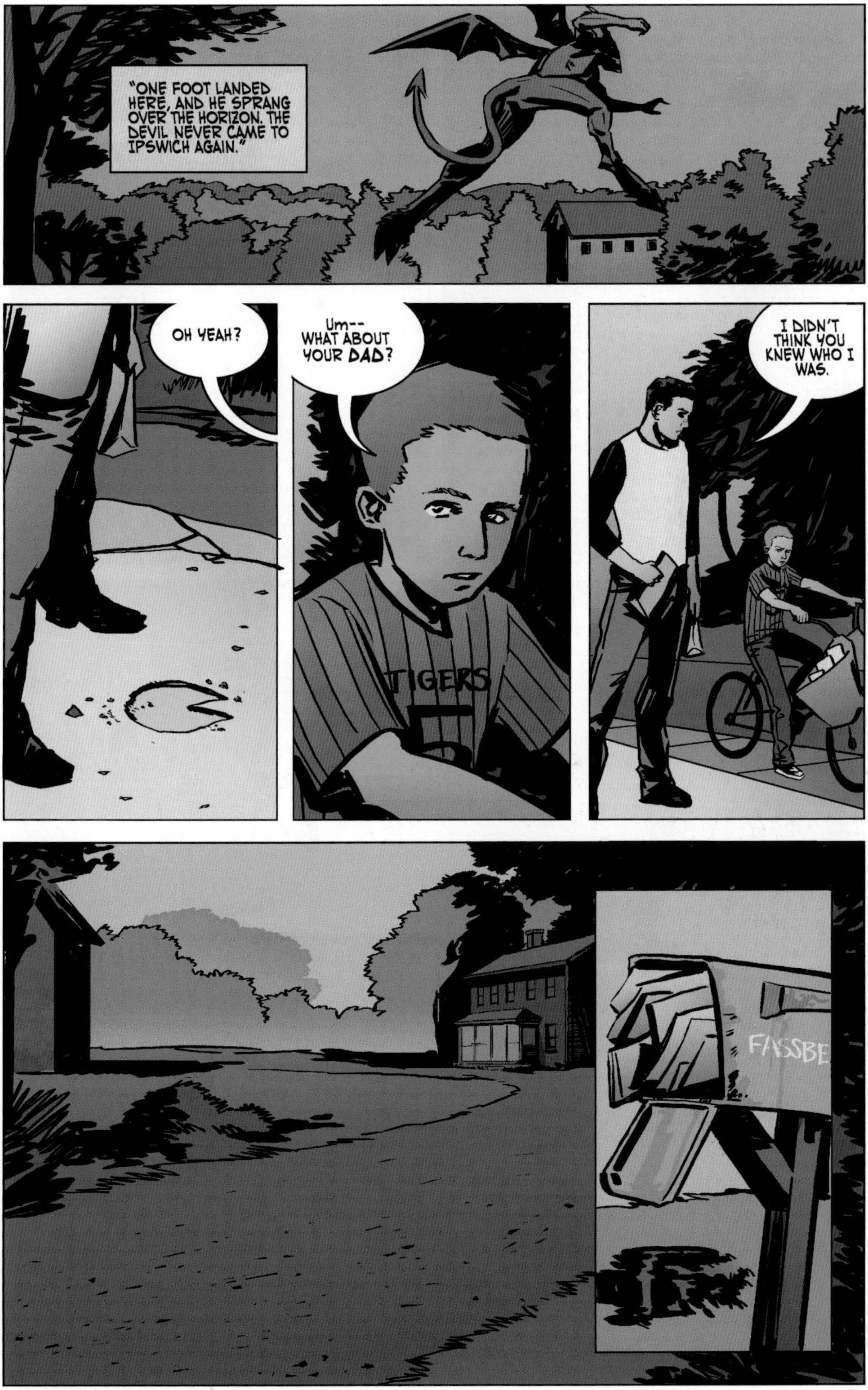
"ONE FOOT LANDED HERE, AND HE SPRANG OVER THE HORIZON. THE DEVIL NEVER CAME TO IPSWICH AGAIN."
OH YEAH?
Um-- WHAT ABOUT YOUR DAD?
TIGERS
I DIDN'T THINK YOU KNEW WHO I WAS.
FASSBE

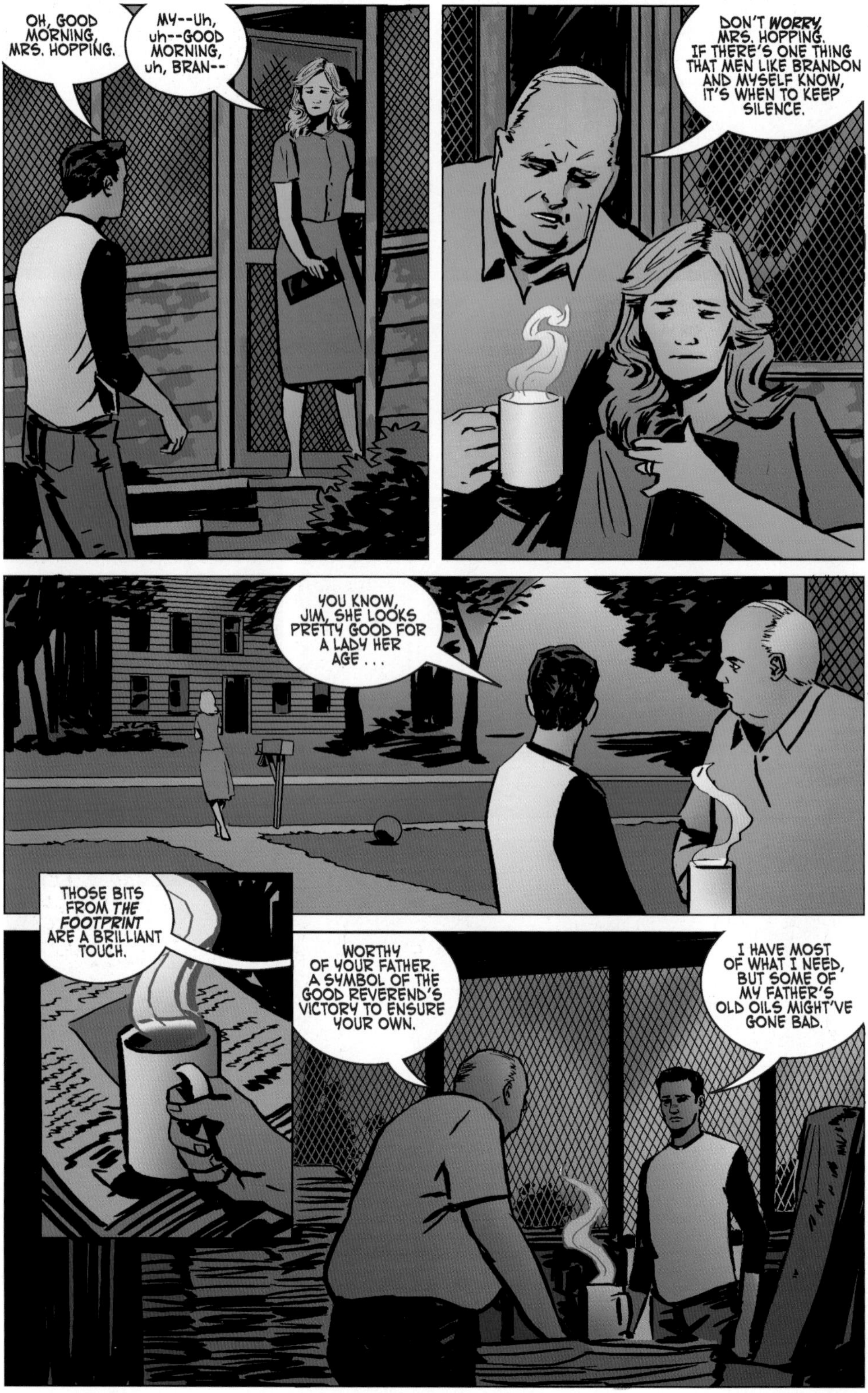

OH, GOOD MORNING, MRS. HOPPING.
MY--uh, uh--GOOD MORNING, uh, BRAN--
DON'T *WORRY,* MRS. HOPPING. IF THERE'S ONE THING THAT MEN LIKE BRANDON AND MYSELF KNOW, IT'S WHEN TO KEEP SILENCE.
YOU KNOW, JIM, SHE LOOKS PRETTY GOOD FOR A LADY HER AGE . . .
THOSE BITS FROM *THE FOOTPRINT* ARE A BRILLIANT TOUCH.
WORTHY OF YOUR FATHER. A SYMBOL OF THE GOOD REVEREND'S VICTORY TO ENSURE YOUR OWN.
I HAVE MOST OF WHAT I NEED, BUT SOME OF MY FATHER'S OLD OILS MIGHT'VE GONE BAD.

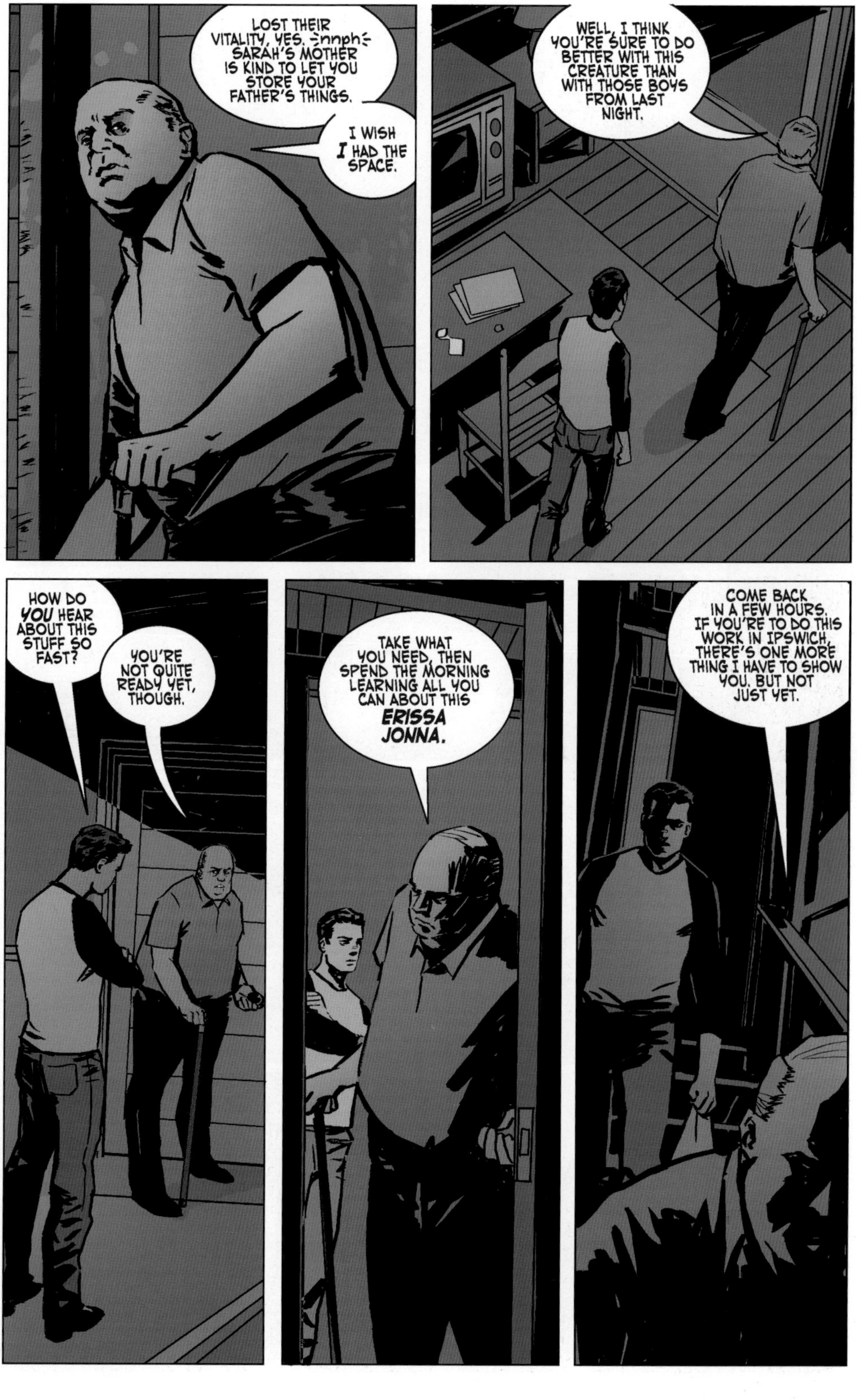
LOST THEIR VITALITY, YES. =nnph= SARAH'S MOTHER IS KIND TO LET YOU STORE YOUR FATHER'S THINGS.
I WISH I HAD THE SPACE.
WELL, I THINK YOU'RE SURE TO DO BETTER WITH THIS CREATURE THAN WITH THOSE BOYS FROM LAST NIGHT.
HOW DO YOU HEAR ABOUT THIS STUFF SO FAST?
YOU'RE NOT QUITE READY YET, THOUGH.
TAKE WHAT YOU NEED, THEN SPEND THE MORNING LEARNING ALL YOU CAN ABOUT THIS ERISSA JONNA.
COME BACK IN A FEW HOURS. IF YOU'RE TO DO THIS WORK IN IPSWICH, THERE'S ONE MORE THING I HAVE TO SHOW YOU. BUT NOT JUST YET.

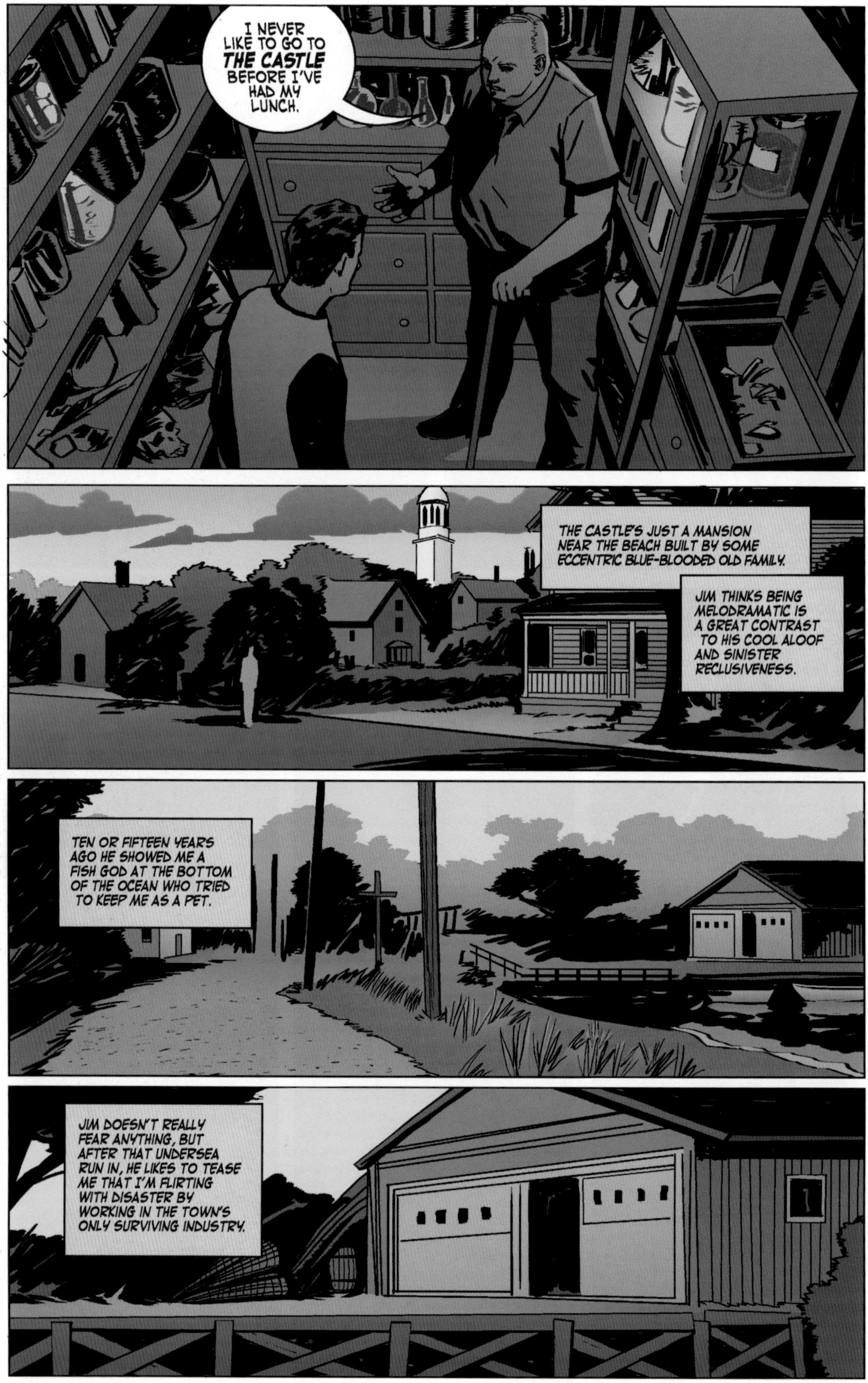
I NEVER LIKE TO GO TO THE CASTLE BEFORE I'VE HAD MY LUNCH.
THE CASTLE'S JUST A MANSION NEAR THE BEACH BUILT BY SOME ECCENTRIC BLUE-BLOODED OLD FAMILY.
JIM THINKS BEING MELODRAMATIC IS A GREAT CONTRAST TO HIS COOL ALOOF AND SINISTER RECLUSIVENESS.
TEN OR FIFTEEN YEARS AGO HE SHOWED ME A FISH GOD AT THE BOTTOM OF THE OCEAN WHO TRIED TO KEEP ME AS A PET.
JIM DOESN'T REALLY FEAR ANYTHING, BUT AFTER THAT UNDERSEA RUN IN, HE LIKES TO TEASE ME THAT I'M FLIRTING WITH DISASTER BY WORKING IN THE TOWN'S ONLY SURVIVING INDUSTRY.

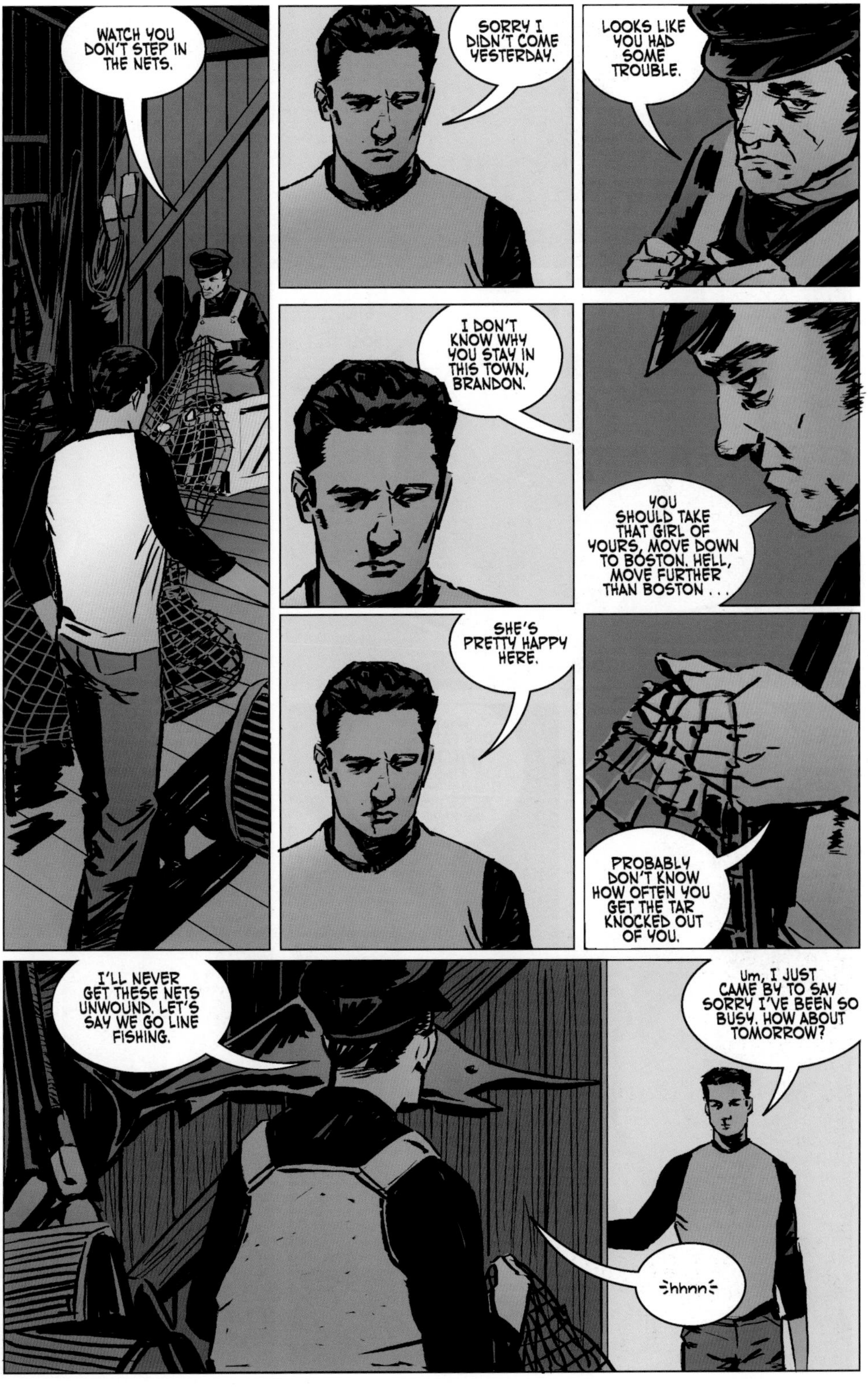
WATCH YOU DON'T STEP IN THE NETS.
SORRY I DIDN'T COME YESTERDAY.
LOOKS LIKE YOU HAD SOME TROUBLE.
I DON'T KNOW WHY YOU STAY IN THIS TOWN, BRANDON.
YOU SHOULD TAKE THAT GIRL OF YOURS, MOVE DOWN TO BOSTON. HELL, MOVE FURTHER THAN BOSTON . . .
SHE'S PRETTY HAPPY HERE.
PROBABLY DON'T KNOW HOW OFTEN YOU GET THE TAR KNOCKED OUT OF YOU.
I'LL NEVER GET THESE NETS UNWOUND. LET'S SAY WE GO LINE FISHING.
Um, I JUST CAME BY TO SAY SORRY I'VE BEEN SO BUSY. HOW ABOUT TOMORROW?
hhnn

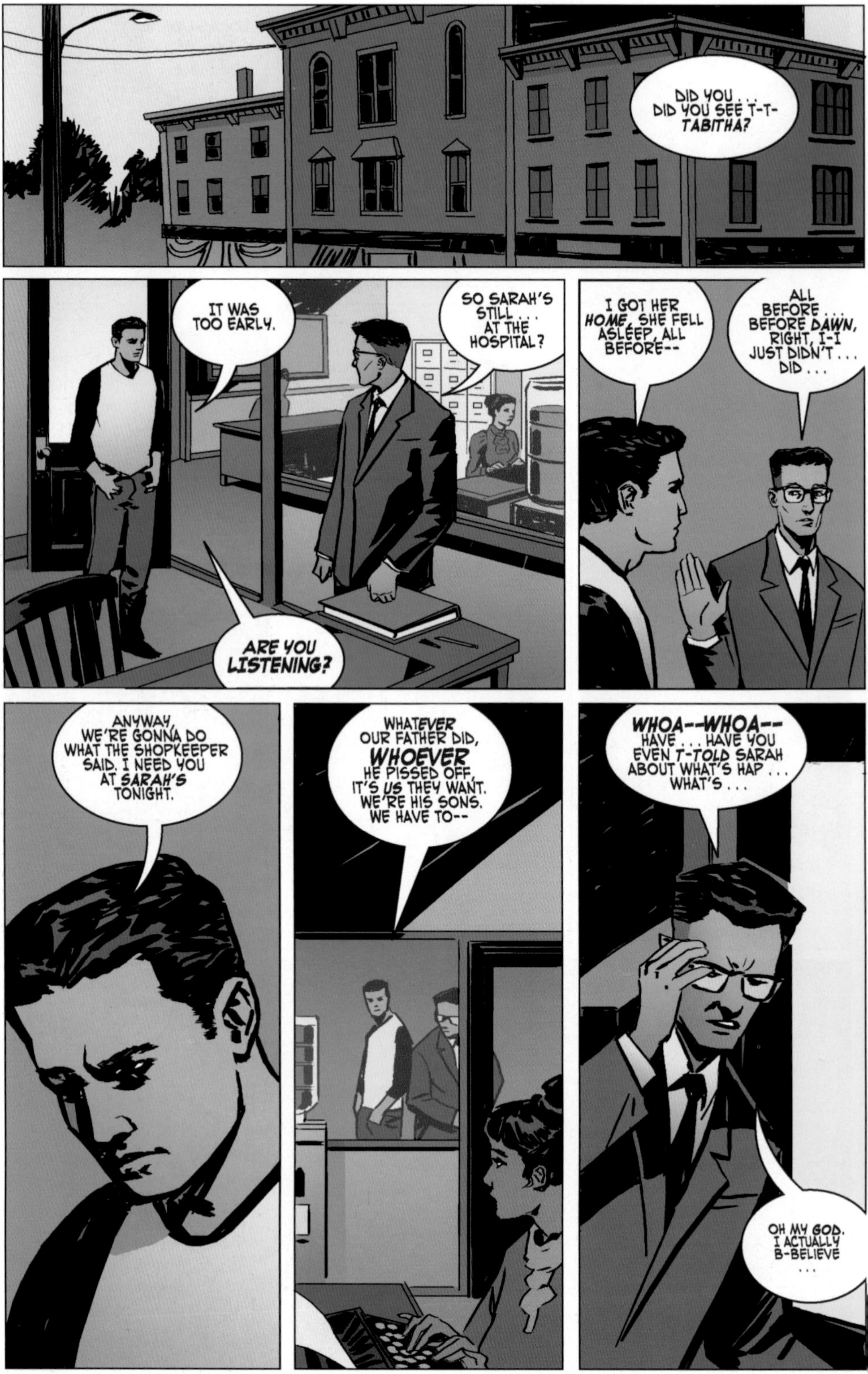
DID YOU . . . DID YOU SEE T-T-TABITHA?
IT WAS TOO EARLY.
SO SARAH'S STILL . . . AT THE HOSPITAL?
ARE YOU LISTENING?
I GOT HER HOME, SHE FELL ASLEEP, ALL BEFORE--
ALL BEFORE . . . BEFORE DAWN, RIGHT, I-I JUST DIDN'T . . . DID . . .
ANYWAY, WE'RE GONNA DO WHAT THE SHOPKEEPER SAID. I NEED YOU AT SARAH'S TONIGHT.
WHATEVER OUR FATHER DID, WHOEVER HE PISSED OFF, IT'S US THEY WANT. WE'RE HIS SONS. WE HAVE TO--
WHOA--WHOA-- HAVE . . . HAVE YOU EVEN T-TOLD SARAH ABOUT WHAT'S HAP . . . WHAT'S . . .
OH MY GOD. I ACTUALLY B-BELIEVE . . .

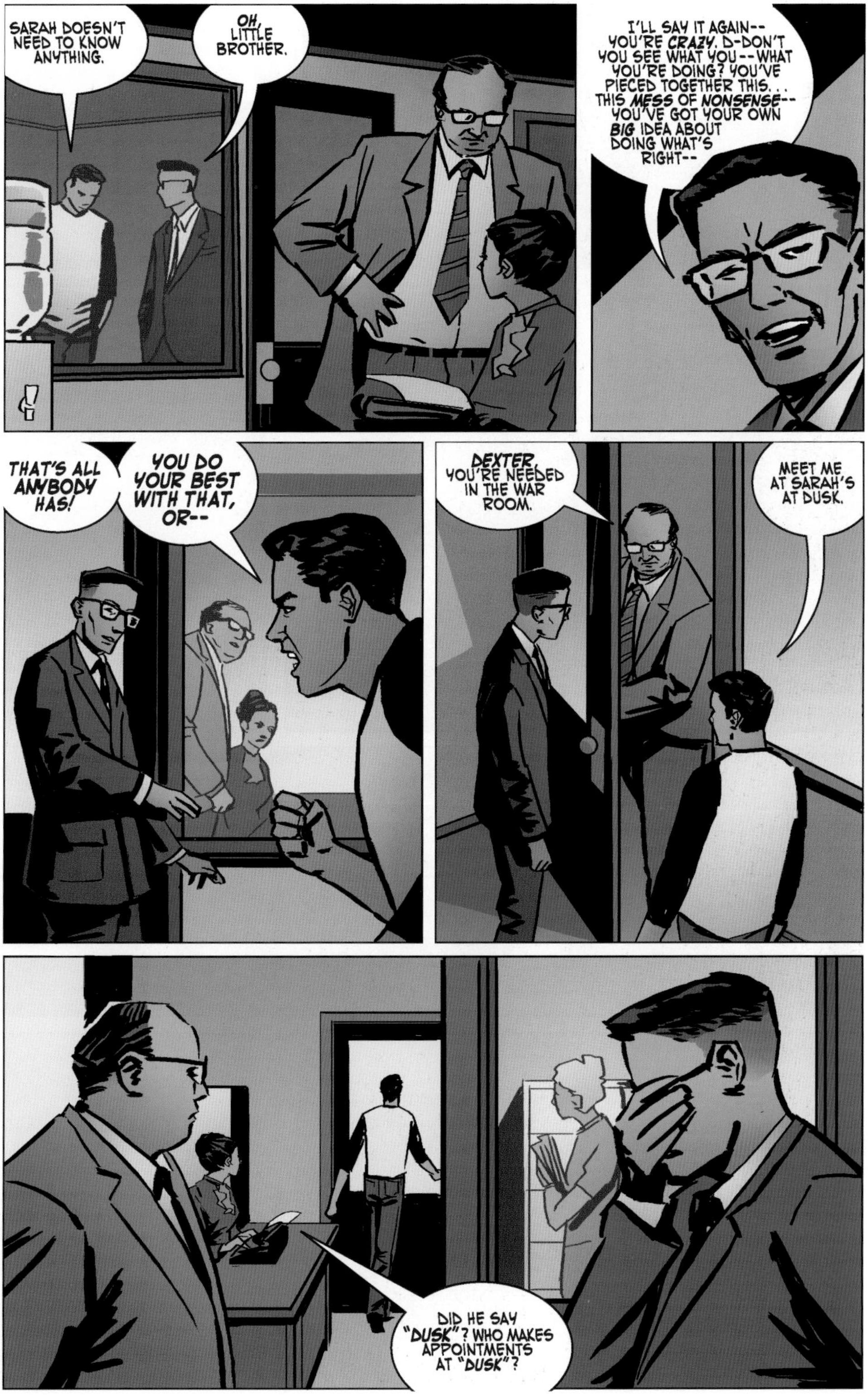

SARAH DOESN'T NEED TO KNOW ANYTHING.
OH, LITTLE BROTHER.
I'LL SAY IT AGAIN-- YOU'RE CRAZY. D-DON'T YOU SEE WHAT YOU--WHAT YOU'RE DOING? YOU'VE PIECED TOGETHER THIS... THIS MESS OF NONSENSE-- YOU'VE GOT YOUR OWN BIG IDEA ABOUT DOING WHAT'S RIGHT--
THAT'S ALL ANYBODY HAS!
YOU DO YOUR BEST WITH THAT, OR--
DEXTER, YOU'RE NEEDED IN THE WAR ROOM.
MEET ME AT SARAH'S AT DUSK.
DID HE SAY "DUSK"? WHO MAKES APPOINTMENTS AT "DUSK"?

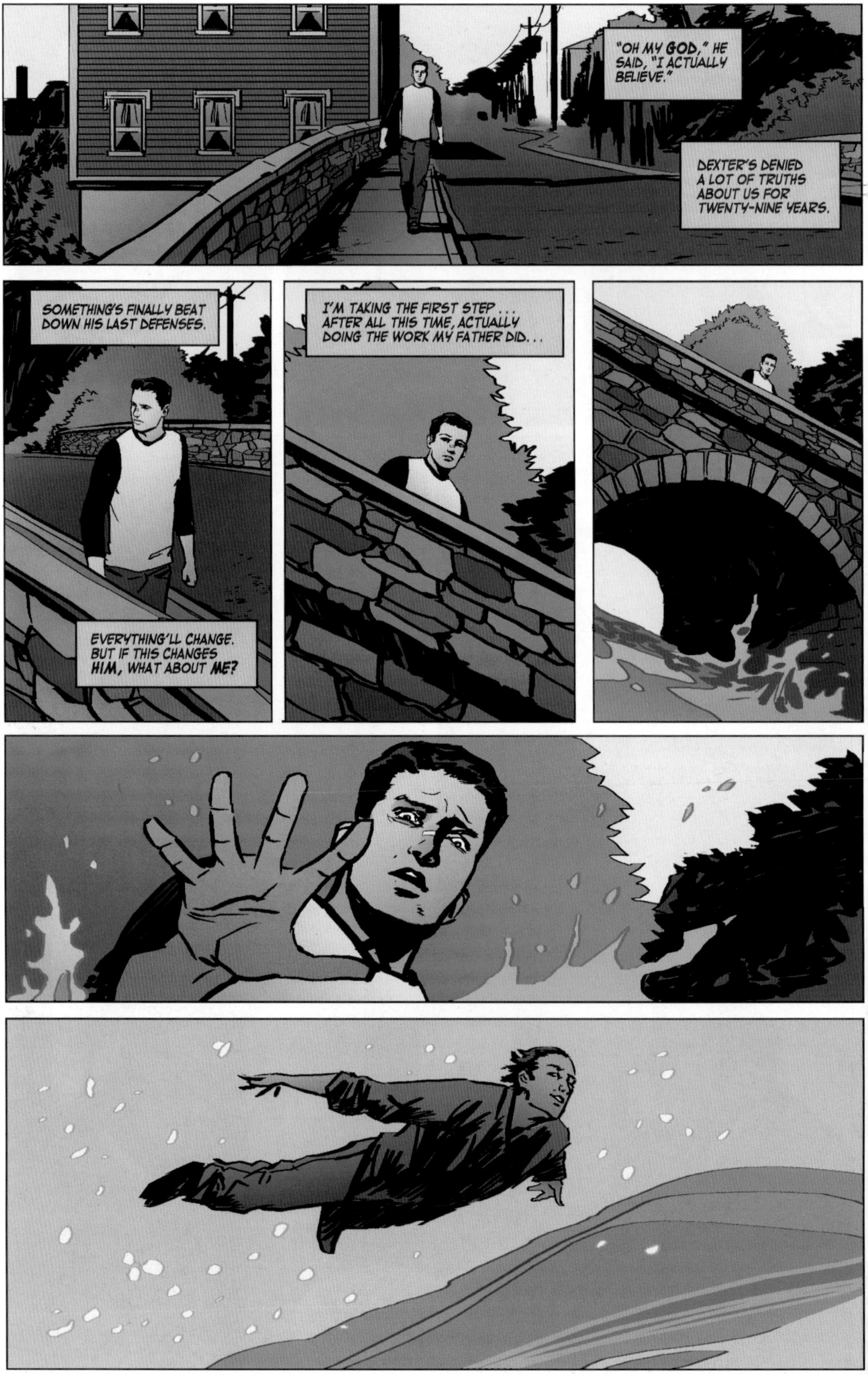
"OH MY GOD," HE SAID, "I ACTUALLY BELIEVE."
DEXTER'S DENIED A LOT OF TRUTHS ABOUT US FOR TWENTY-NINE YEARS.
SOMETHING'S FINALLY BEAT DOWN HIS LAST DEFENSES.
EVERYTHING'LL CHANGE. BUT IF THIS CHANGES HIM, WHAT ABOUT ME?
I'M TAKING THE FIRST STEP . . . AFTER ALL THIS TIME, ACTUALLY DOING THE WORK MY FATHER DID . . .

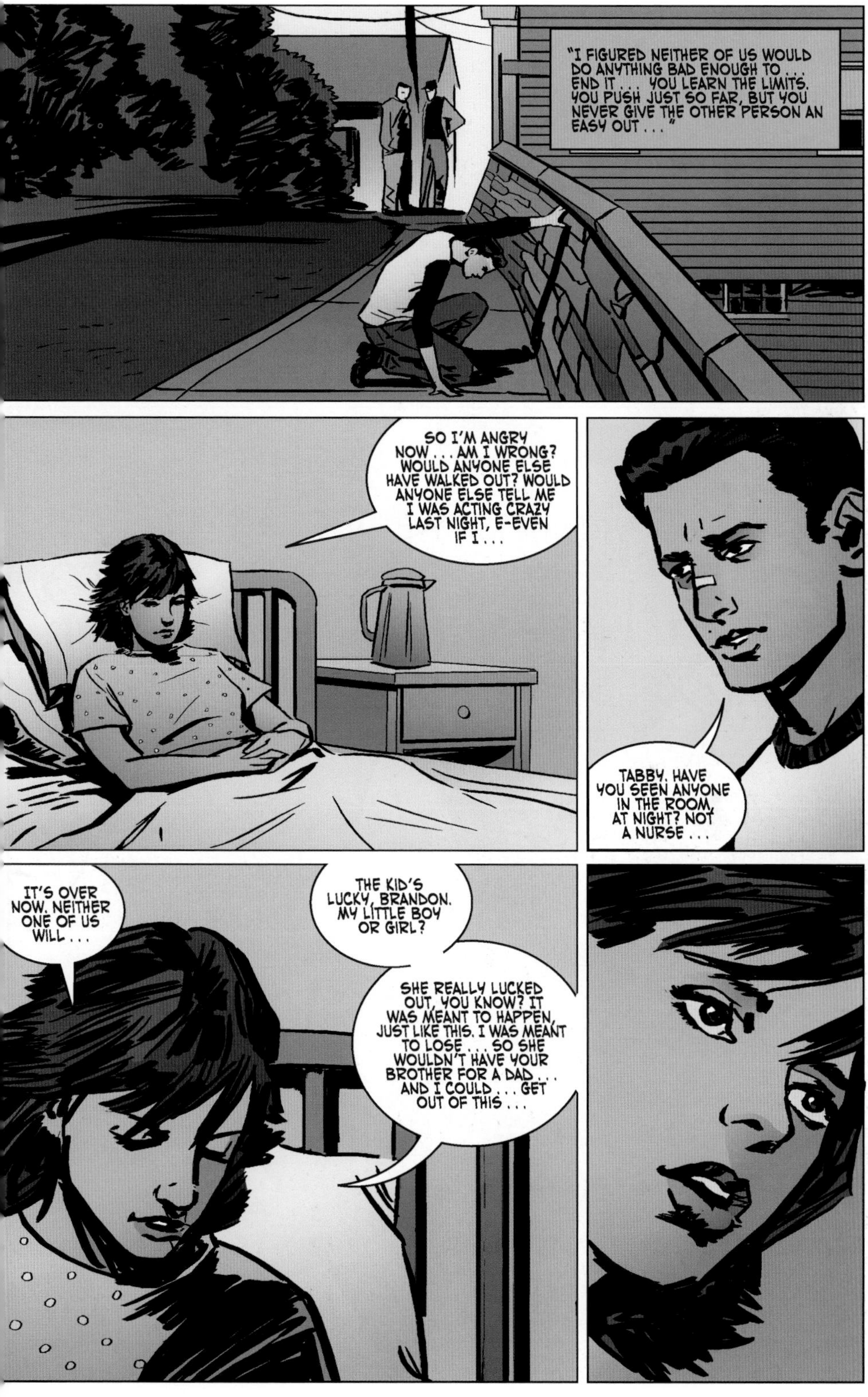
"I FIGURED NEITHER OF US WOULD DO ANYTHING BAD ENOUGH TO . . . END IT . . . YOU LEARN THE LIMITS. YOU PUSH JUST SO FAR, BUT YOU NEVER GIVE THE OTHER PERSON AN EASY OUT . . ."
SO I'M ANGRY NOW . . . AM I WRONG? WOULD ANYONE ELSE HAVE WALKED OUT? WOULD ANYONE ELSE TELL ME I WAS ACTING CRAZY LAST NIGHT, E-EVEN IF I . . .
TABBY. HAVE YOU SEEN ANYONE IN THE ROOM, AT NIGHT? NOT A NURSE . . .
IT'S OVER NOW. NEITHER ONE OF US WILL . . .
THE KID'S LUCKY, BRANDON. MY LITTLE BOY OR GIRL?
SHE REALLY LUCKED OUT, YOU KNOW? IT WAS MEANT TO HAPPEN, JUST LIKE THIS. I WAS MEANT TO LOSE . . . SO SHE WOULDN'T HAVE YOUR BROTHER FOR A DAD . . . AND I COULD . . . GET OUT OF THIS . . .

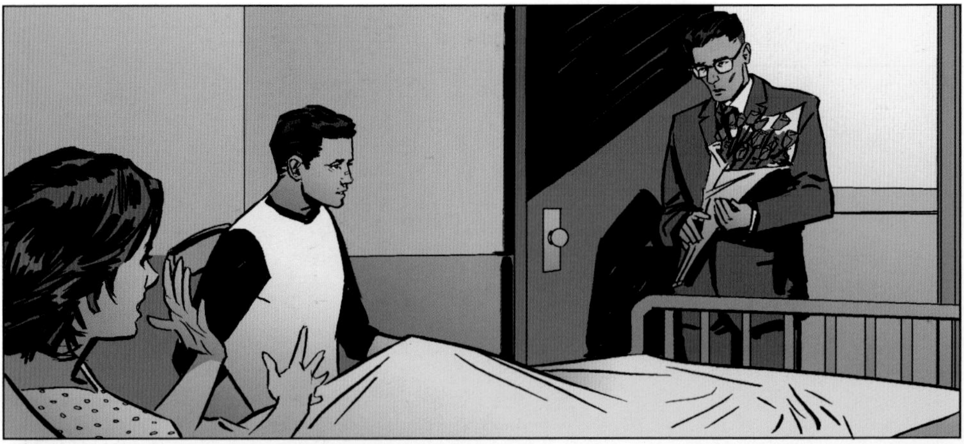

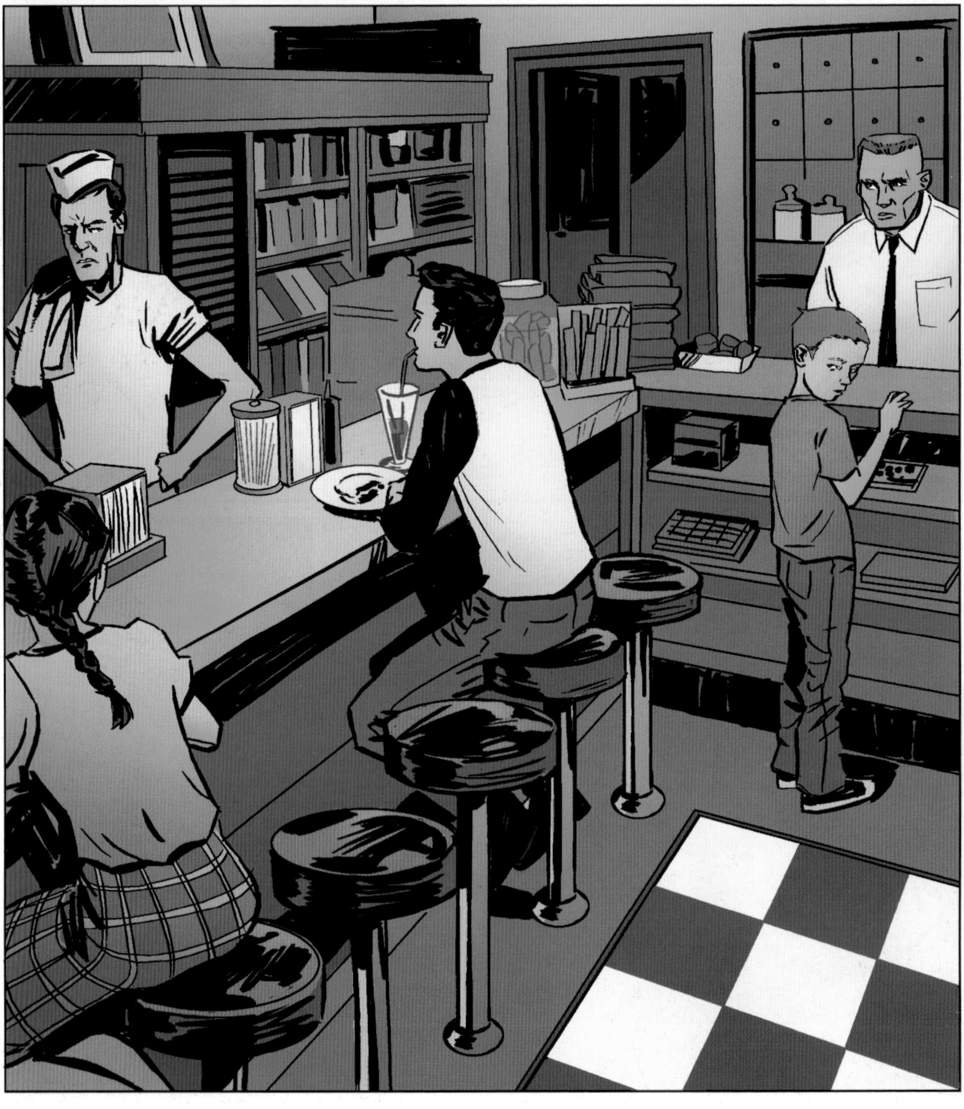

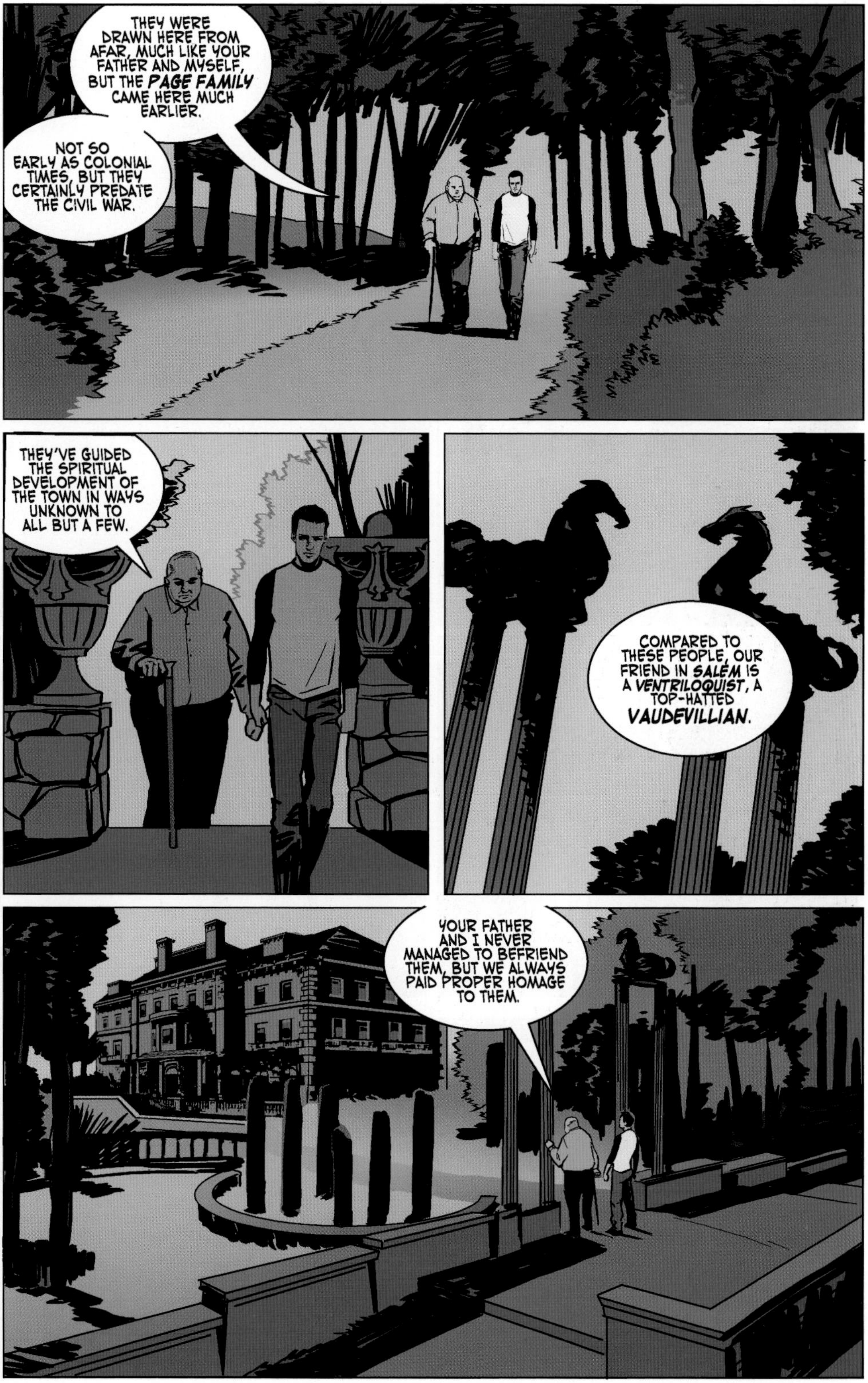
THEY WERE DRAWN HERE FROM AFAR, MUCH LIKE YOUR FATHER AND MYSELF, BUT THE PAGE FAMILY CAME HERE MUCH EARLIER.
NOT SO EARLY AS COLONIAL TIMES, BUT THEY CERTAINLY PREDATE THE CIVIL WAR.
THEY'VE GUIDED THE SPIRITUAL DEVELOPMENT OF THE TOWN IN WAYS UNKNOWN TO ALL BUT A FEW.
COMPARED TO THESE PEOPLE, OUR FRIEND IN SALEM IS A VENTRILOQUIST, A TOP-HATTED VAUDEVILLIAN.
YOUR FATHER AND I NEVER MANAGED TO BEFRIEND THEM, BUT WE ALWAYS PAID PROPER HOMAGE TO THEM.

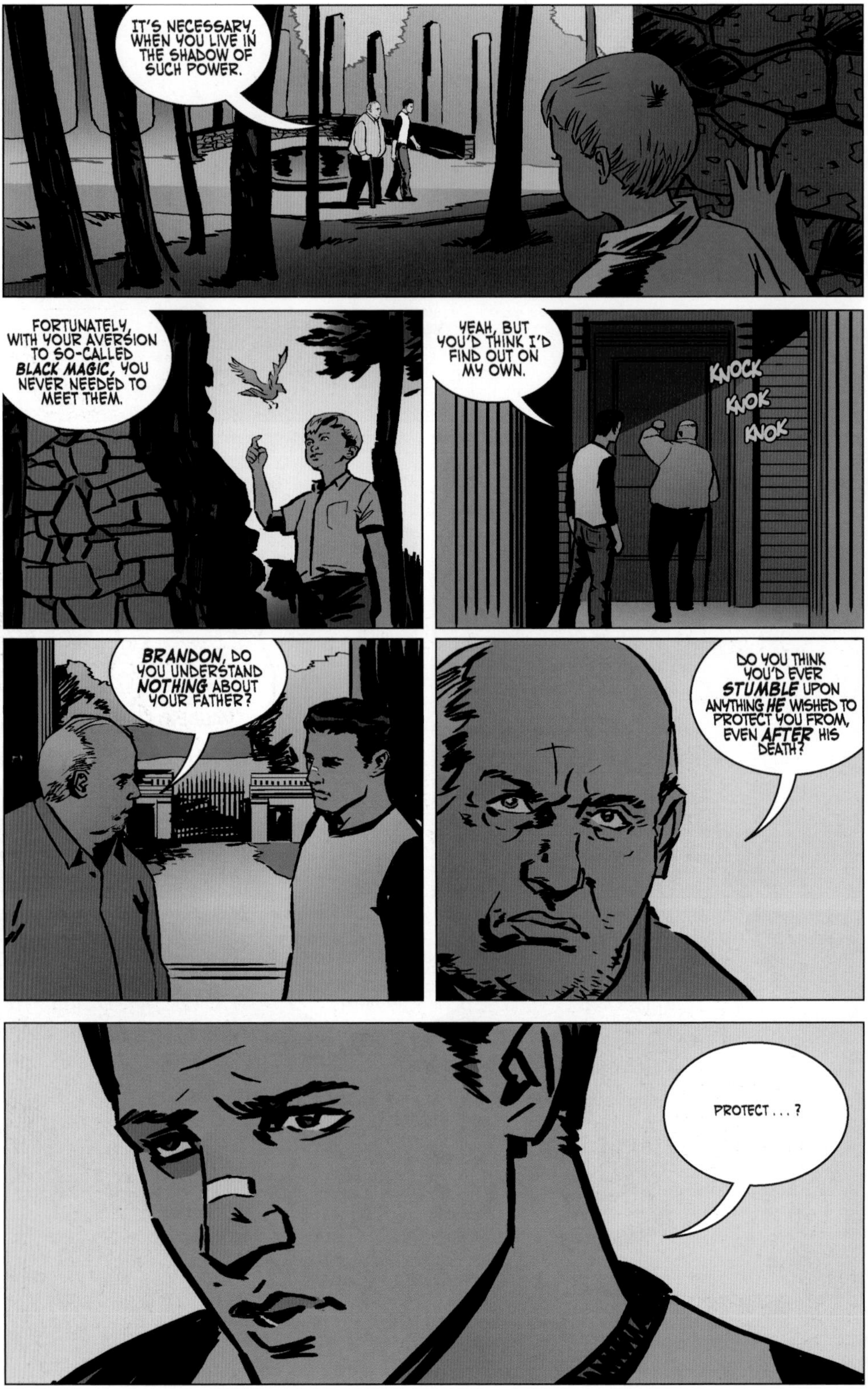
IT'S NECESSARY, WHEN YOU LIVE IN THE SHADOW OF SUCH POWER.
FORTUNATELY, WITH YOUR AVERSION TO SO-CALLED BLACK MAGIC, YOU NEVER NEEDED TO MEET THEM.
YEAH, BUT YOU'D THINK I'D FIND OUT ON MY OWN.
KNOCK
KNOK
KNOK
BRANDON, DO YOU UNDERSTAND NOTHING ABOUT YOUR FATHER?
DO YOU THINK YOU'D EVER STUMBLE UPON ANYTHING HE WISHED TO PROTECT YOU FROM, EVEN AFTER HIS DEATH?
PROTECT . . . ?

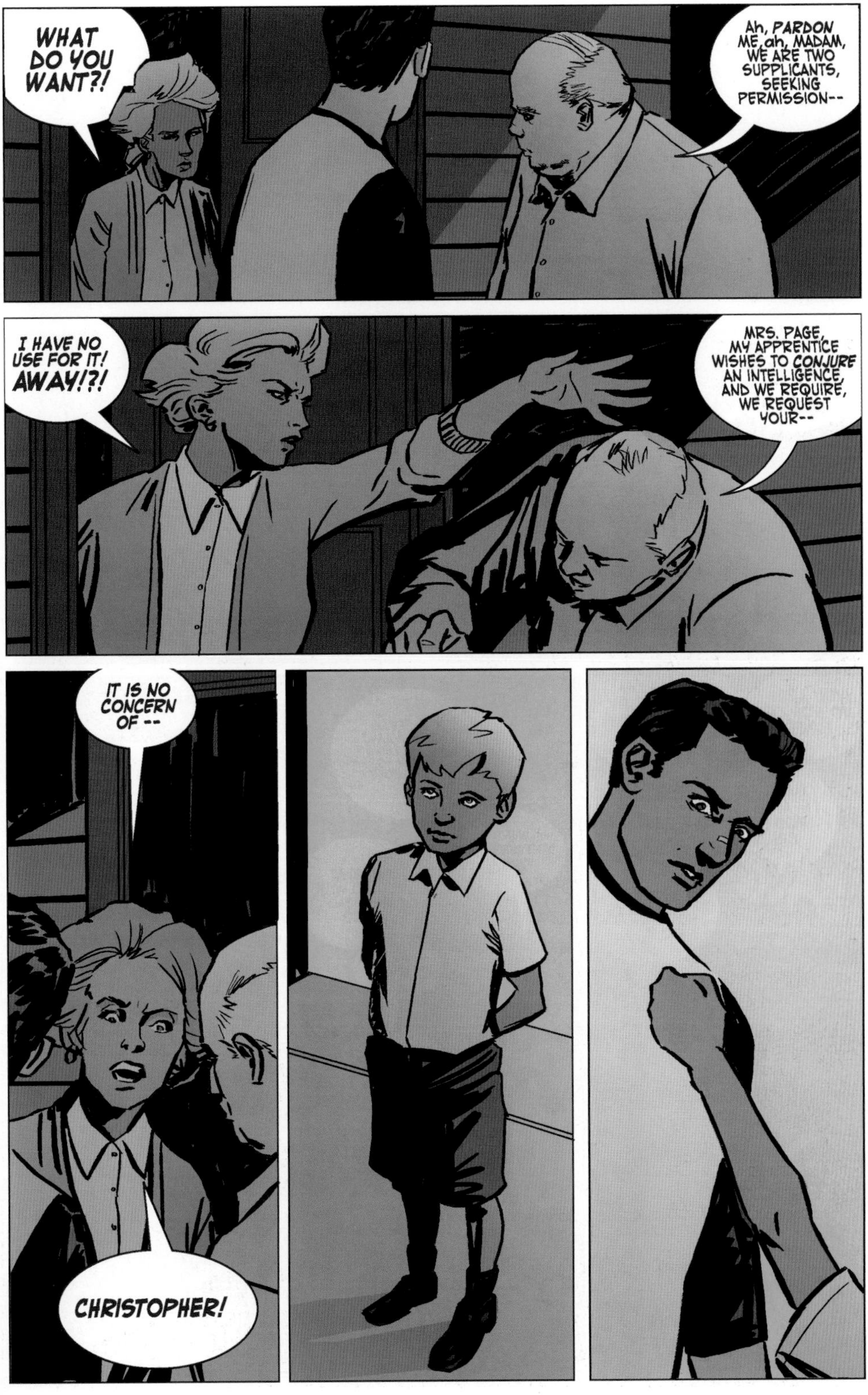
WHAT DO YOU WANT?!
Ah, PARDON ME, ah, MADAM, WE ARE TWO SUPPLICANTS, SEEKING PERMISSION--
I HAVE NO USE FOR IT! AWAY!?!
MRS. PAGE, MY APPRENTICE WISHES TO CONJURE AN INTELLIGENCE, AND WE REQUIRE, WE REQUEST YOUR--
IT IS NO CONCERN OF --
CHRISTOPHER!

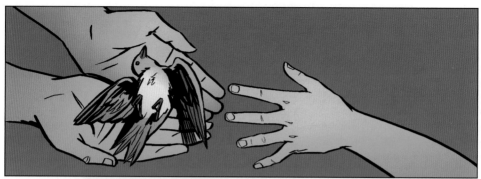

THAT IS THE FINAL STRAW, YOU FILTHY BEAST!

YOU ARE NO SON OF MINE!

LEFT UPON THE STAIR BY MUD-DWELLING VISION TOADS!

BACK TO THEM SHALL YOU GO, CHILD!

BANG

WELL, SHE DIDN'T TELL YOU *NOT* TO DO IT . . .

OH, SPEAK! DAMMIT! HAVE YOU NOTHING TO SAY FOR YOURSELF?!

WHAT DO I DO WITH *THIS?*

DO WHAT YOU DO WITH ANY DEAD THING.

YOU BURY IT.

SO YOU ≶ koff ≶ WENT TO THE HOSPITAL TWICE TODAY?

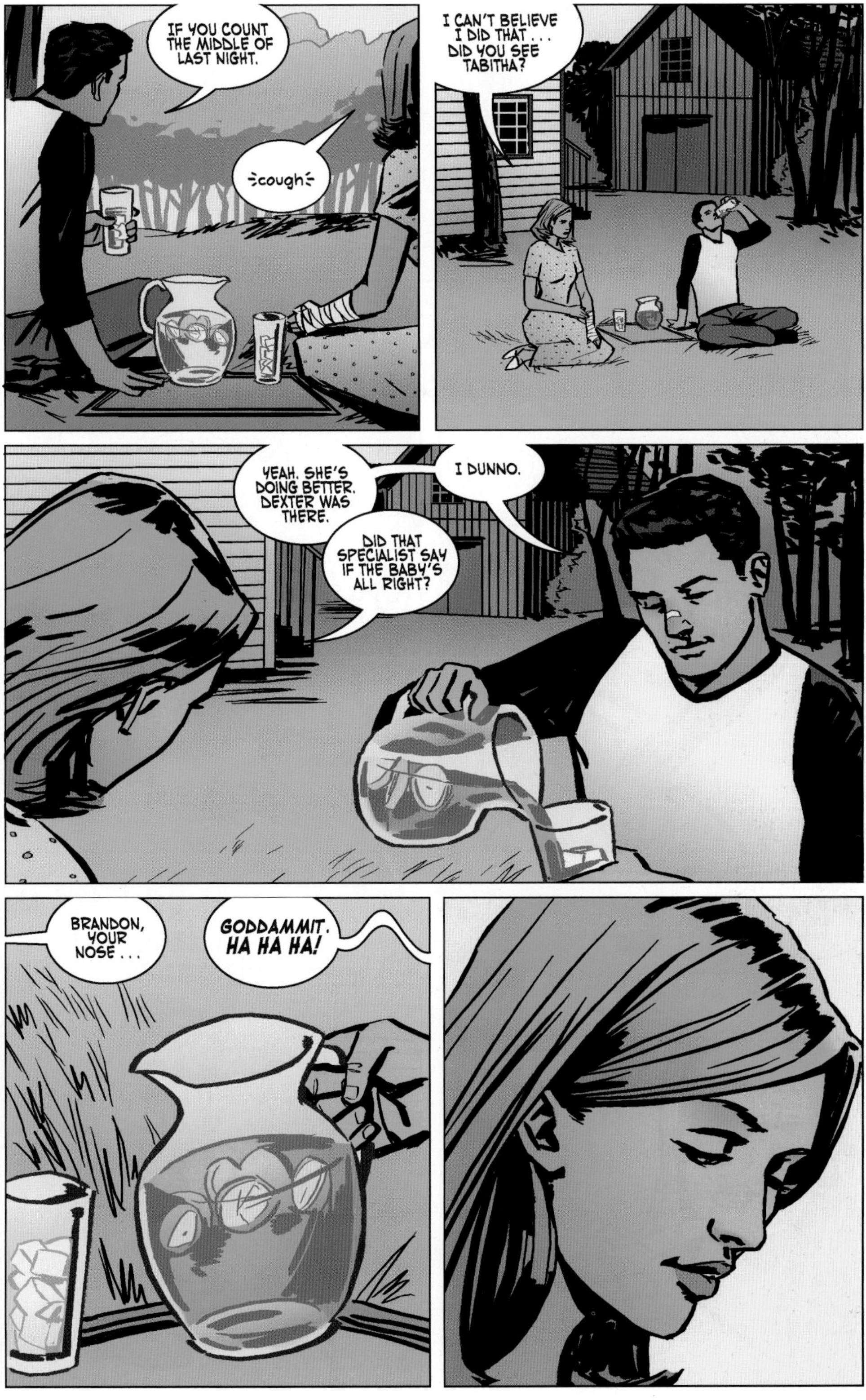
IF YOU COUNT THE MIDDLE OF LAST NIGHT.
cough
I CAN'T BELIEVE I DID THAT . . . DID YOU SEE TABITHA?
YEAH. SHE'S DOING BETTER. DEXTER WAS THERE.
I DUNNO.
DID THAT SPECIALIST SAY IF THE BABY'S ALL RIGHT?
BRANDON, YOUR NOSE . . .
GODDAMMIT. HA HA HA!

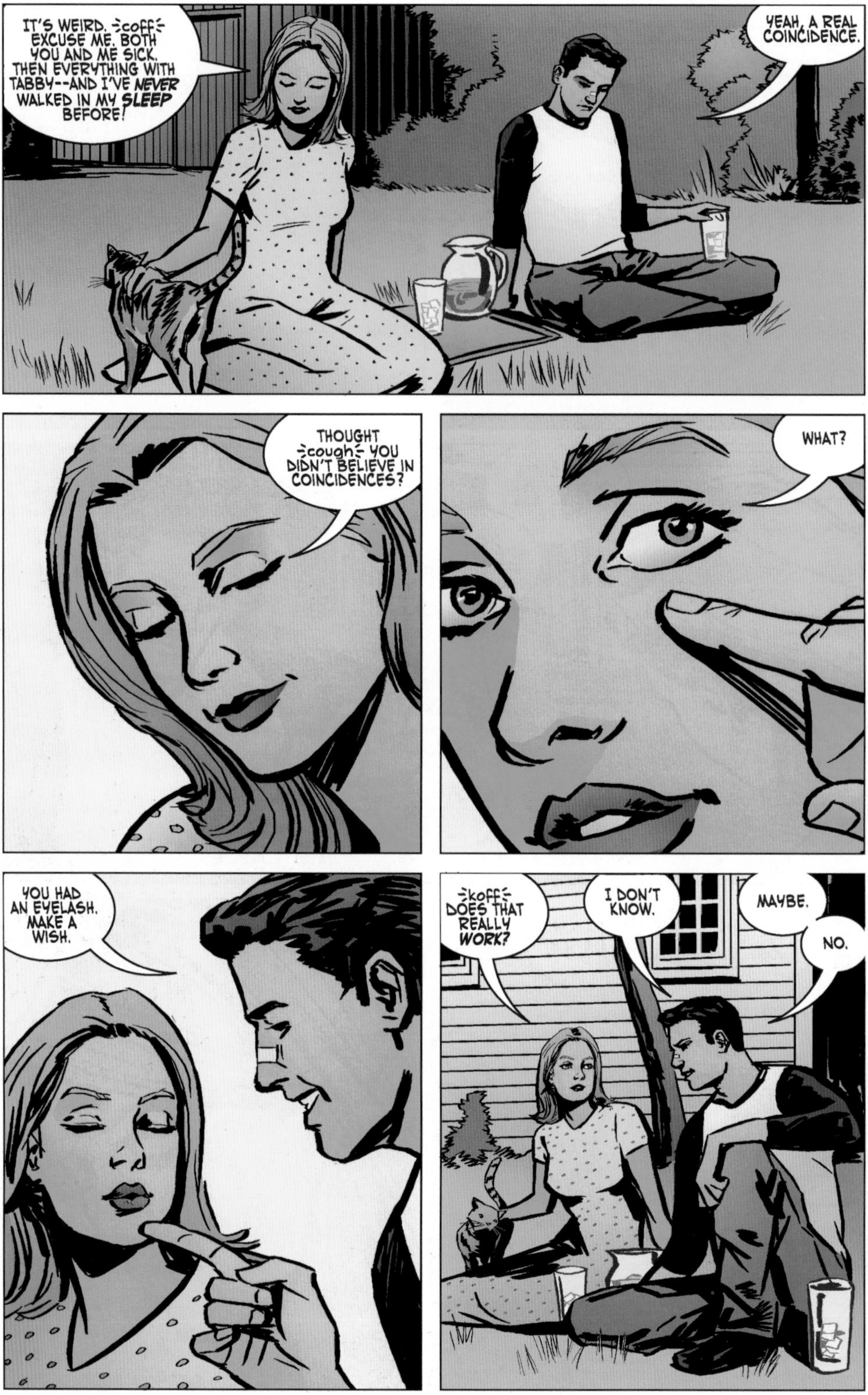
IT'S WEIRD. ≈coff≈ EXCUSE ME. BOTH YOU AND ME SICK. THEN EVERYTHING WITH TABBY--AND I'VE *NEVER* WALKED IN MY *SLEEP* BEFORE!
YEAH, A REAL COINCIDENCE.
THOUGHT ≈cough≈ YOU DIDN'T BELIEVE IN COINCIDENCES?
WHAT?
YOU HAD AN EYELASH. MAKE A WISH.
≈koff≈ DOES THAT REALLY *WORK?*
I DON'T KNOW.
MAYBE.
NO.

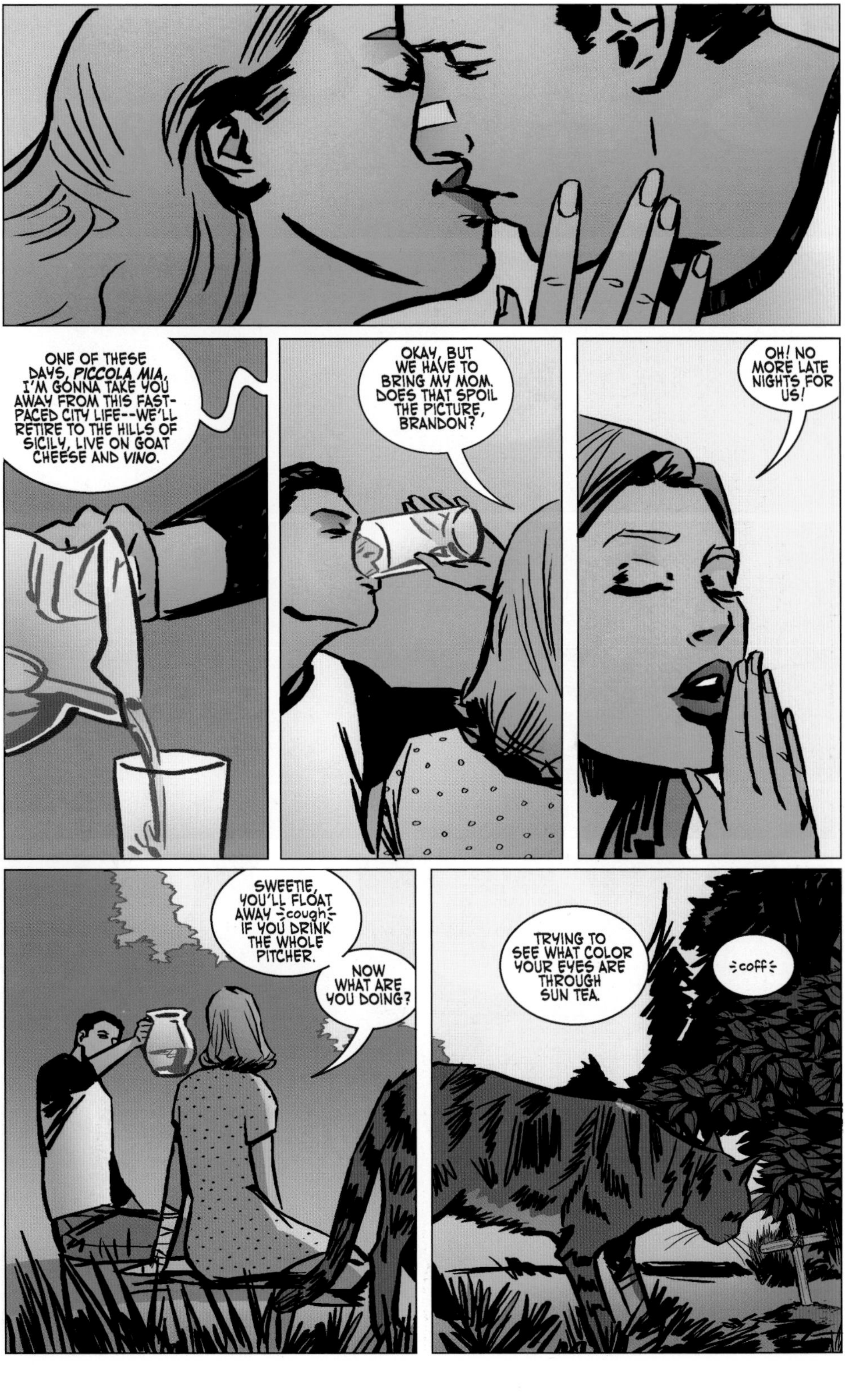
ONE OF THESE DAYS, *PICCOLA MIA*, I'M GONNA TAKE YOU AWAY FROM THIS FAST-PACED CITY LIFE--WE'LL RETIRE TO THE HILLS OF SICILY, LIVE ON GOAT CHEESE AND *VINO*.
OKAY, BUT WE HAVE TO BRING MY MOM. DOES THAT SPOIL THE PICTURE, BRANDON?
OH! NO MORE LATE NIGHTS FOR US!
SWEETIE, YOU'LL FLOAT AWAY *cough* IF YOU DRINK THE WHOLE PITCHER.
NOW WHAT ARE YOU DOING?
TRYING TO SEE WHAT COLOR YOUR EYES ARE THROUGH SUN TEA.
coff

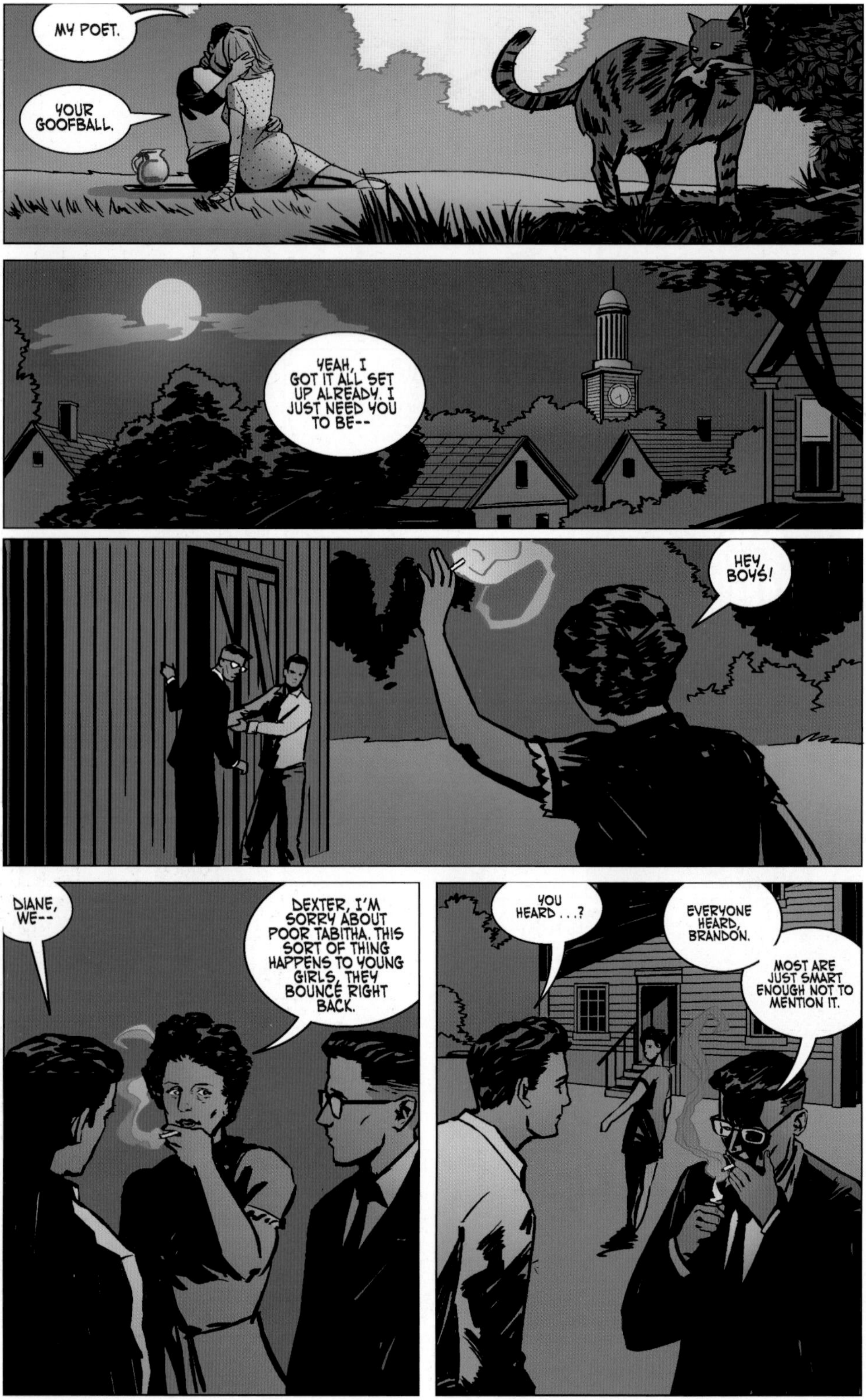
MY POET.
YOUR GOOFBALL.
YEAH, I GOT IT ALL SET UP ALREADY. I JUST NEED YOU TO BE--
HEY, BOYS!
DIANE, WE--
DEXTER, I'M SORRY ABOUT POOR TABITHA. THIS SORT OF THING HAPPENS TO YOUNG GIRLS. THEY BOUNCE RIGHT BACK.
YOU HEARD...?
EVERYONE HEARD, BRANDON.
MOST ARE JUST SMART ENOUGH NOT TO MENTION IT.

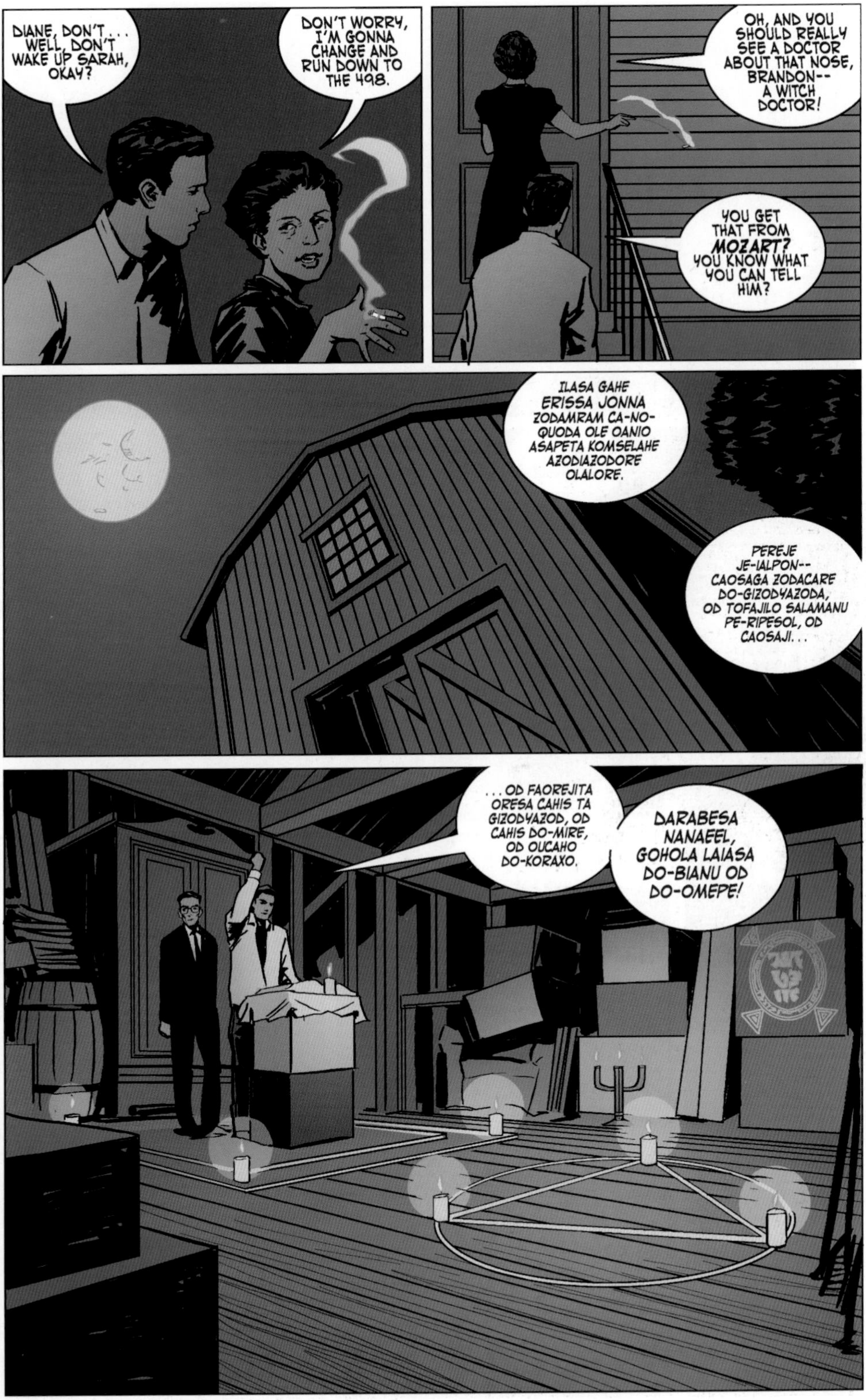
DIANE, DON'T . . . WELL, DON'T WAKE UP SARAH, OKAY?
DON'T WORRY, I'M GONNA CHANGE AND RUN DOWN TO THE 498.
OH, AND YOU SHOULD REALLY SEE A DOCTOR ABOUT THAT NOSE, BRANDON-- A WITCH DOCTOR!
YOU GET THAT FROM MOZART? YOU KNOW WHAT YOU CAN TELL HIM?
ILASA GAHE ERISSA JONNA ZODAMRAM CA-NO-QUODA OLE OANIO ASAPETA KOMSELAHE AZODIAZODORE OLALORE.
PEREJE JE-IALPON-- CAOSAGA ZODACARE DO-GIZODYAZODA, OD TOFAJILO SALAMANU PE-RIPESOL, OD CAOSAJI . . .
. . . OD FAOREJITA ORESA CAHIS TA GIZODYAZOD, OD CAHIS DO-MIRE, OD OUCAHO DO-KORAXO.
DARABESA NANAEEL, GOHOLA LAIASA DO-BIANU OD DO-OMEPE!

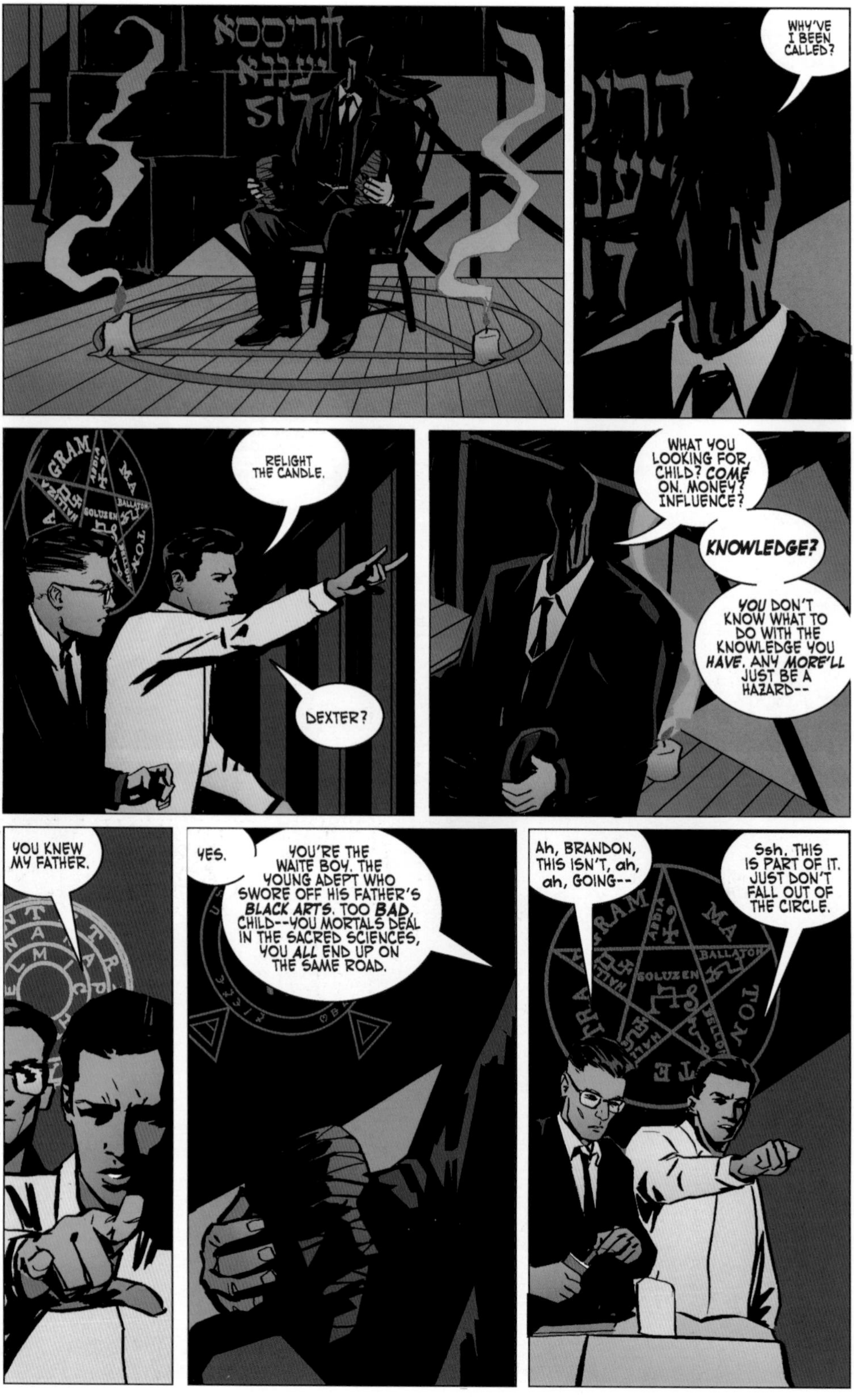
WHY'VE I BEEN CALLED?
RELIGHT THE CANDLE.
DEXTER?
WHAT YOU LOOKING FOR, CHILD? COME ON. MONEY? INFLUENCE?
KNOWLEDGE?
YOU DON'T KNOW WHAT TO DO WITH THE KNOWLEDGE YOU HAVE. ANY MORE'LL JUST BE A HAZARD--
YOU KNEW MY FATHER.
YES.
YOU'RE THE WAITE BOY. THE YOUNG ADEPT WHO SWORE OFF HIS FATHER'S BLACK ARTS. TOO BAD, CHILD--YOU MORTALS DEAL IN THE SACRED SCIENCES, YOU ALL END UP ON THE SAME ROAD.
Ah, BRANDON, THIS ISN'T, ah, ah, GOING--
Ssh. THIS IS PART OF IT. JUST DON'T FALL OUT OF THE CIRCLE.

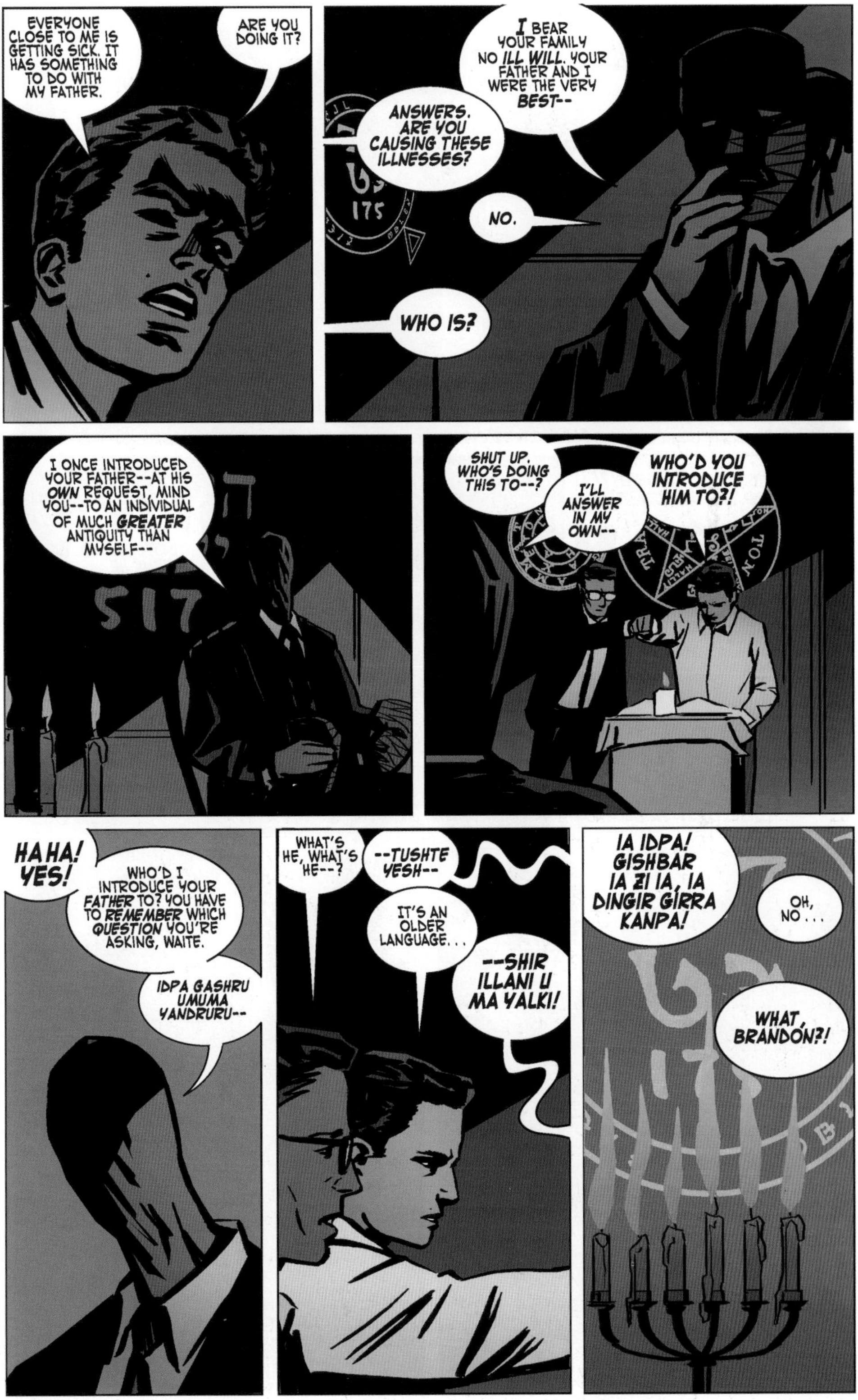
EVERYONE CLOSE TO ME IS GETTING SICK. IT HAS SOMETHING TO DO WITH MY FATHER.
ARE YOU DOING IT?
I BEAR YOUR FAMILY NO ILL WILL. YOUR FATHER AND I WERE THE VERY BEST--
ANSWERS. ARE YOU CAUSING THESE ILLNESSES?
NO.
WHO IS?
I ONCE INTRODUCED YOUR FATHER--AT HIS OWN REQUEST, MIND YOU--TO AN INDIVIDUAL OF MUCH GREATER ANTIQUITY THAN MYSELF--
SHUT UP. WHO'S DOING THIS TO--?
I'LL ANSWER IN MY OWN--
WHO'D YOU INTRODUCE HIM TO?!
HA HA! YES!
WHO'D I INTRODUCE YOUR FATHER TO? YOU HAVE TO REMEMBER WHICH QUESTION YOU'RE ASKING, WAITE.
IDPA GASHRU UMUMA YANDRURU--
WHAT'S HE, WHAT'S HE--?
--TUSHTE YESH--
IT'S AN OLDER LANGUAGE. . .
--SHIR ILLANI U MA YALKI!
IA IDPA! GISHBAR IA ZI IA, IA DINGIR GIRRA KANPA!
OH, NO . . .
WHAT, BRANDON?!

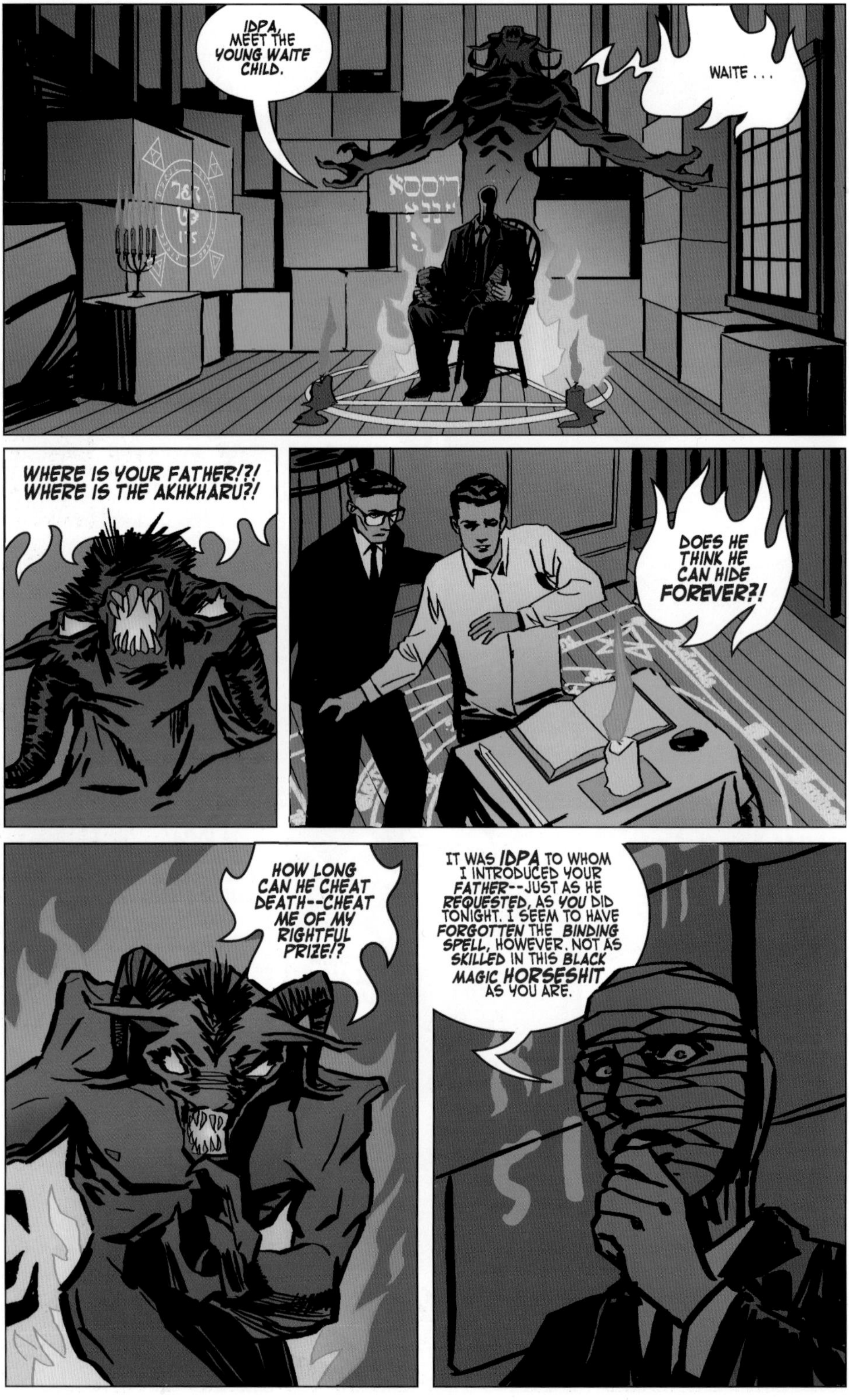
IDPA, MEET THE YOUNG WAITE CHILD.
WAITE . . .
WHERE IS YOUR FATHER!?! WHERE IS THE AKHKHARU?!
DOES HE THINK HE CAN HIDE FOREVER?!
HOW LONG CAN HE CHEAT DEATH--CHEAT ME OF MY RIGHTFUL PRIZE!?
IT WAS IDPA TO WHOM I INTRODUCED YOUR FATHER--JUST AS HE REQUESTED, AS YOU DID TONIGHT. I SEEM TO HAVE FORGOTTEN THE BINDING SPELL, HOWEVER. NOT AS SKILLED IN THIS BLACK MAGIC HORSESHIT AS YOU ARE.

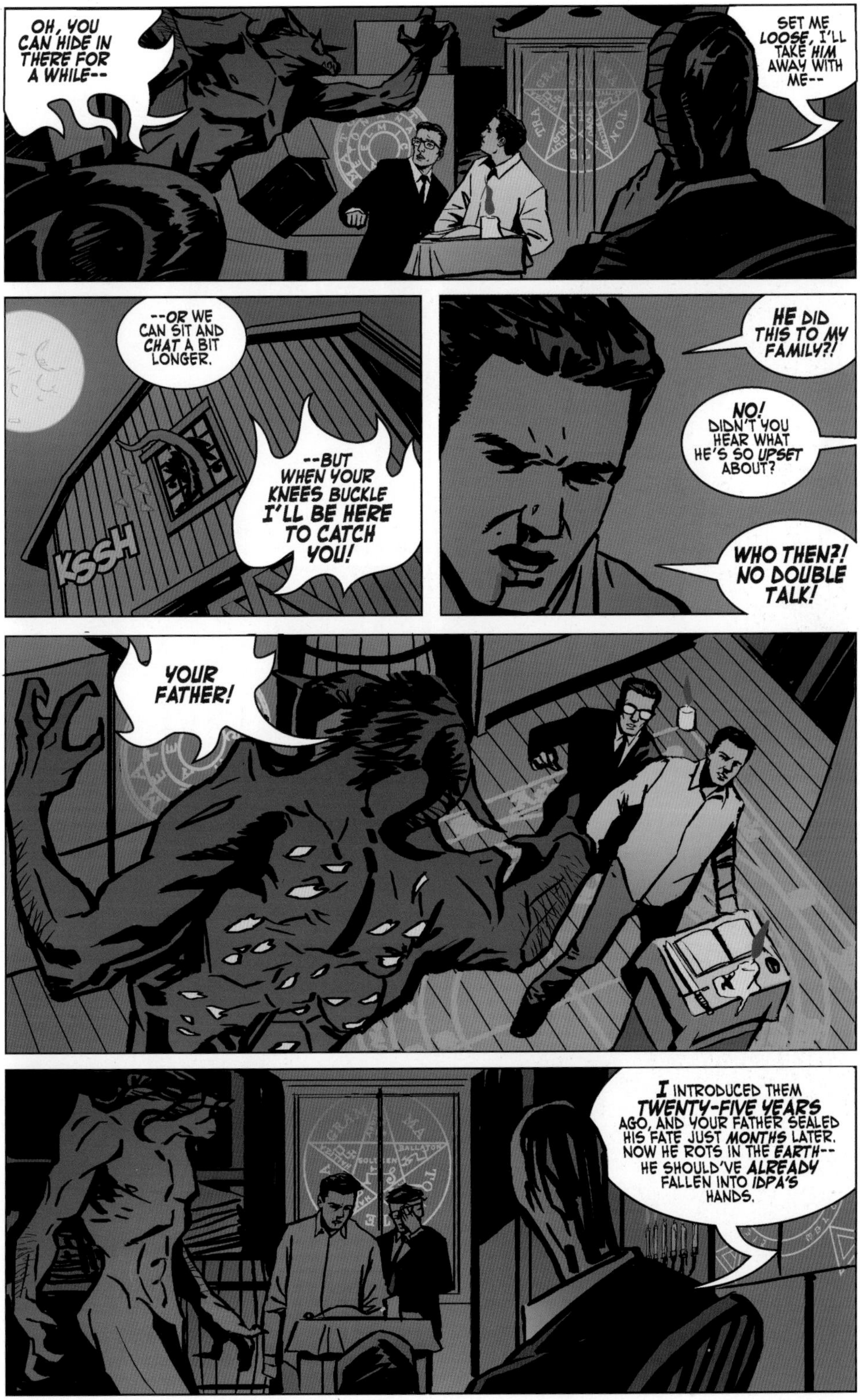

OH, YOU CAN HIDE IN THERE FOR A WHILE--
SET ME LOOSE, I'LL TAKE HIM AWAY WITH ME--
--OR WE CAN SIT AND CHAT A BIT LONGER.
--BUT WHEN YOUR KNEES BUCKLE I'LL BE HERE TO CATCH YOU!
KSSH
HE DID THIS TO MY FAMILY?!
NO! DIDN'T YOU HEAR WHAT HE'S SO UPSET ABOUT?
WHO THEN?! NO DOUBLE TALK!
YOUR FATHER!
I INTRODUCED THEM TWENTY-FIVE YEARS AGO, AND YOUR FATHER SEALED HIS FATE JUST MONTHS LATER. NOW HE ROTS IN THE EARTH-- HE SHOULD'VE ALREADY FALLEN INTO IDPA'S HANDS.

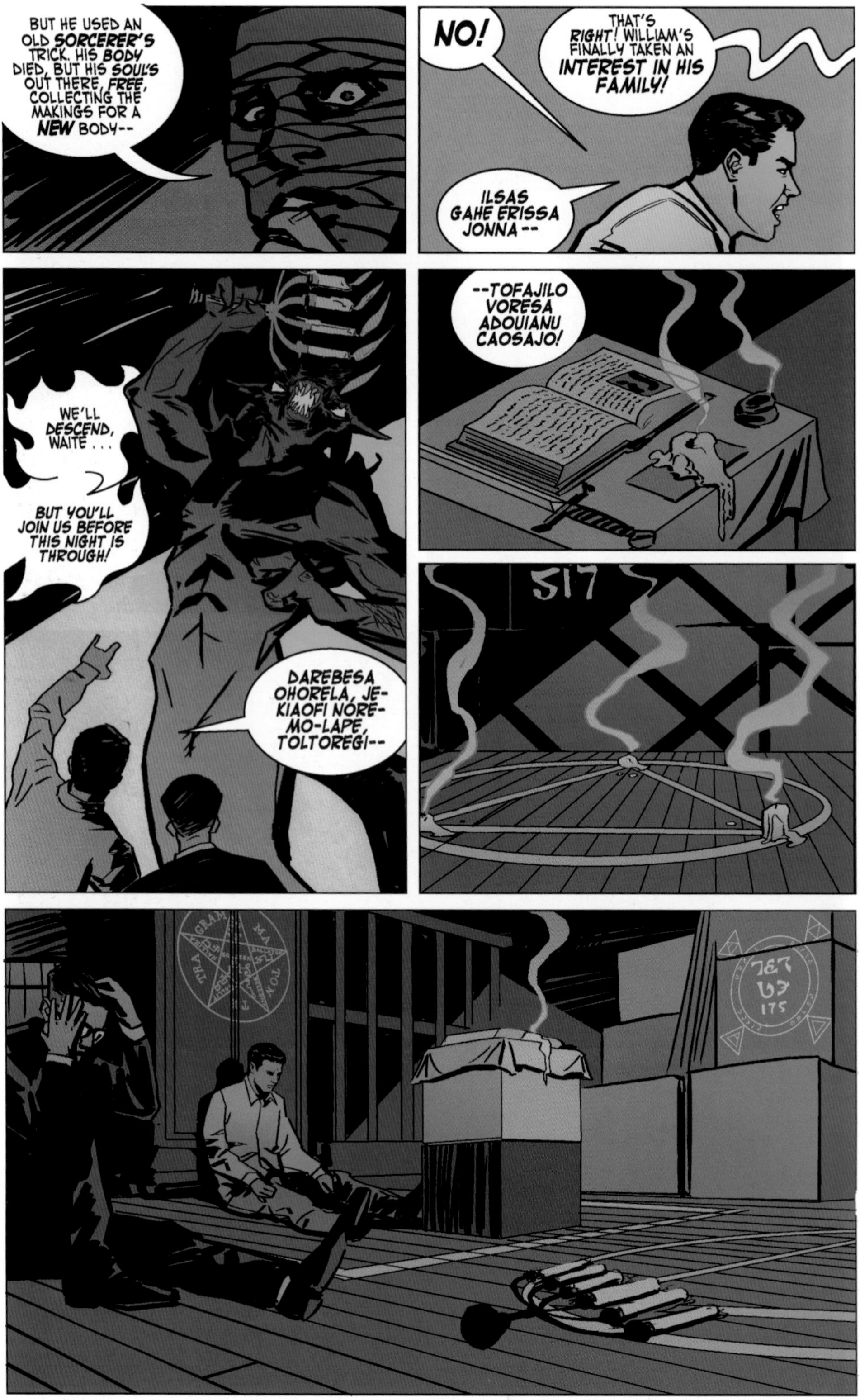

BUT HE USED AN OLD SORCERER'S TRICK. HIS BODY DIED, BUT HIS SOUL'S OUT THERE, FREE, COLLECTING THE MAKINGS FOR A NEW BODY--
NO!
THAT'S RIGHT! WILLIAM'S FINALLY TAKEN AN INTEREST IN HIS FAMILY!
ILSAS GAHE ERISSA JONNA --
WE'LL DESCEND, WAITE . . .
BUT YOU'LL JOIN US BEFORE THIS NIGHT IS THROUGH!
DAREBESA OHORELA, JE-KIAOFI NÓRE-MO-LAPE, TOLTOREGI--
--TOFAJILO VORESA ADOUIANU CAOSAJO!
517

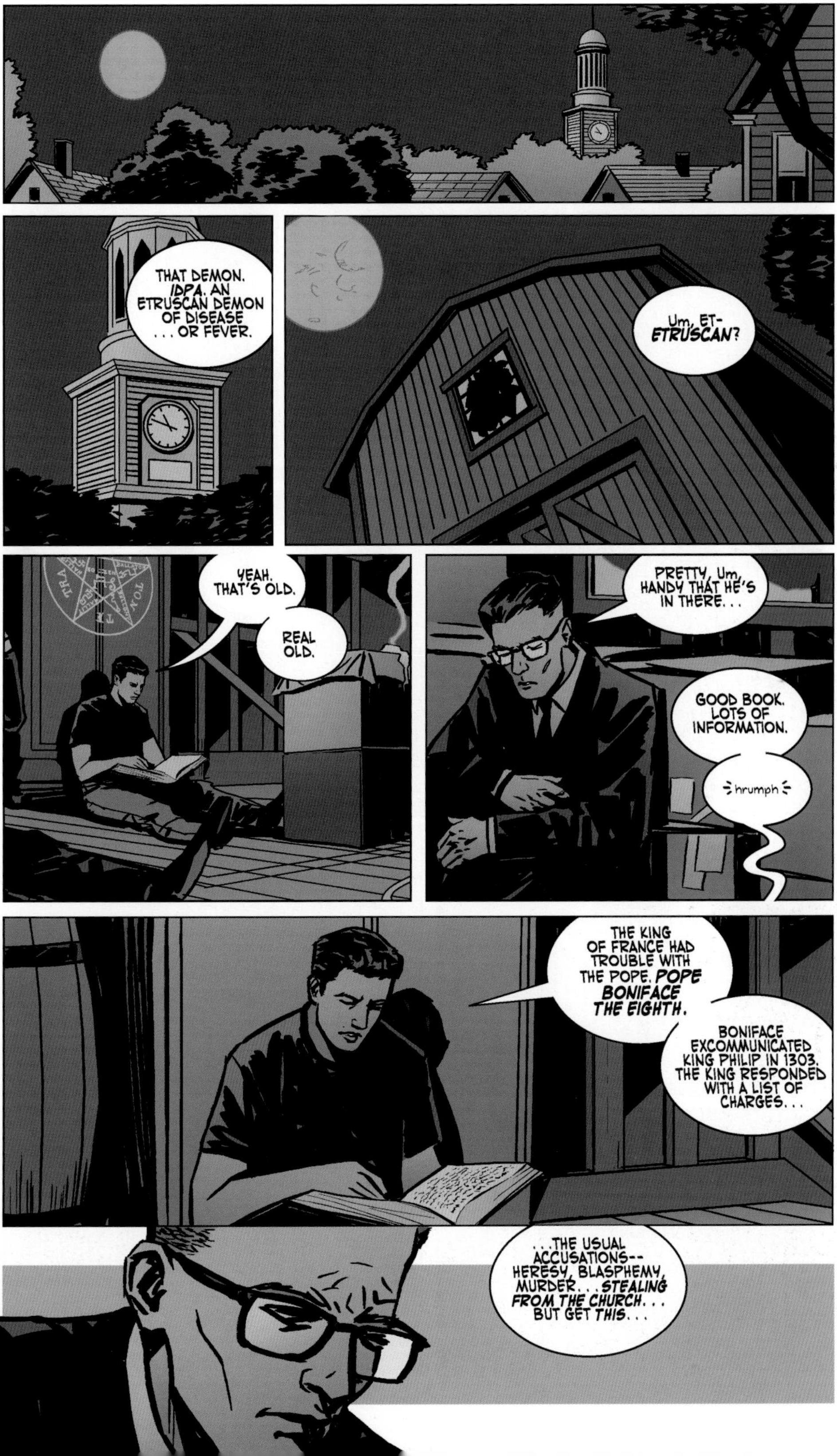
THAT DEMON. IDPA. AN ETRUSCAN DEMON OF DISEASE . . . OR FEVER.
Um, ET-ETRUSCAN?
YEAH. THAT'S OLD.
REAL OLD.
PRETTY, Um, HANDY THAT HE'S IN THERE. . .
GOOD BOOK. LOTS OF INFORMATION.
hrumph
THE KING OF FRANCE HAD TROUBLE WITH THE POPE. POPE BONIFACE THE EIGHTH.
BONIFACE EXCOMMUNICATED KING PHILIP IN 1303. THE KING RESPONDED WITH A LIST OF CHARGES. . .
. . .THE USUAL ACCUSATIONS-- HERESY, BLASPHEMY, MURDER. . . STEALING FROM THE CHURCH. . . BUT GET THIS. . .

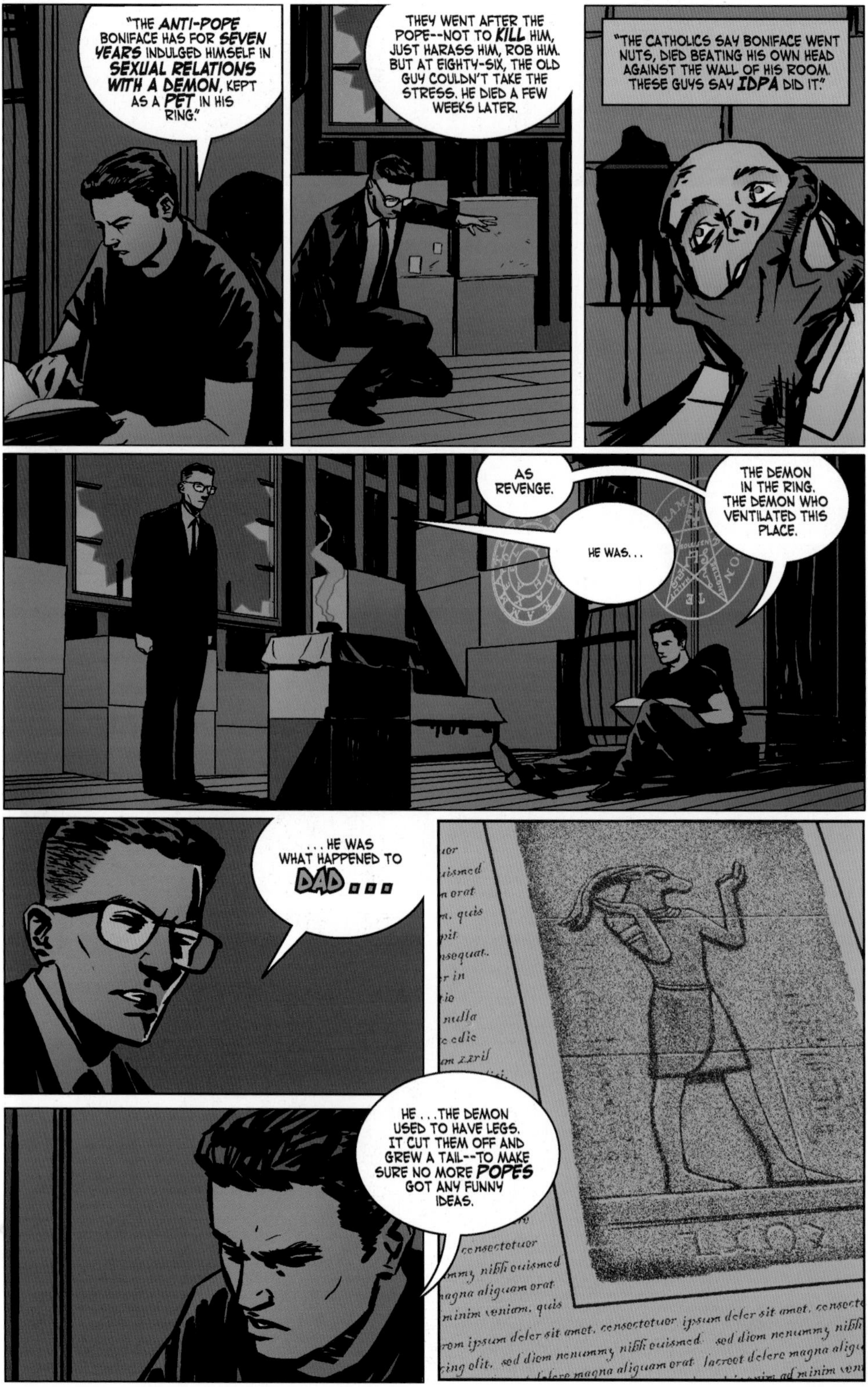

"THE ANTI-POPE BONIFACE HAS FOR SEVEN YEARS INDULGED HIMSELF IN SEXUAL RELATIONS WITH A DEMON, KEPT AS A PET IN HIS RING."
THEY WENT AFTER THE POPE--NOT TO KILL HIM, JUST HARASS HIM, ROB HIM. BUT AT EIGHTY-SIX, THE OLD GUY COULDN'T TAKE THE STRESS. HE DIED A FEW WEEKS LATER.
"THE CATHOLICS SAY BONIFACE WENT NUTS, DIED BEATING HIS OWN HEAD AGAINST THE WALL OF HIS ROOM. THESE GUYS SAY IDPA DID IT."
AS REVENGE.
THE DEMON IN THE RING. THE DEMON WHO VENTILATED THIS PLACE.
HE WAS. . .
. . . HE WAS WHAT HAPPENED TO DAD . . .
HE . . . THE DEMON USED TO HAVE LEGS. IT CUT THEM OFF AND GREW A TAIL--TO MAKE SURE NO MORE POPES GOT ANY FUNNY IDEAS.

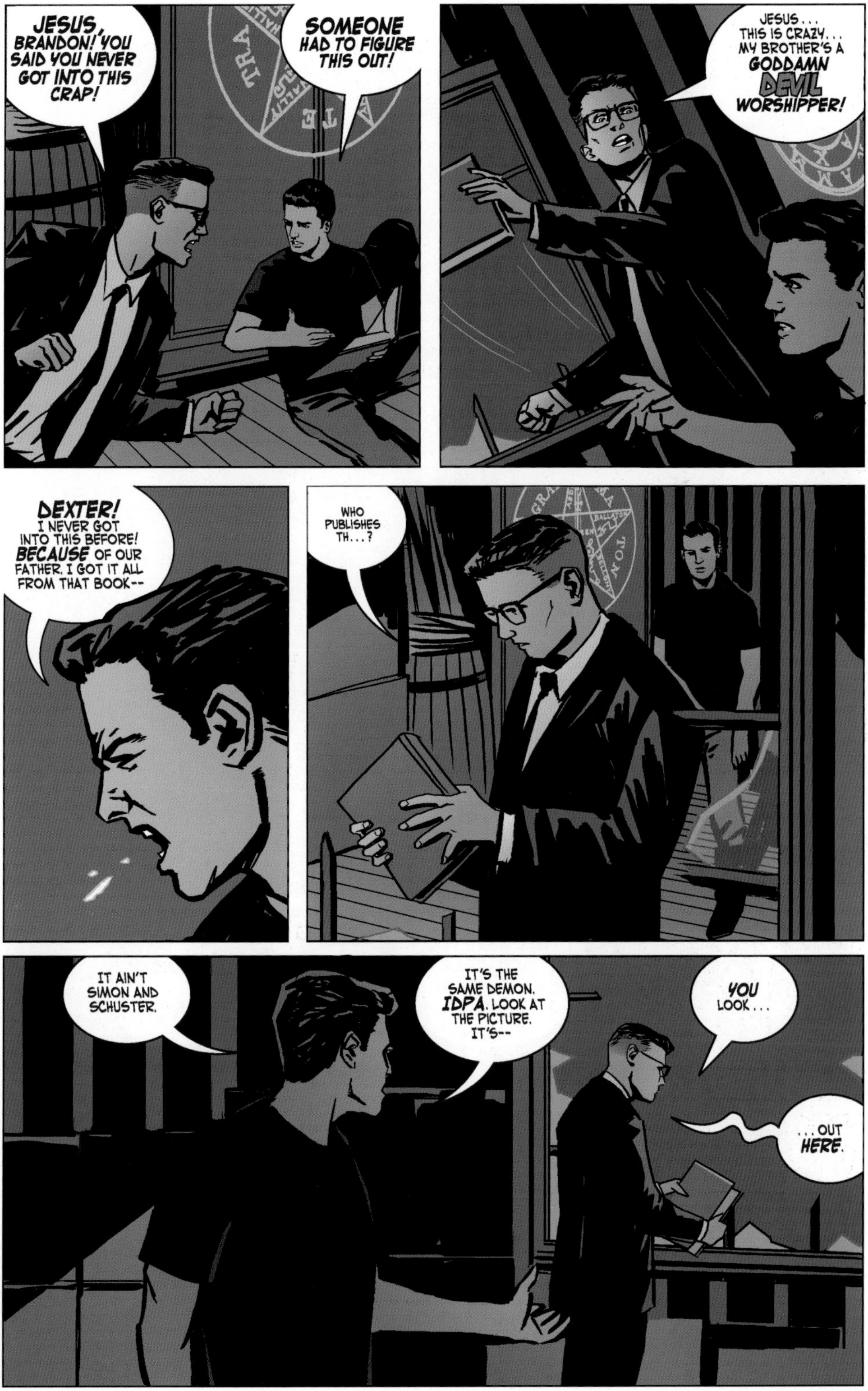
JESUS, BRANDON! YOU SAID YOU NEVER GOT INTO THIS CRAP!
SOMEONE HAD TO FIGURE THIS OUT!
JESUS... THIS IS CRAZY... MY BROTHER'S A GODDAMN DEVIL WORSHIPPER!
DEXTER! I NEVER GOT INTO THIS BEFORE! BECAUSE OF OUR FATHER. I GOT IT ALL FROM THAT BOOK--
WHO PUBLISHES TH...?
IT AIN'T SIMON AND SCHUSTER.
IT'S THE SAME DEMON, IDPA. LOOK AT THE PICTURE. IT'S--
YOU LOOK...
...OUT HERE.

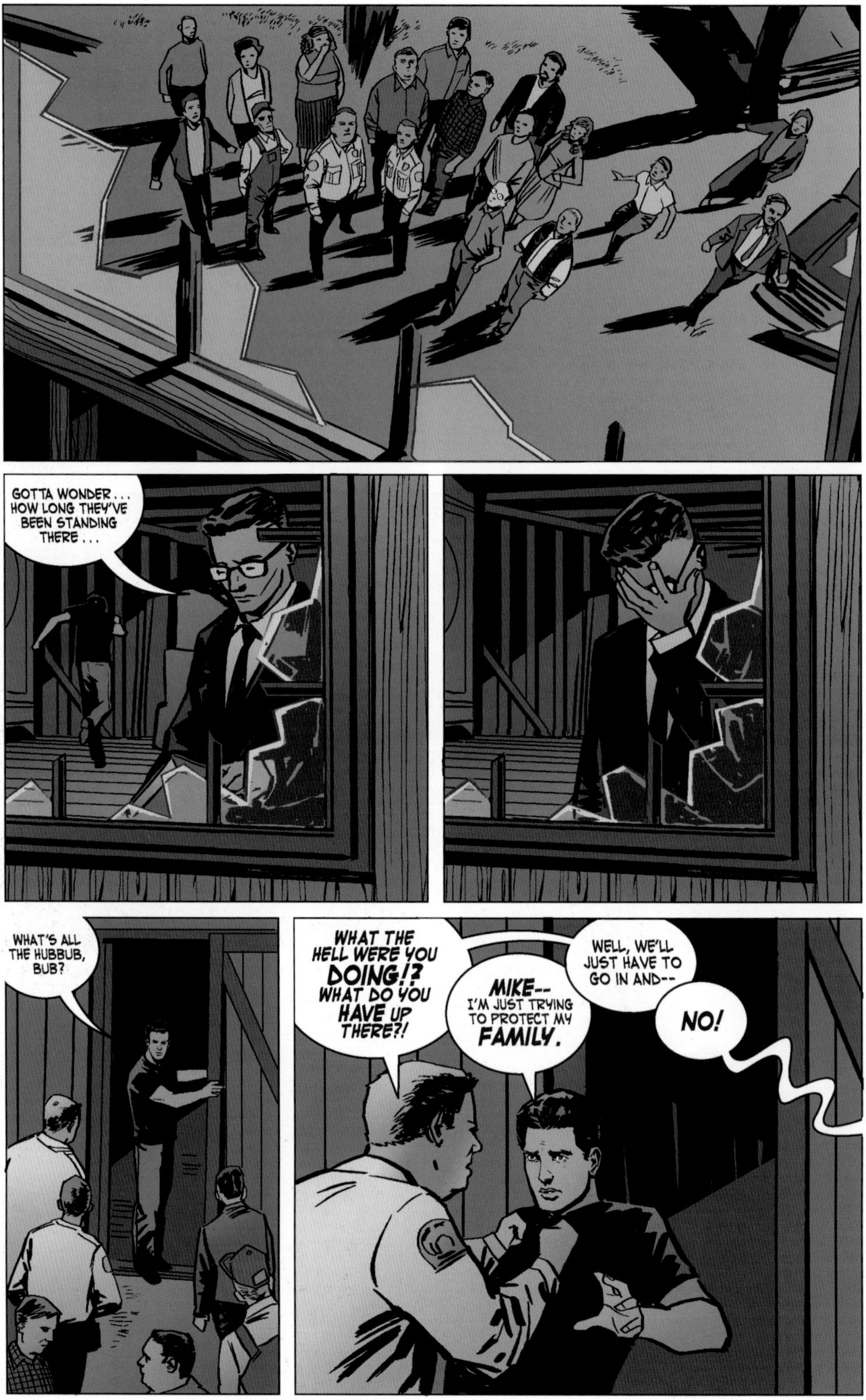
GOTTA WONDER . . . HOW LONG THEY'VE BEEN STANDING THERE . . .
WHAT'S ALL THE HUBBUB, BUB?
WHAT THE HELL WERE YOU DOING!? WHAT DO YOU HAVE UP THERE?!
MIKE-- I'M JUST TRYING TO PROTECT MY FAMILY.
WELL, WE'LL JUST HAVE TO GO IN AND--
NO!

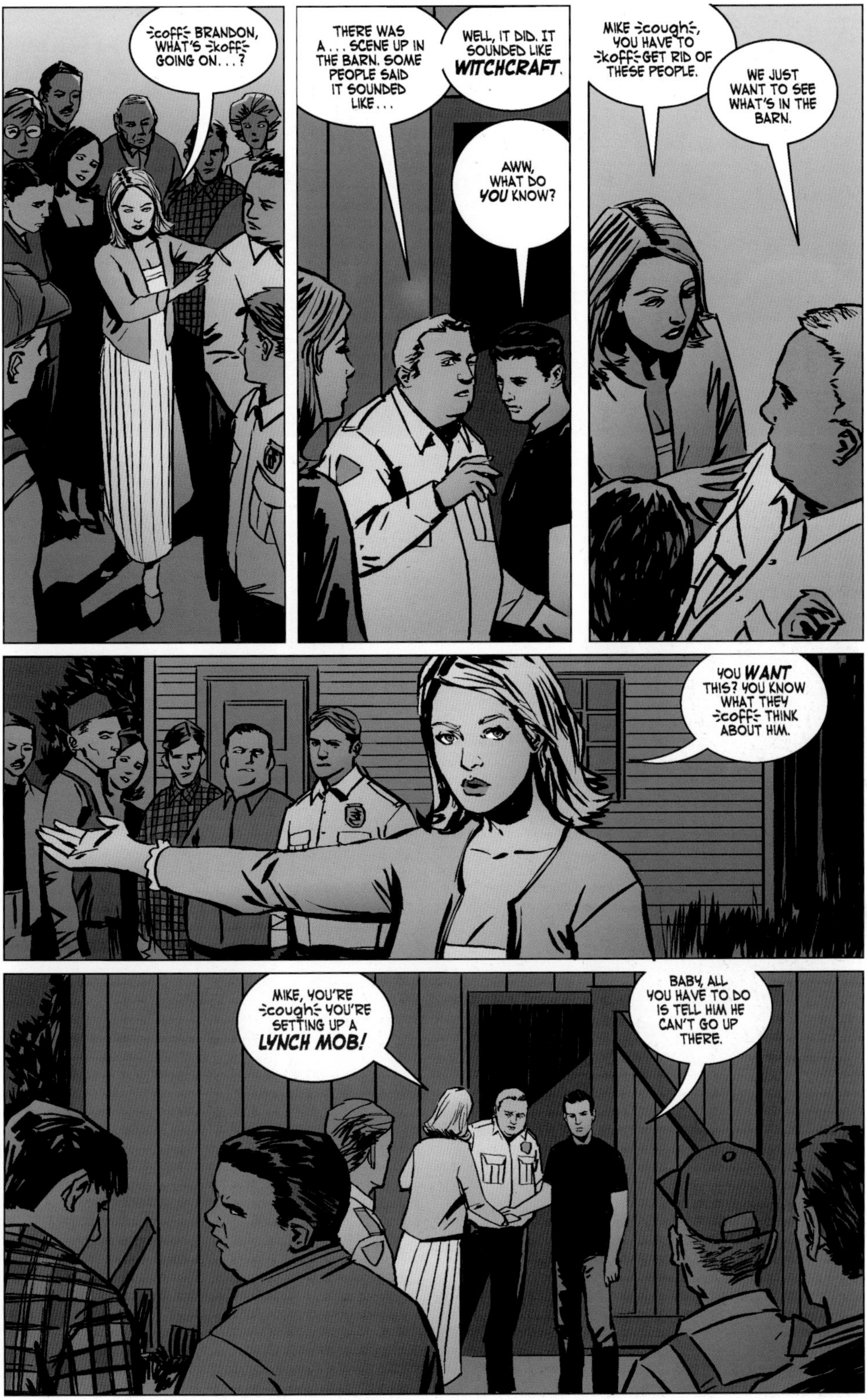

-coff- BRANDON, WHAT'S -koff- GOING ON. . . ?
THERE WAS A . . . SCENE UP IN THE BARN. SOME PEOPLE SAID IT SOUNDED LIKE . . .
WELL, IT DID. IT SOUNDED LIKE WITCHCRAFT.
AWW, WHAT DO YOU KNOW?
MIKE -cough-, YOU HAVE TO -koff- GET RID OF THESE PEOPLE.
WE JUST WANT TO SEE WHAT'S IN THE BARN.
YOU WANT THIS? YOU KNOW WHAT THEY -coff- THINK ABOUT HIM.
MIKE, YOU'RE -cough- YOU'RE SETTING UP A LYNCH MOB!
BABY, ALL YOU HAVE TO DO IS TELL HIM HE CAN'T GO UP THERE.

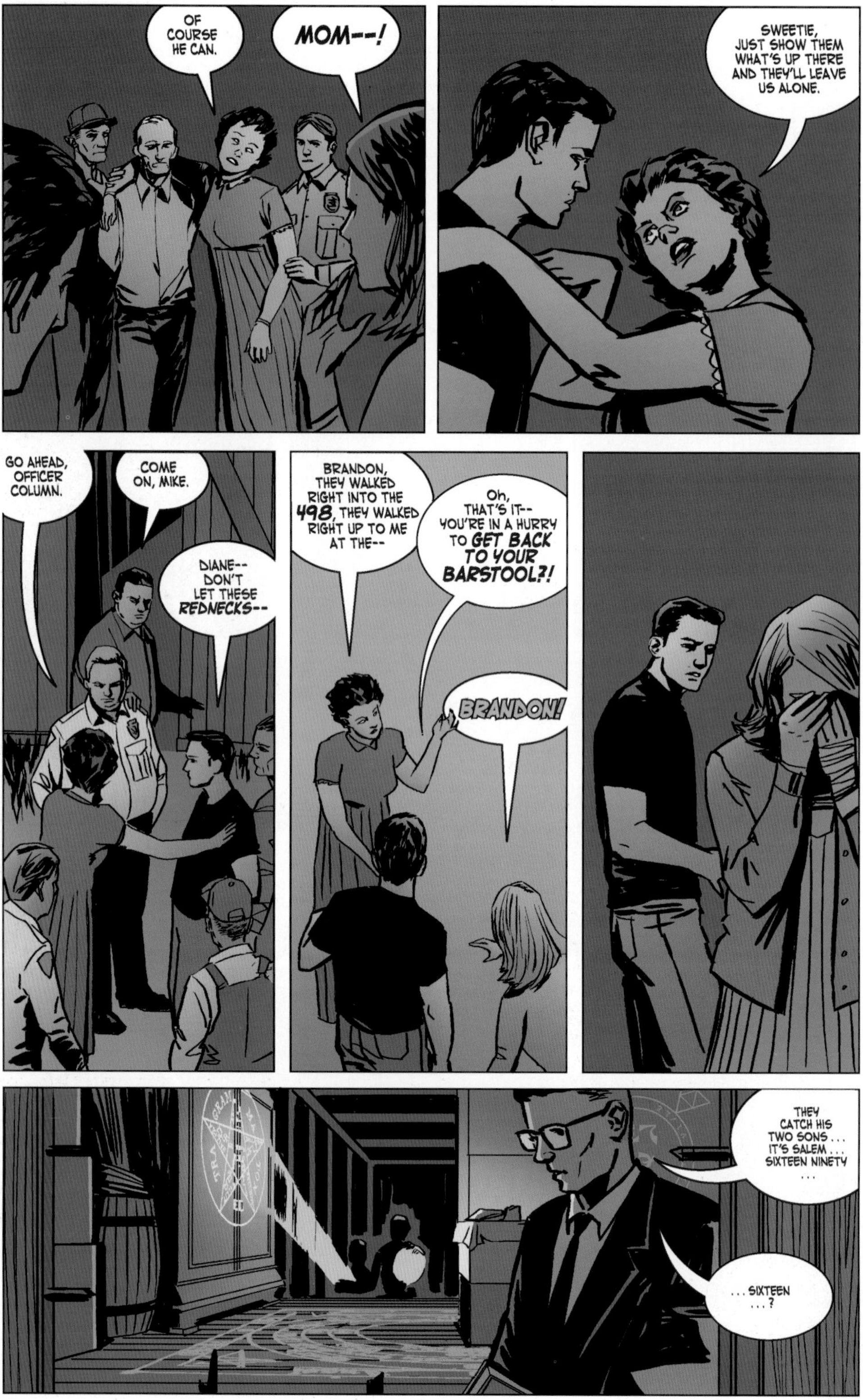
OF COURSE HE CAN.
MOM--!
SWEETIE, JUST SHOW THEM WHAT'S UP THERE AND THEY'LL LEAVE US ALONE.
GO AHEAD, OFFICER COLUMN.
COME ON, MIKE.
DIANE-- DON'T LET THESE REDNECKS--
BRANDON, THEY WALKED RIGHT INTO THE 498, THEY WALKED RIGHT UP TO ME AT THE--
Oh, THAT'S IT-- YOU'RE IN A HURRY TO GET BACK TO YOUR BARSTOOL?!
BRANDON!
THEY CATCH HIS TWO SONS . . . IT'S SALEM . . . SIXTEEN NINETY . . .
. . . SIXTEEN . . . ?

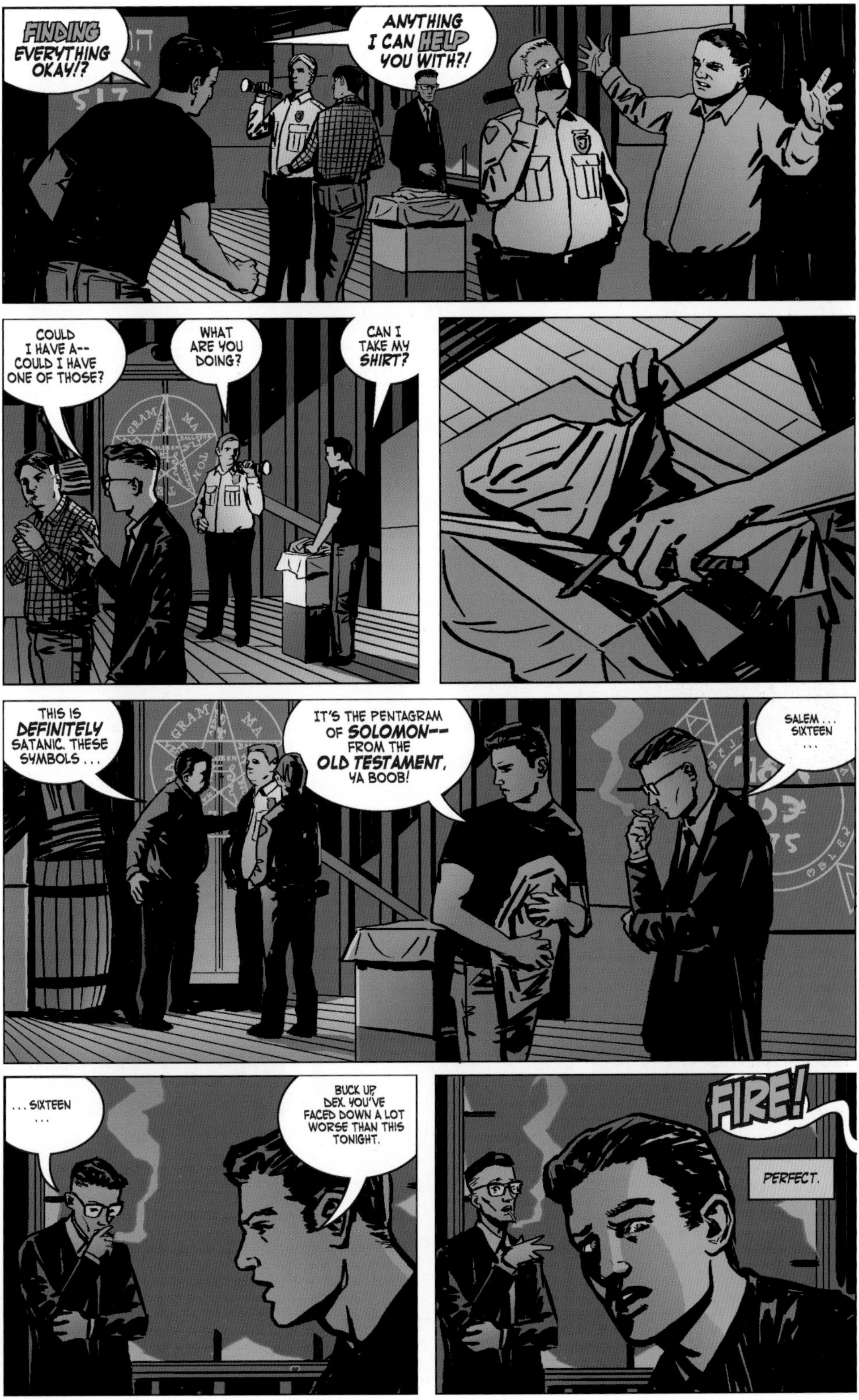
FINDING EVERYTHING OKAY!?
ANYTHING I CAN HELP YOU WITH?!
COULD I HAVE A-- COULD I HAVE ONE OF THOSE?
WHAT ARE YOU DOING?
CAN I TAKE MY SHIRT?
THIS IS DEFINITELY SATANIC. THESE SYMBOLS . . .
IT'S THE PENTAGRAM OF SOLOMON-- FROM THE OLD TESTAMENT, YA BOOB!
SALEM . . . SIXTEEN . . .
. . . SIXTEEN . . .
BUCK UP, DEX. YOU'VE FACED DOWN A LOT WORSE THAN THIS TONIGHT.
FIRE!
PERFECT.

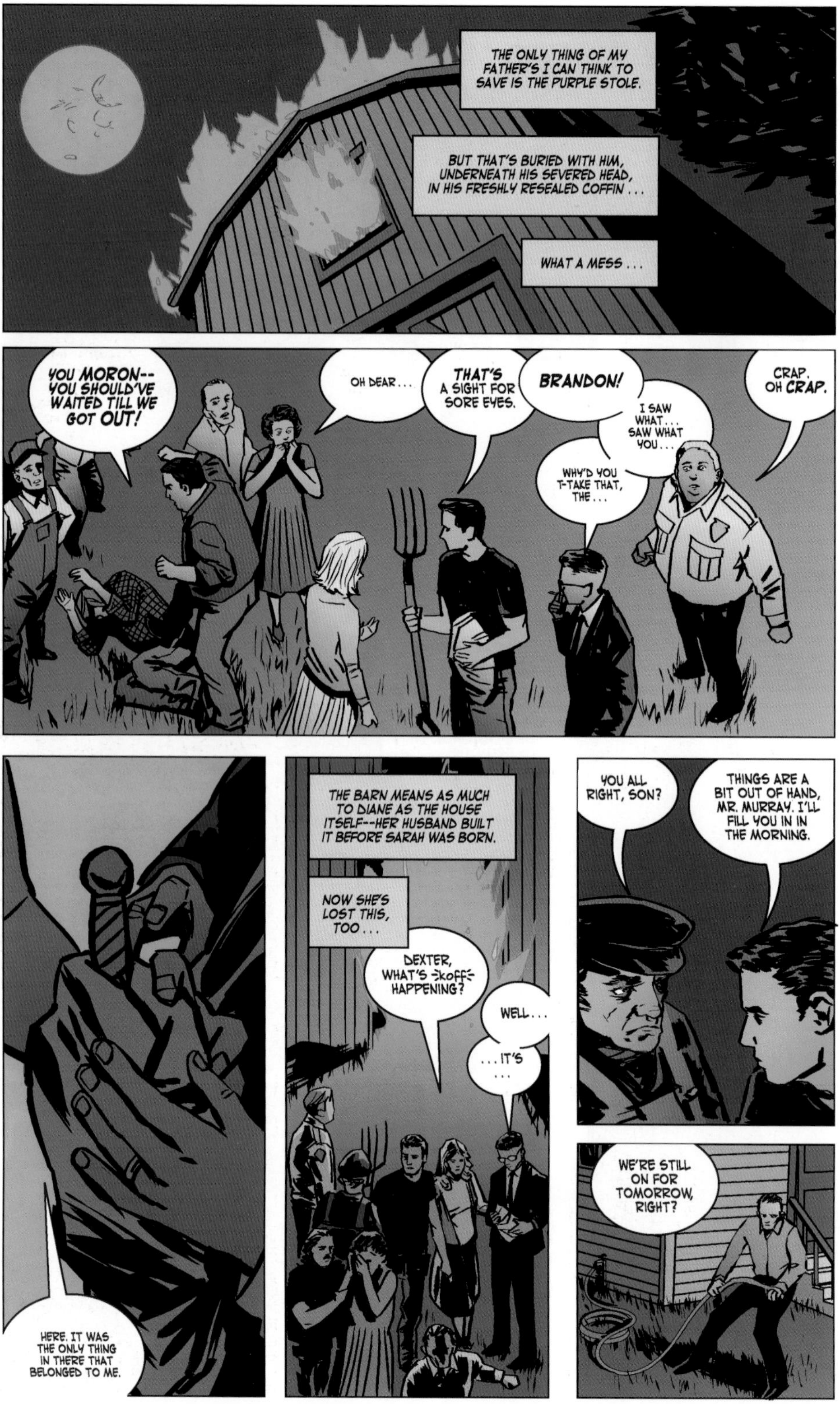
THE ONLY THING OF MY FATHER'S I CAN THINK TO SAVE IS THE PURPLE STOLE.
BUT THAT'S BURIED WITH HIM, UNDERNEATH HIS SEVERED HEAD, IN HIS FRESHLY RESEALED COFFIN . . .
WHAT A MESS . . .
YOU MORON-- YOU SHOULD'VE WAITED TILL WE GOT OUT!
OH DEAR . . .
THAT'S A SIGHT FOR SORE EYES.
BRANDON!
I SAW WHAT . . . SAW WHAT YOU . . .
WHY'D YOU T-TAKE THAT, THE . . .
CRAP. OH CRAP.
HERE. IT WAS THE ONLY THING IN THERE THAT BELONGED TO ME.
THE BARN MEANS AS MUCH TO DIANE AS THE HOUSE ITSELF--HER HUSBAND BUILT IT BEFORE SARAH WAS BORN.
NOW SHE'S LOST THIS, TOO . . .
DEXTER, WHAT'S -koff- HAPPENING?
WELL . . .
. . . IT'S . . .
YOU ALL RIGHT, SON?
THINGS ARE A BIT OUT OF HAND, MR. MURRAY. I'LL FILL YOU IN IN THE MORNING.
WE'RE STILL ON FOR TOMORROW, RIGHT?

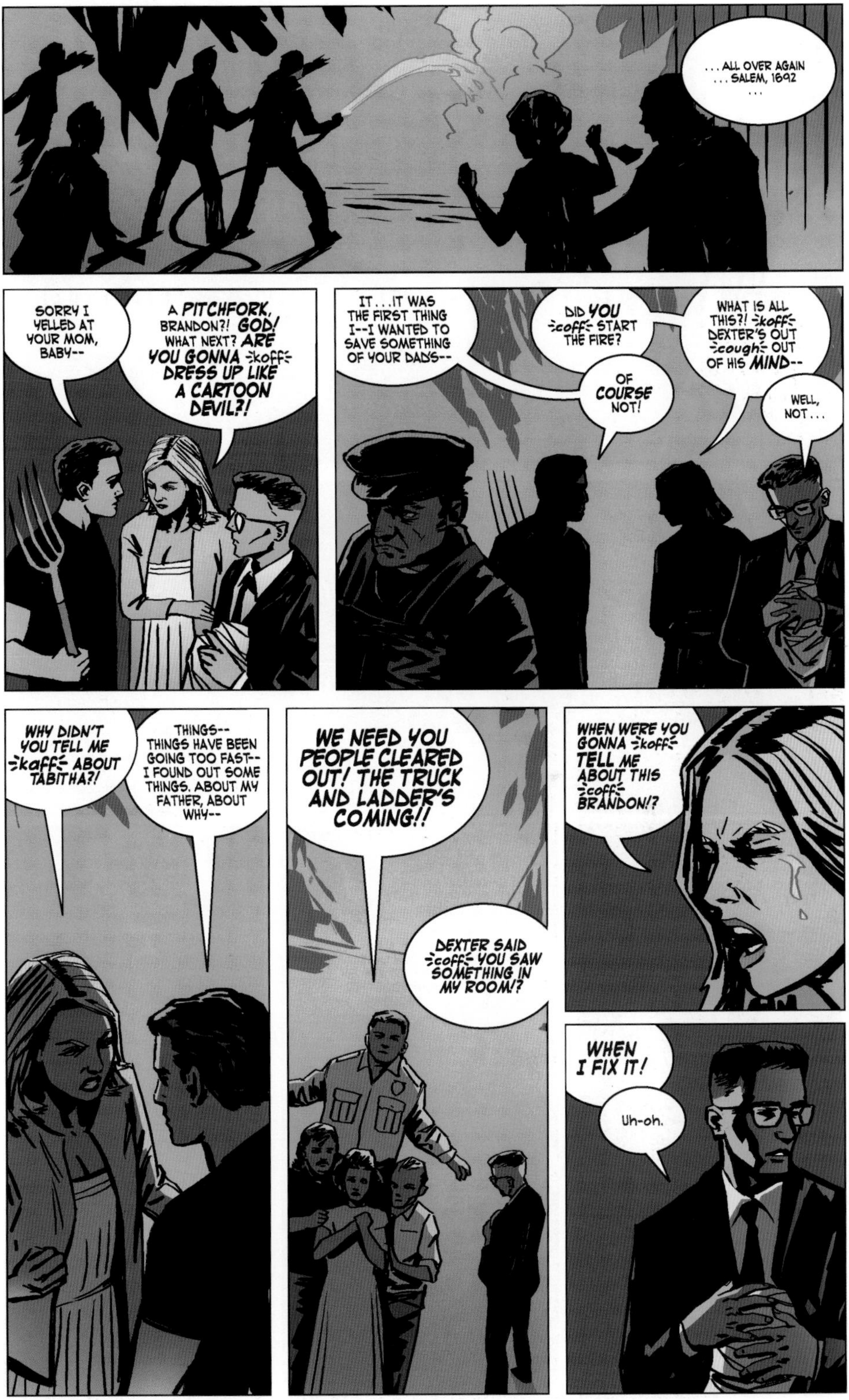
. . . ALL OVER AGAIN . . . SALEM, 1692 . . .
SORRY I YELLED AT YOUR MOM, BABY--
A PITCHFORK, BRANDON?! GOD! WHAT NEXT? ARE YOU GONNA -koff- DRESS UP LIKE A CARTOON DEVIL?!
IT . . . IT WAS THE FIRST THING I--I WANTED TO SAVE SOMETHING OF YOUR DAD'S--
DID YOU -coff- START THE FIRE?
OF COURSE NOT!
WHAT IS ALL THIS?! -koff- DEXTER'S OUT -cough- OUT OF HIS MIND--
WELL, NOT . . .
WHY DIDN'T YOU TELL ME -kaff- ABOUT TABITHA?!
THINGS-- THINGS HAVE BEEN GOING TOO FAST-- I FOUND OUT SOME THINGS. ABOUT MY FATHER, ABOUT WHY--
WE NEED YOU PEOPLE CLEARED OUT! THE TRUCK AND LADDER'S COMING!!
DEXTER SAID -coff- YOU SAW SOMETHING IN MY ROOM!?
WHEN WERE YOU GONNA -koff- TELL ME ABOUT THIS -coff- BRANDON!?
WHEN I FIX IT!
Uh-oh.

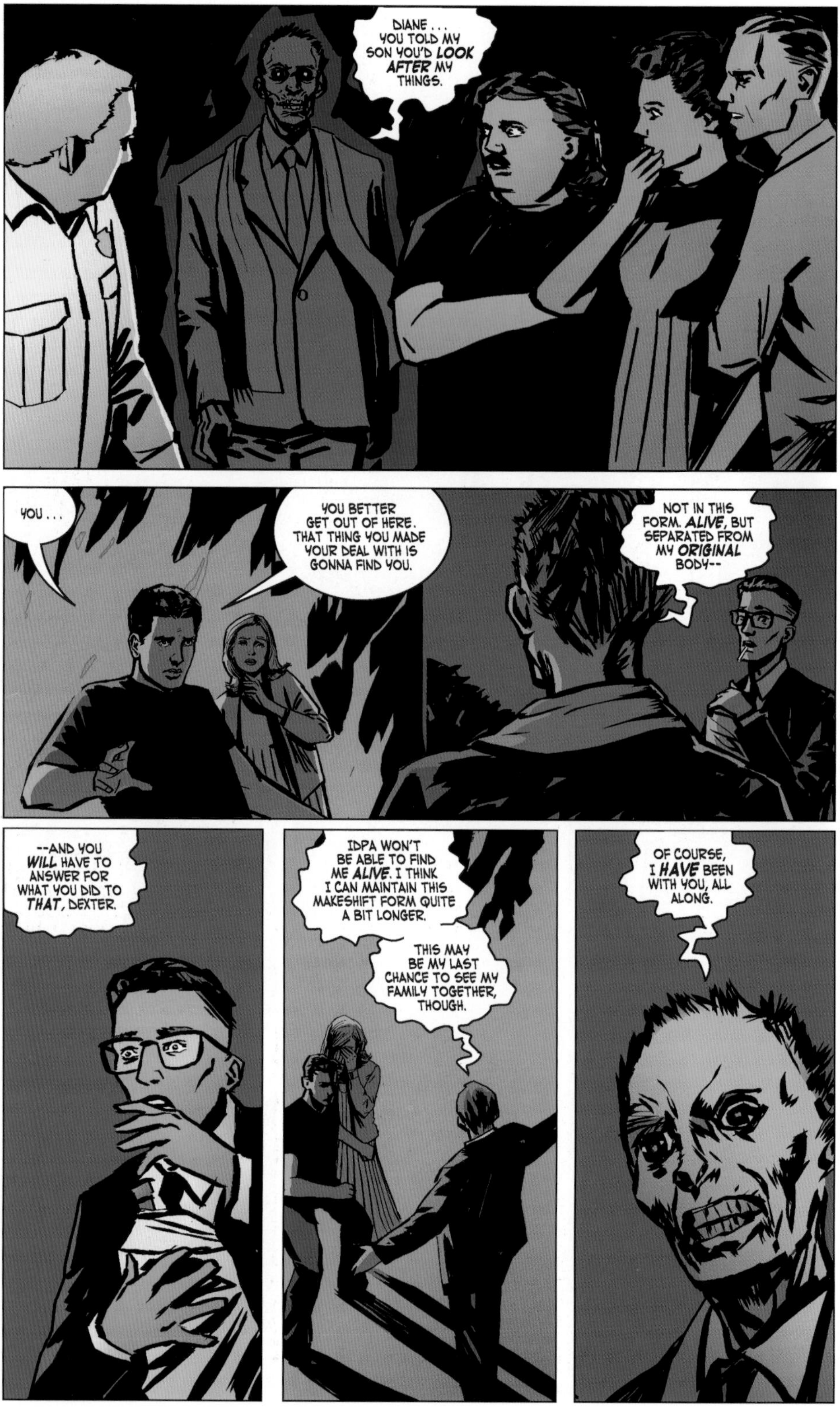
DIANE . . . YOU TOLD MY SON YOU'D LOOK AFTER MY THINGS.
YOU . . .
YOU BETTER GET OUT OF HERE. THAT THING YOU MADE YOUR DEAL WITH IS GONNA FIND YOU.
NOT IN THIS FORM. ALIVE, BUT SEPARATED FROM MY ORIGINAL BODY--
--AND YOU WILL HAVE TO ANSWER FOR WHAT YOU DID TO THAT, DEXTER.
IDPA WON'T BE ABLE TO FIND ME ALIVE. I THINK I CAN MAINTAIN THIS MAKESHIFT FORM QUITE A BIT LONGER.
THIS MAY BE MY LAST CHANCE TO SEE MY FAMILY TOGETHER, THOUGH.
OF COURSE, I HAVE BEEN WITH YOU, ALL ALONG.

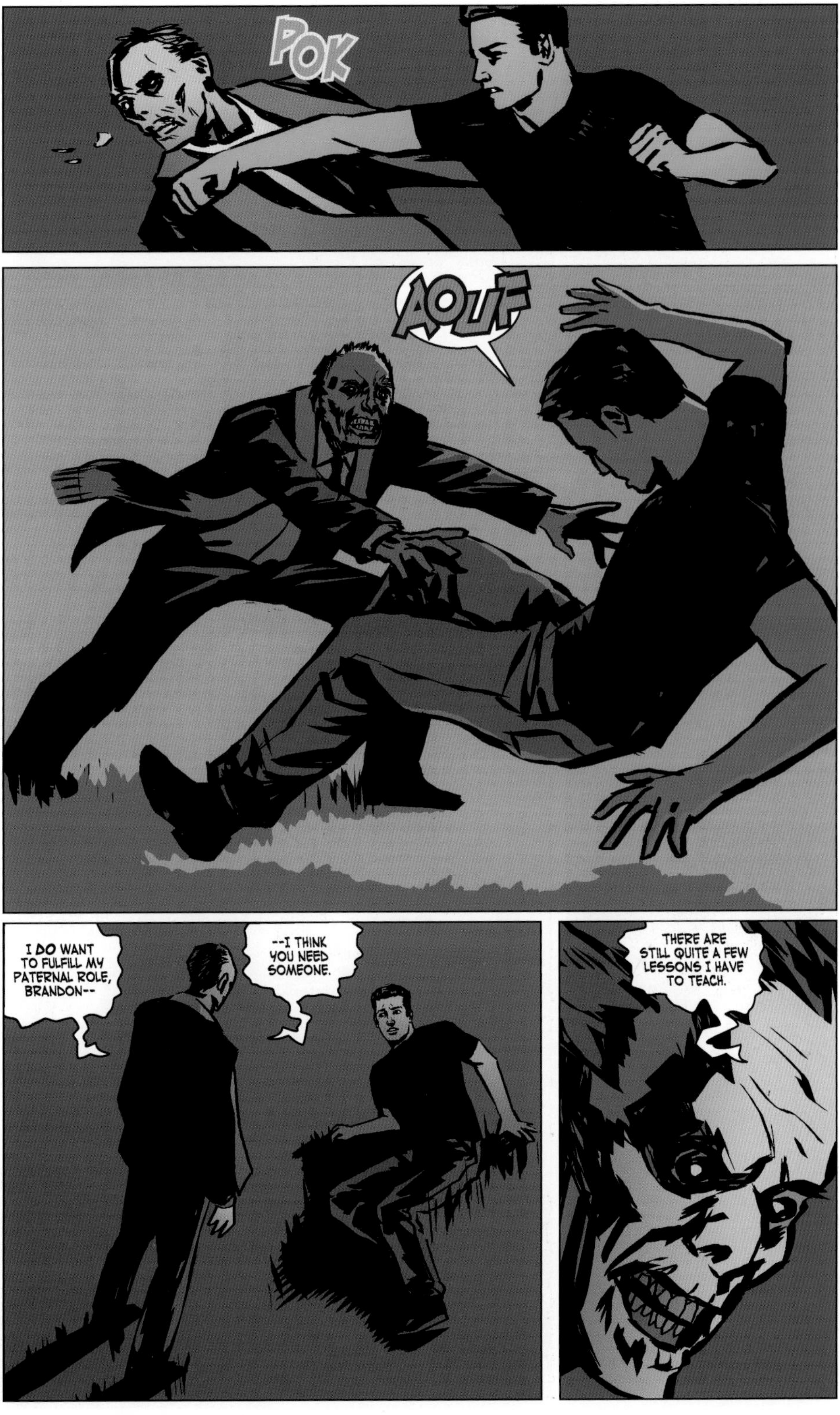
POK
AOUF
I DO WANT TO FULFILL MY PATERNAL ROLE, BRANDON--
--I THINK YOU NEED SOMEONE.
THERE ARE STILL QUITE A FEW LESSONS I HAVE TO TEACH.

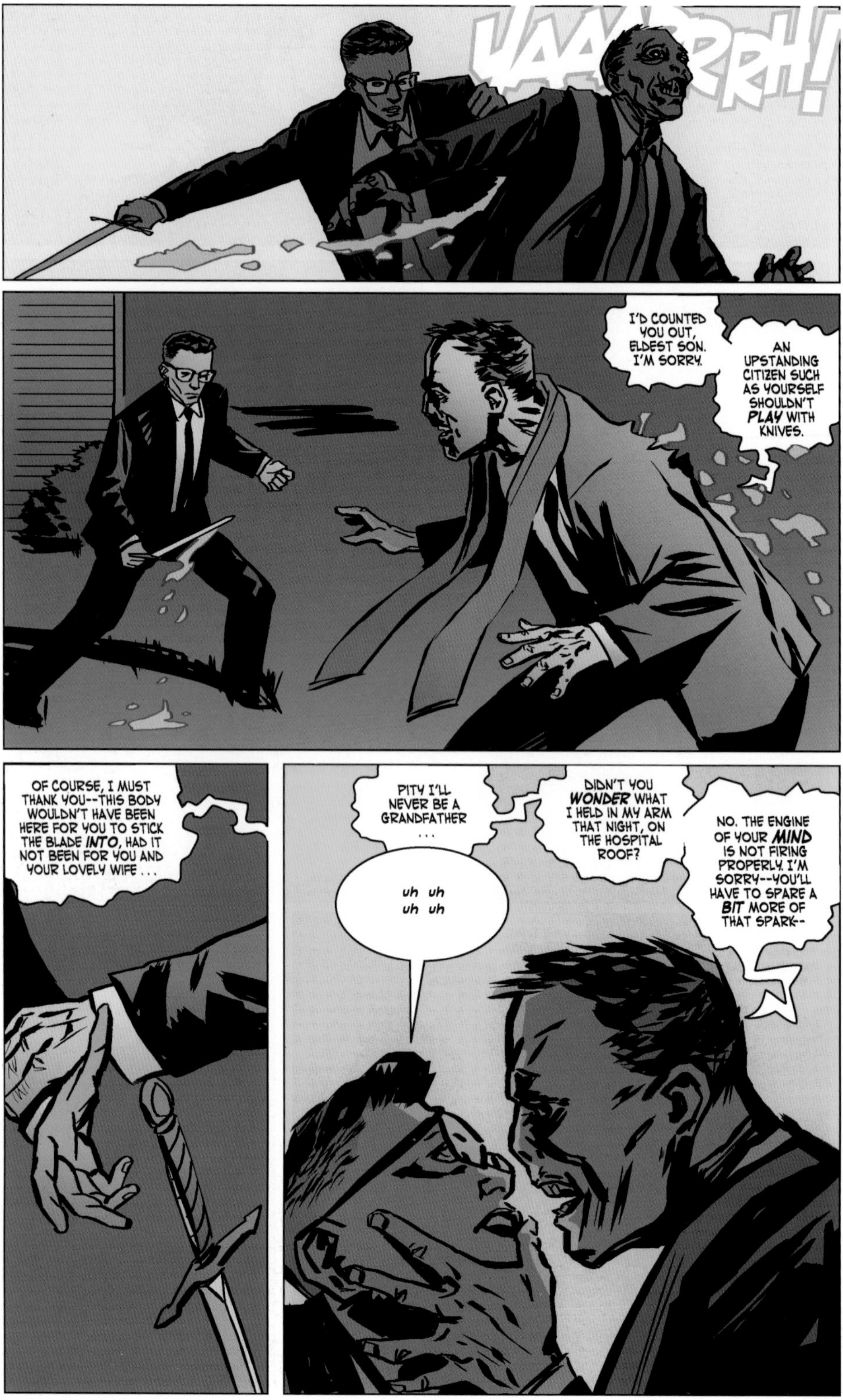

UAA RRH!
I'D COUNTED YOU OUT, ELDEST SON. I'M SORRY.
AN UPSTANDING CITIZEN SUCH AS YOURSELF SHOULDN'T *PLAY* WITH KNIVES.
OF COURSE, I MUST THANK YOU--THIS BODY WOULDN'T HAVE BEEN HERE FOR YOU TO STICK THE BLADE *INTO*, HAD IT NOT BEEN FOR YOU AND YOUR LOVELY WIFE . . .
PITY I'LL NEVER BE A GRANDFATHER . . .
uh uh uh uh
DIDN'T YOU *WONDER* WHAT I HELD IN MY ARM THAT NIGHT, ON THE HOSPITAL ROOF?
NO. THE ENGINE OF YOUR *MIND* IS NOT FIRING PROPERLY. I'M SORRY--YOU'LL HAVE TO SPARE A *BIT* MORE OF THAT SPARK--

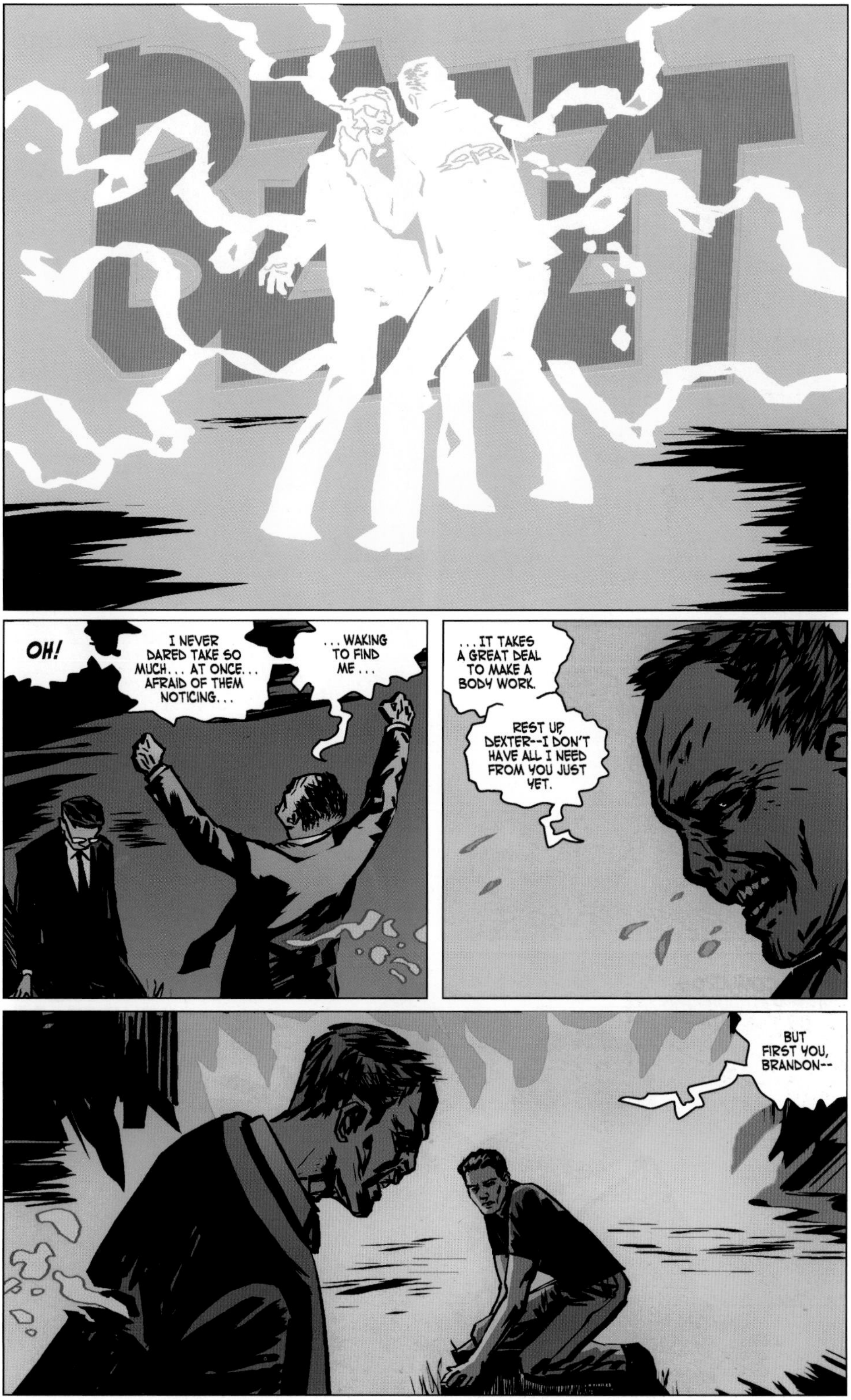
OH!
I NEVER DARED TAKE SO MUCH... AT ONCE... AFRAID OF THEM NOTICING...
...WAKING TO FIND ME...
...IT TAKES A GREAT DEAL TO MAKE A BODY WORK.
REST UP, DEXTER--I DON'T HAVE ALL I NEED FROM YOU JUST YET.
BUT FIRST YOU, BRANDON--

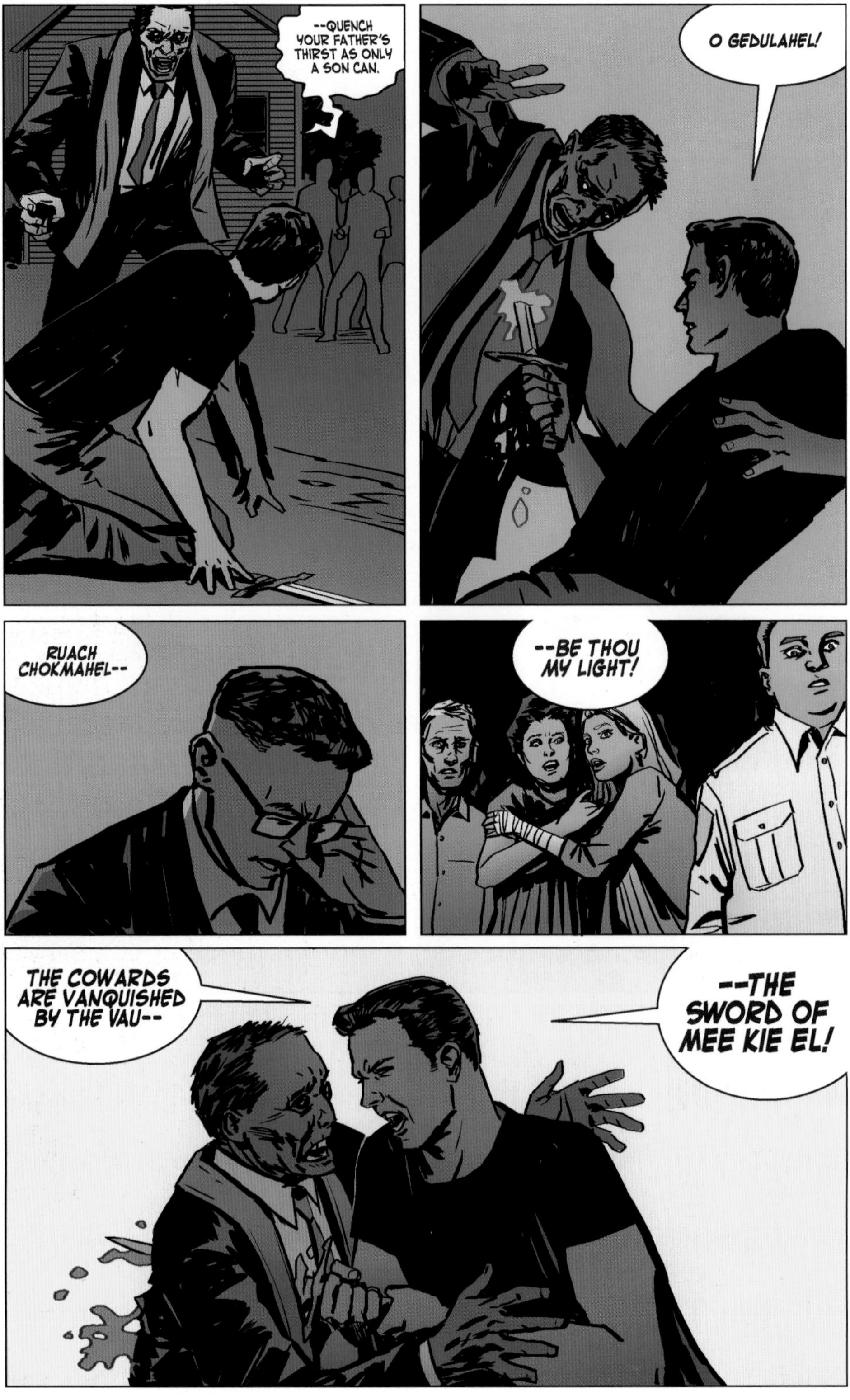
--QUENCH YOUR FATHER'S THIRST AS ONLY A SON CAN.
O GEDULAHEL!
RUACH CHOKMAHEL--
--BE THOU MY LIGHT!
THE COWARDS ARE VANQUISHED BY THE VAU--
--THE SWORD OF MEE KIE EL!

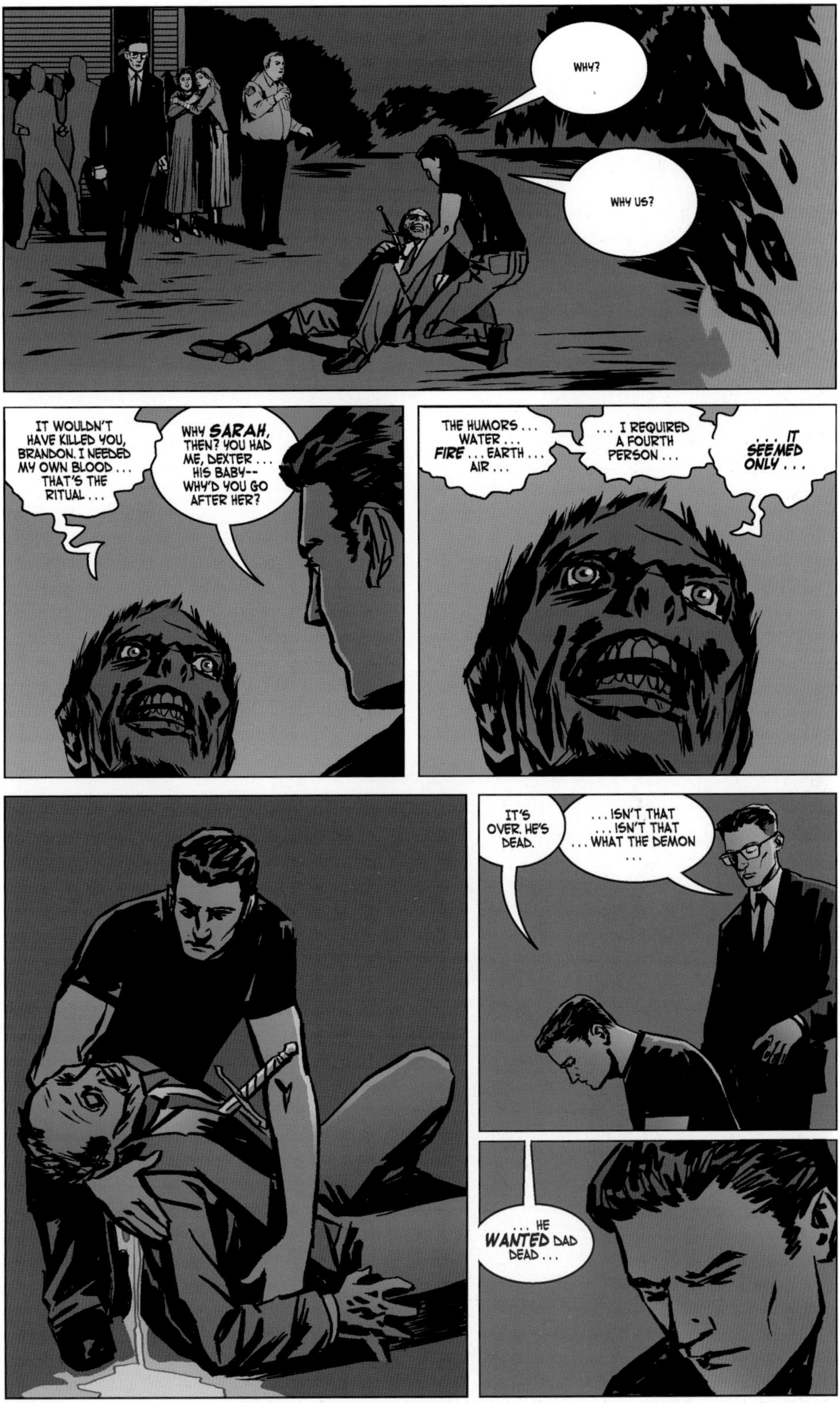
WHY?
WHY US?
IT WOULDN'T HAVE KILLED YOU, BRANDON. I NEEDED MY OWN BLOOD . . . THAT'S THE RITUAL . . .
WHY SARAH, THEN? YOU HAD ME, DEXTER . . . HIS BABY-- WHY'D YOU GO AFTER HER?
THE HUMORS . . . WATER . . . FIRE . . . EARTH . . . AIR . . .
. . . I REQUIRED A FOURTH PERSON . . .
. . . IT SEEMED ONLY . . .
IT'S OVER. HE'S DEAD.
. . . ISN'T THAT . . . ISN'T THAT . . . WHAT THE DEMON . . .
. . . HE WANTED DAD DEAD . . .

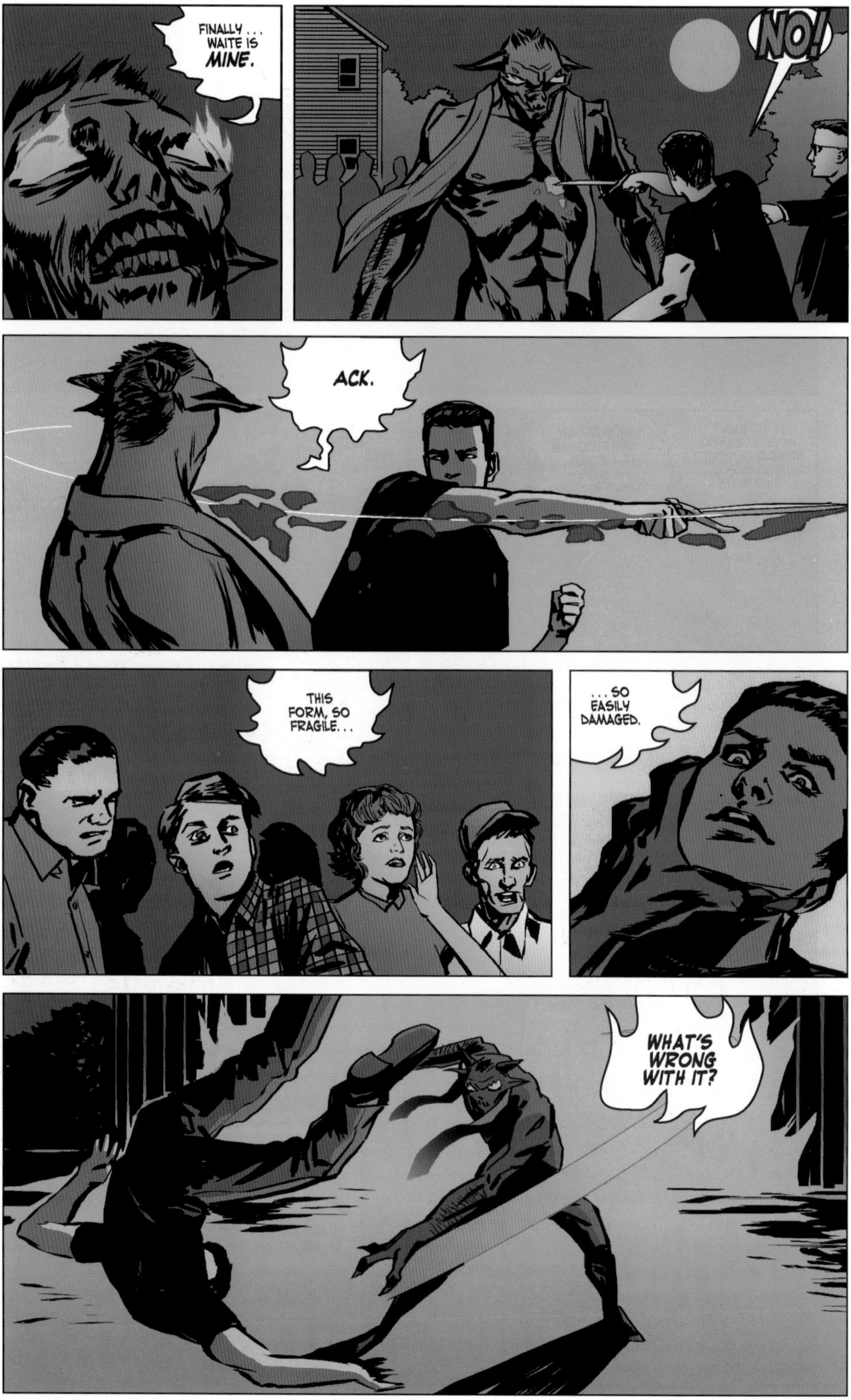
FINALLY . . . WAITE IS MINE.
NO!
ACK.
THIS FORM, SO FRAGILE. . .
. . . SO EASILY DAMAGED.
WHAT'S WRONG WITH IT?

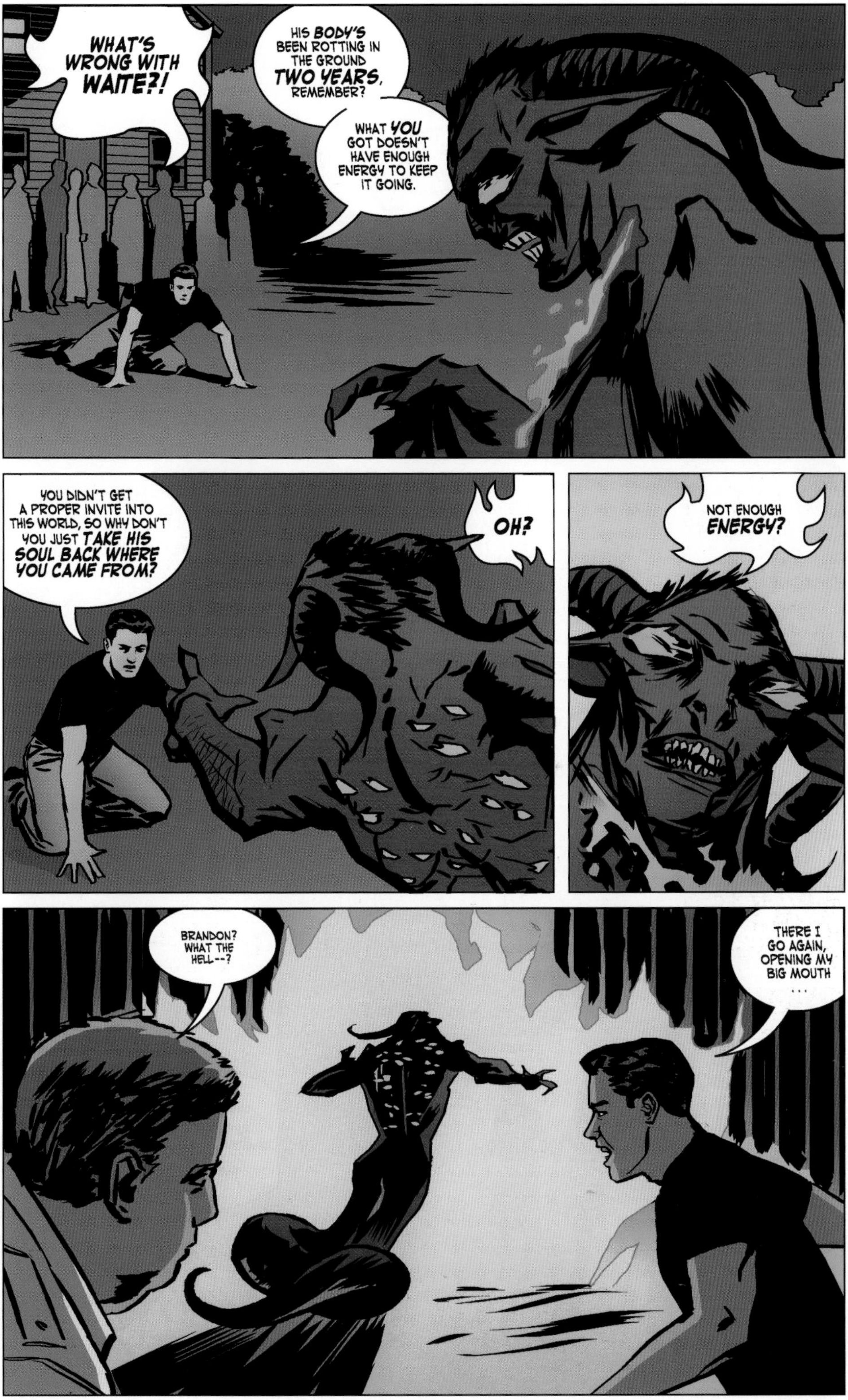
WHAT'S WRONG WITH WAITE?!
HIS BODY'S BEEN ROTTING IN THE GROUND TWO YEARS, REMEMBER?
WHAT YOU GOT DOESN'T HAVE ENOUGH ENERGY TO KEEP IT GOING.
YOU DIDN'T GET A PROPER INVITE INTO THIS WORLD, SO WHY DON'T YOU JUST TAKE HIS SOUL BACK WHERE YOU CAME FROM?
OH?
NOT ENOUGH ENERGY?
BRANDON? WHAT THE HELL--?
THERE I GO AGAIN, OPENING MY BIG MOUTH . . .

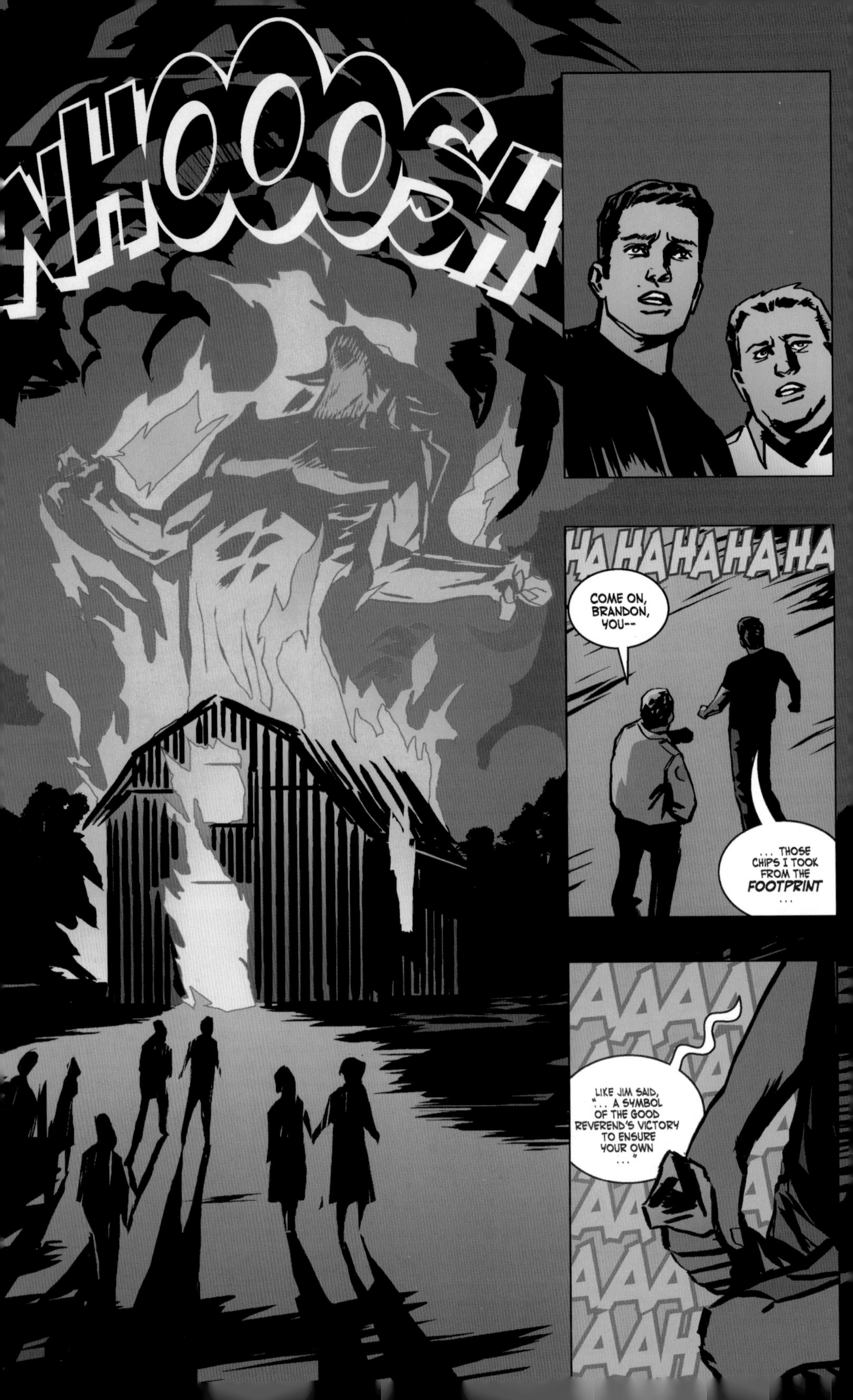
WHOOOSH
HA HA HA HA HA HA
COME ON, BRANDON, YOU--
. . . THOSE CHIPS I TOOK FROM THE *FOOTPRINT* . . .
AAAAAAAH
LIKE JIM SAID, ". . . A SYMBOL OF THE GOOD REVEREND'S VICTORY TO ENSURE YOUR OWN . . ."

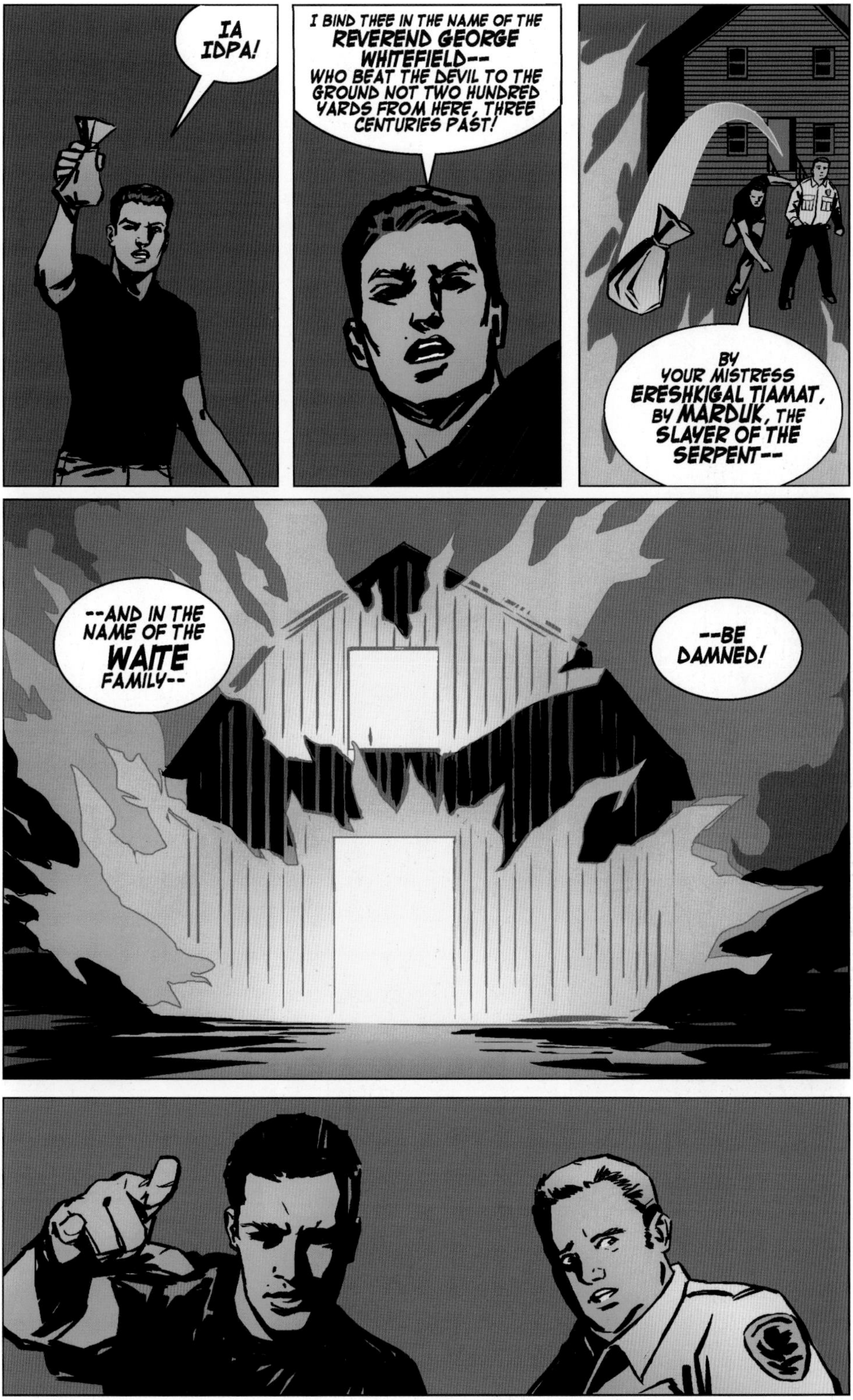
IA IDPA!
I BIND THEE IN THE NAME OF THE REVEREND GEORGE WHITEFIELD-- WHO BEAT THE DEVIL TO THE GROUND NOT TWO HUNDRED YARDS FROM HERE, THREE CENTURIES PAST!
BY YOUR MISTRESS ERESHKIGAL TIAMAT, BY MARDUK, THE SLAYER OF THE SERPENT--
--AND IN THE NAME OF THE WAITE FAMILY--
--BE DAMNED!

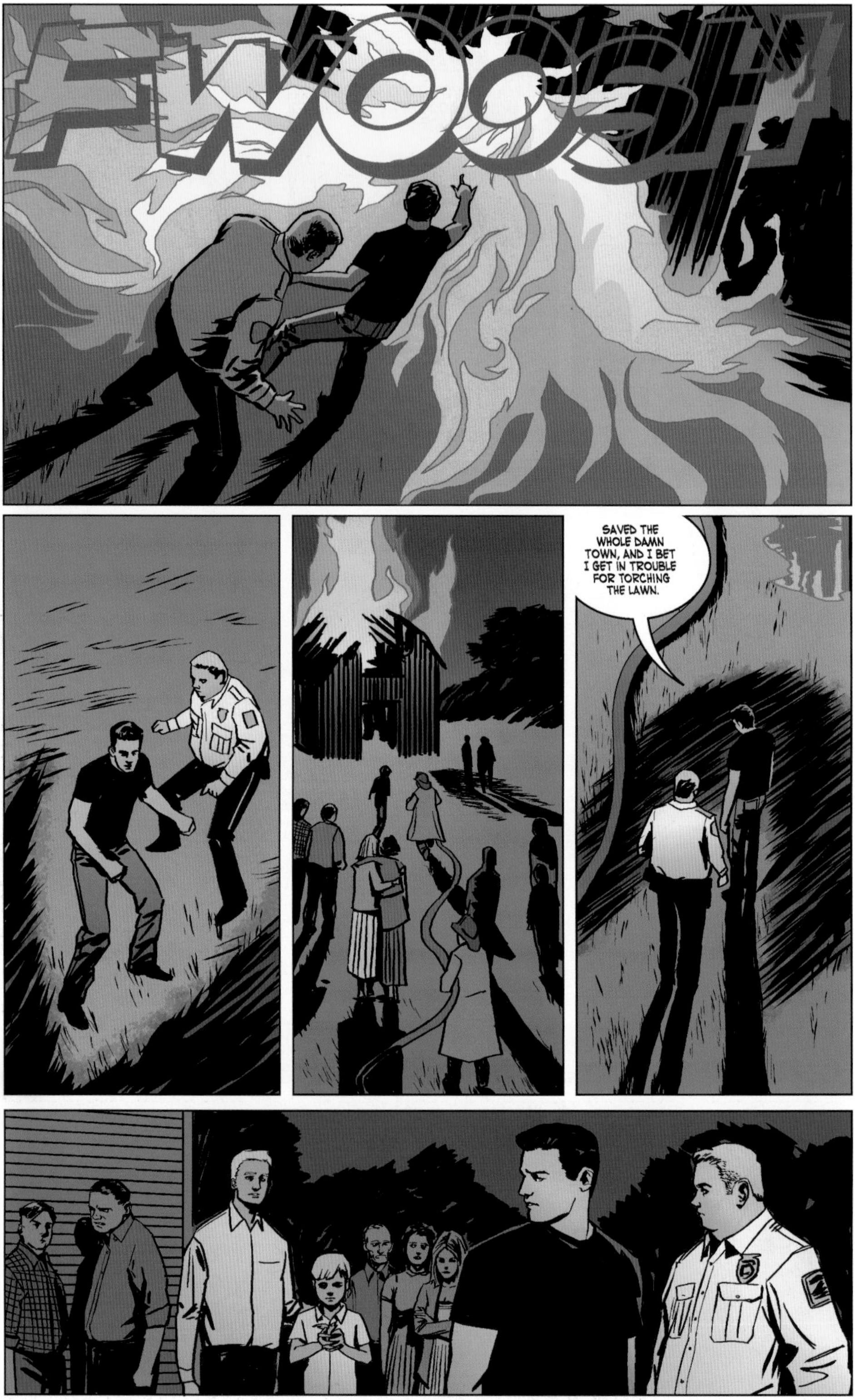
FWOOSH!
SAVED THE WHOLE DAMN TOWN, AND I BET I GET IN TROUBLE FOR TORCHING THE LAWN.

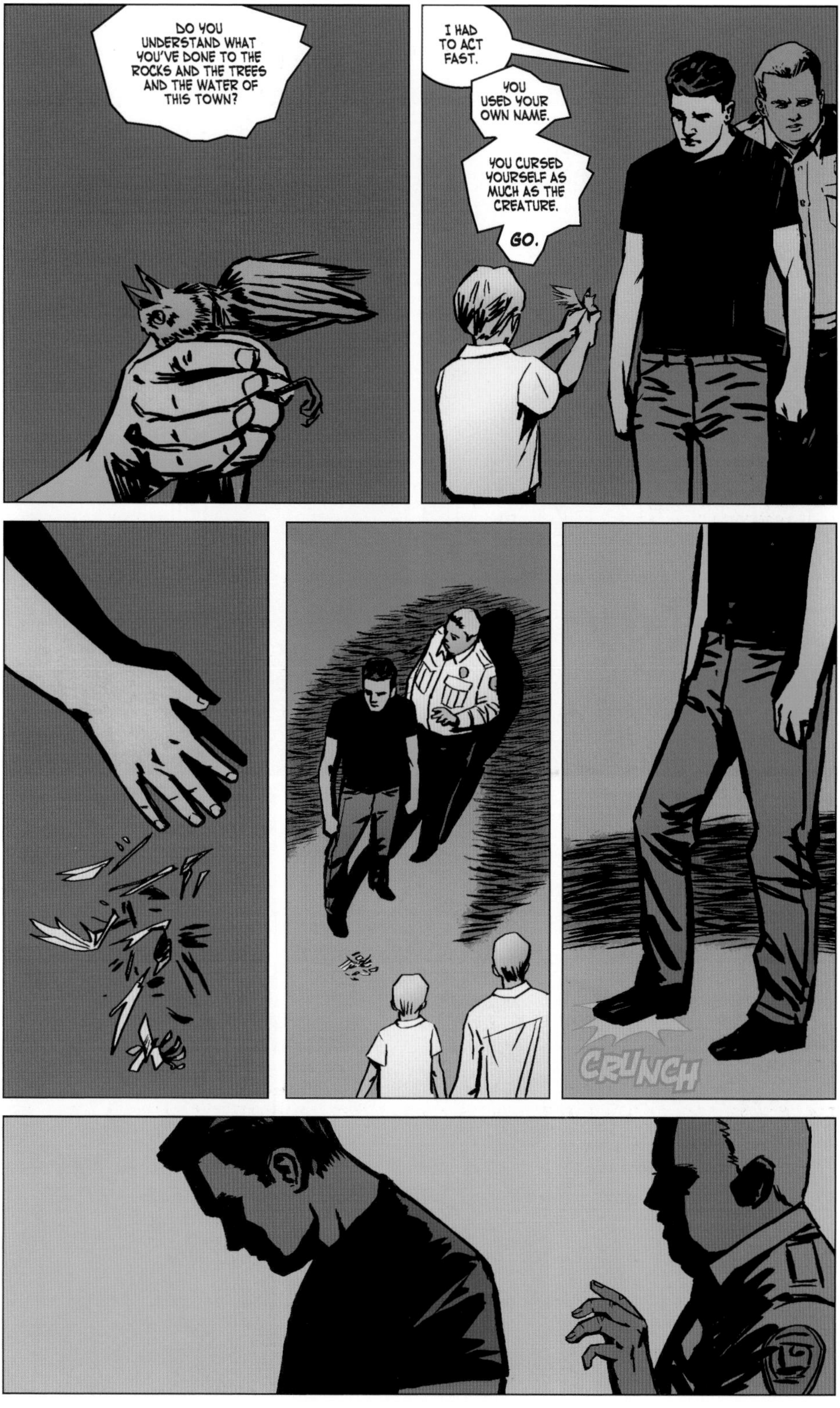
DO YOU UNDERSTAND WHAT YOU'VE DONE TO THE ROCKS AND THE TREES AND THE WATER OF THIS TOWN?
I HAD TO ACT FAST.
YOU USED YOUR OWN NAME.
YOU CURSED YOURSELF AS MUCH AS THE CREATURE.
GO.
CRUNCH

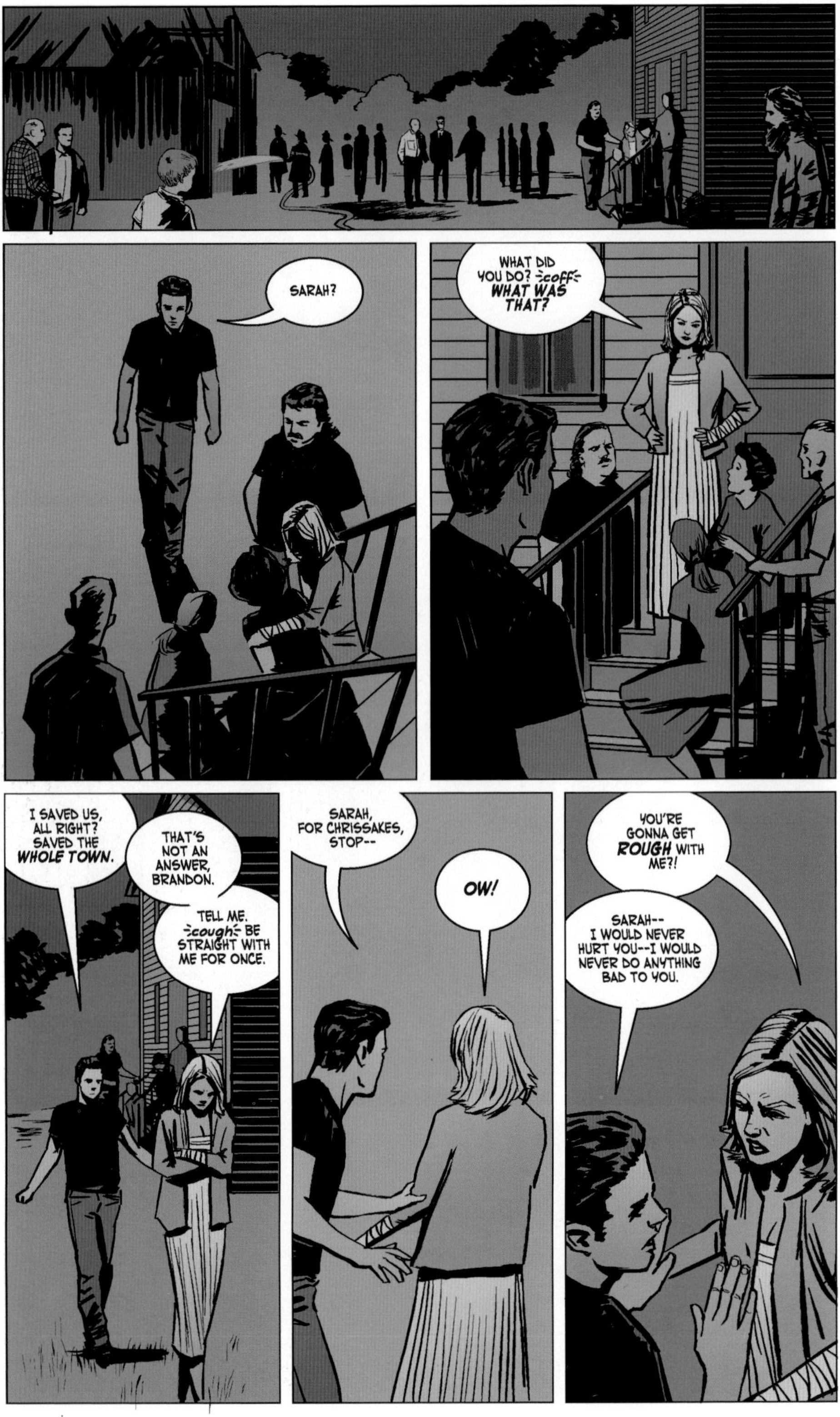
SARAH?
WHAT DID YOU DO? -coff- WHAT WAS THAT?
I SAVED US, ALL RIGHT? SAVED THE WHOLE TOWN.
THAT'S NOT AN ANSWER, BRANDON.
TELL ME. -cough- BE STRAIGHT WITH ME FOR ONCE.
SARAH, FOR CHRISSAKES, STOP--
OW!
YOU'RE GONNA GET ROUGH WITH ME?!
SARAH-- I WOULD NEVER HURT YOU--I WOULD NEVER DO ANYTHING BAD TO YOU.

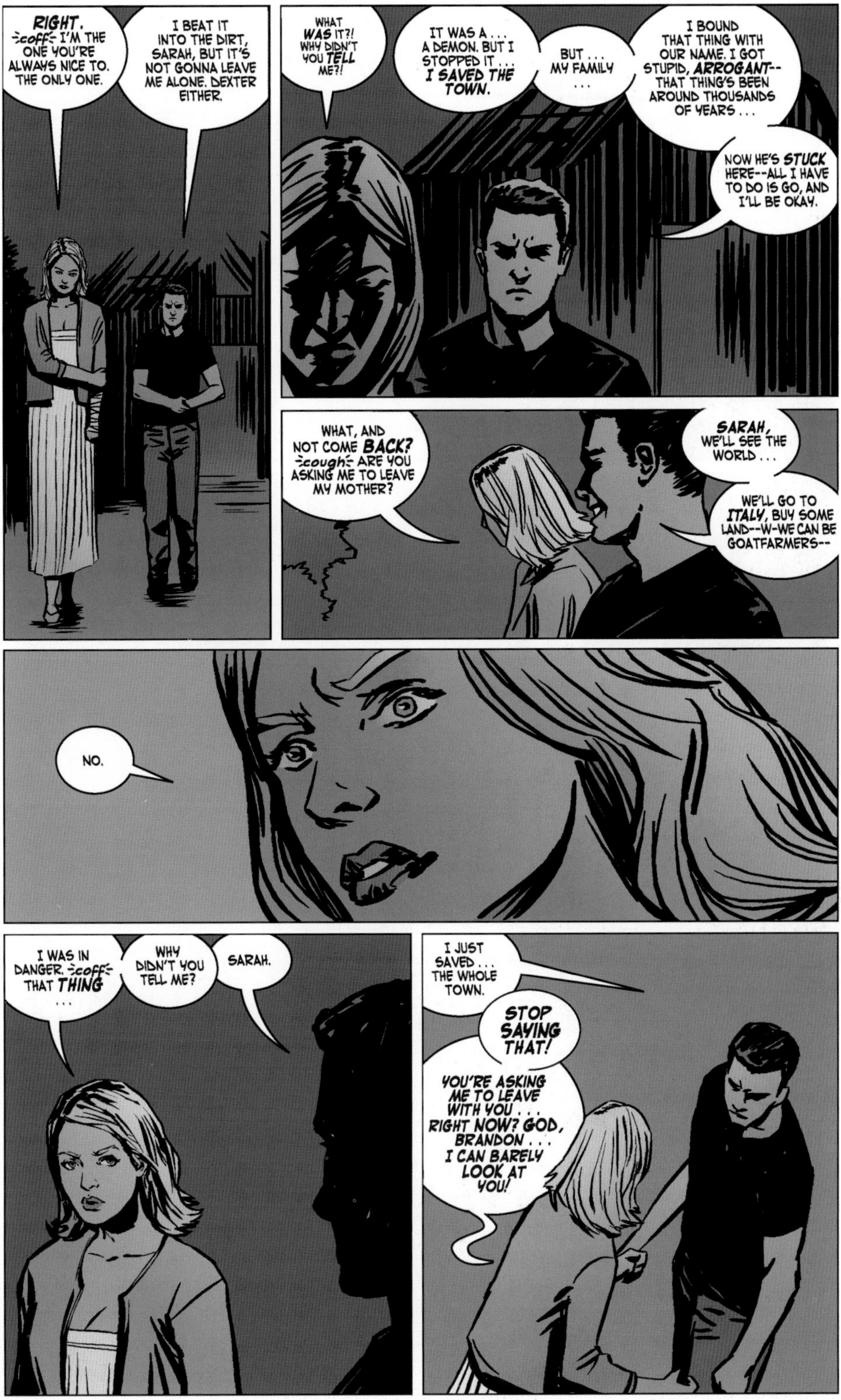
RIGHT. *COFF* I'M THE ONE YOU'RE ALWAYS NICE TO. THE ONLY ONE.
I BEAT IT INTO THE DIRT, SARAH, BUT IT'S NOT GONNA LEAVE ME ALONE. DEXTER EITHER.
WHAT WAS IT?! WHY DIDN'T YOU TELL ME?!
IT WAS A . . . A DEMON. BUT I STOPPED IT . . . I SAVED THE TOWN.
BUT . . . MY FAMILY . . .
I BOUND THAT THING WITH OUR NAME. I GOT STUPID, ARROGANT-- THAT THING'S BEEN AROUND THOUSANDS OF YEARS . . .
NOW HE'S STUCK HERE--ALL I HAVE TO DO IS GO, AND I'LL BE OKAY.
WHAT, AND NOT COME BACK? *COUGH* ARE YOU ASKING ME TO LEAVE MY MOTHER?
SARAH, WE'LL SEE THE WORLD . . .
WE'LL GO TO ITALY, BUY SOME LAND--W-WE CAN BE GOATFARMERS--
NO.
I WAS IN DANGER. *COFF* THAT THING . . .
WHY DIDN'T YOU TELL ME?
SARAH.
I JUST SAVED . . . THE WHOLE TOWN.
STOP SAYING THAT!
YOU'RE ASKING ME TO LEAVE WITH YOU . . . RIGHT NOW? GOD, BRANDON . . . I CAN BARELY LOOK AT YOU!

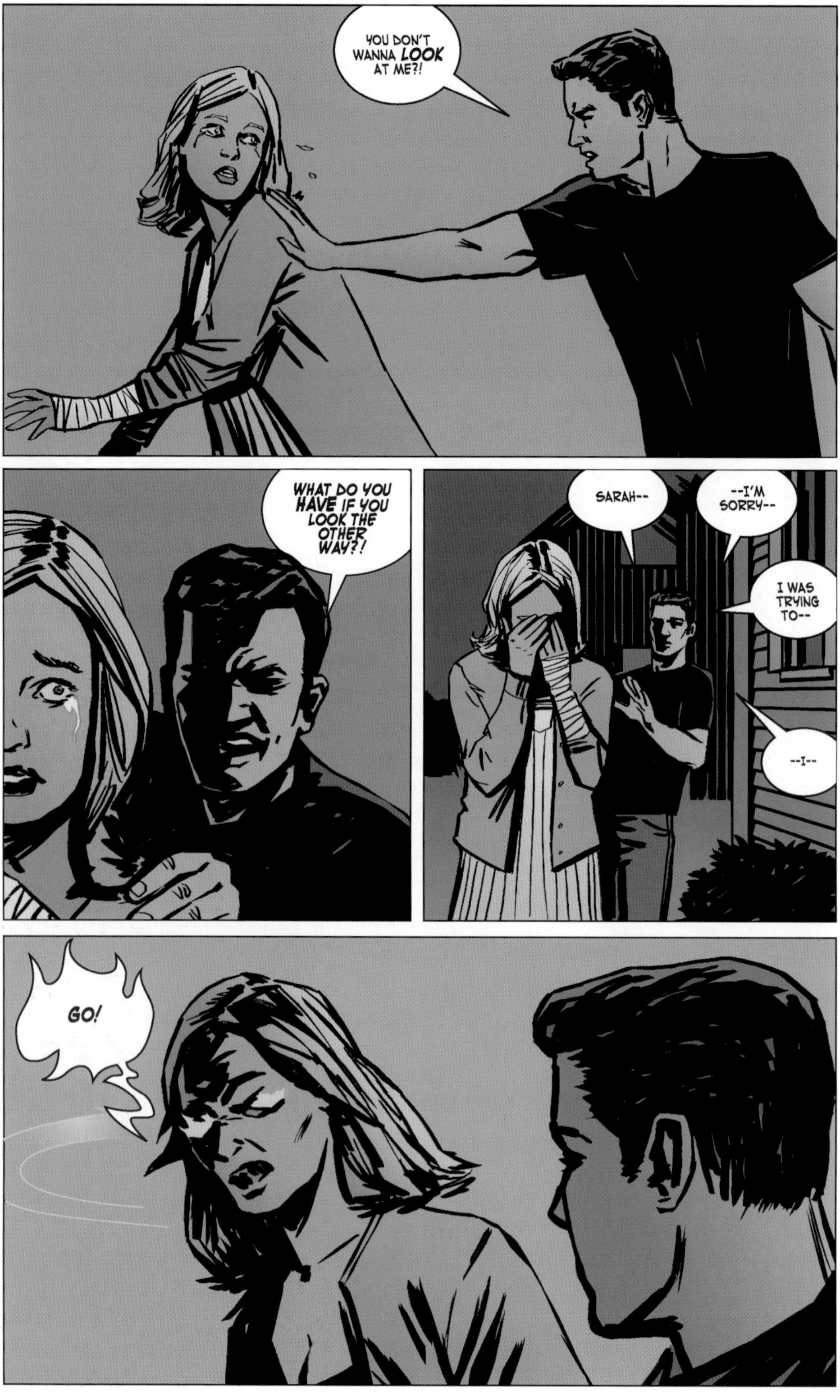
YOU DON'T WANNA LOOK AT ME?!
WHAT DO YOU HAVE IF YOU LOOK THE OTHER WAY?!
SARAH--
--I'M SORRY--
I WAS TRYING TO--
--I--
GO!

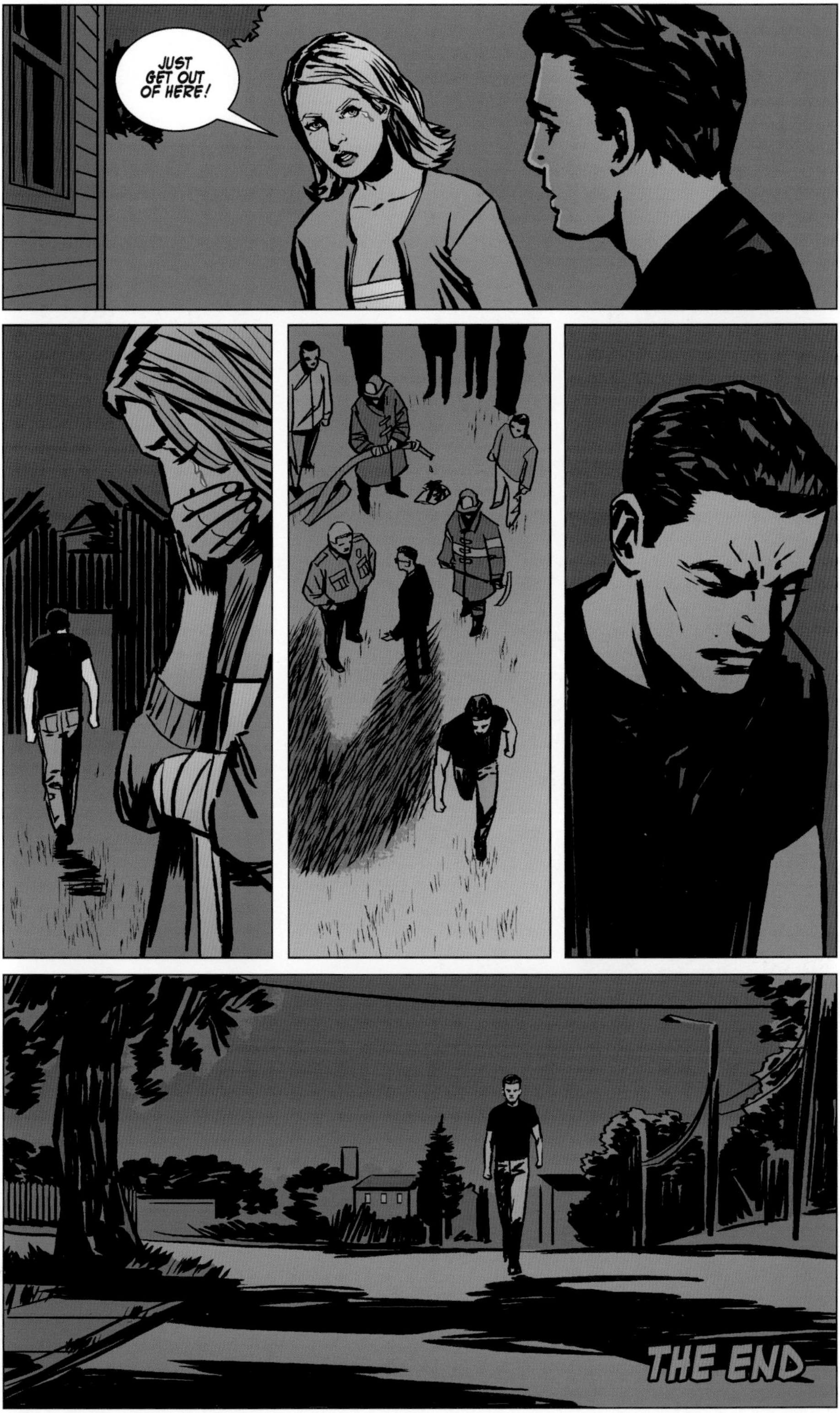
JUST GET OUT OF HERE!
THE END

DEMONOLOGY

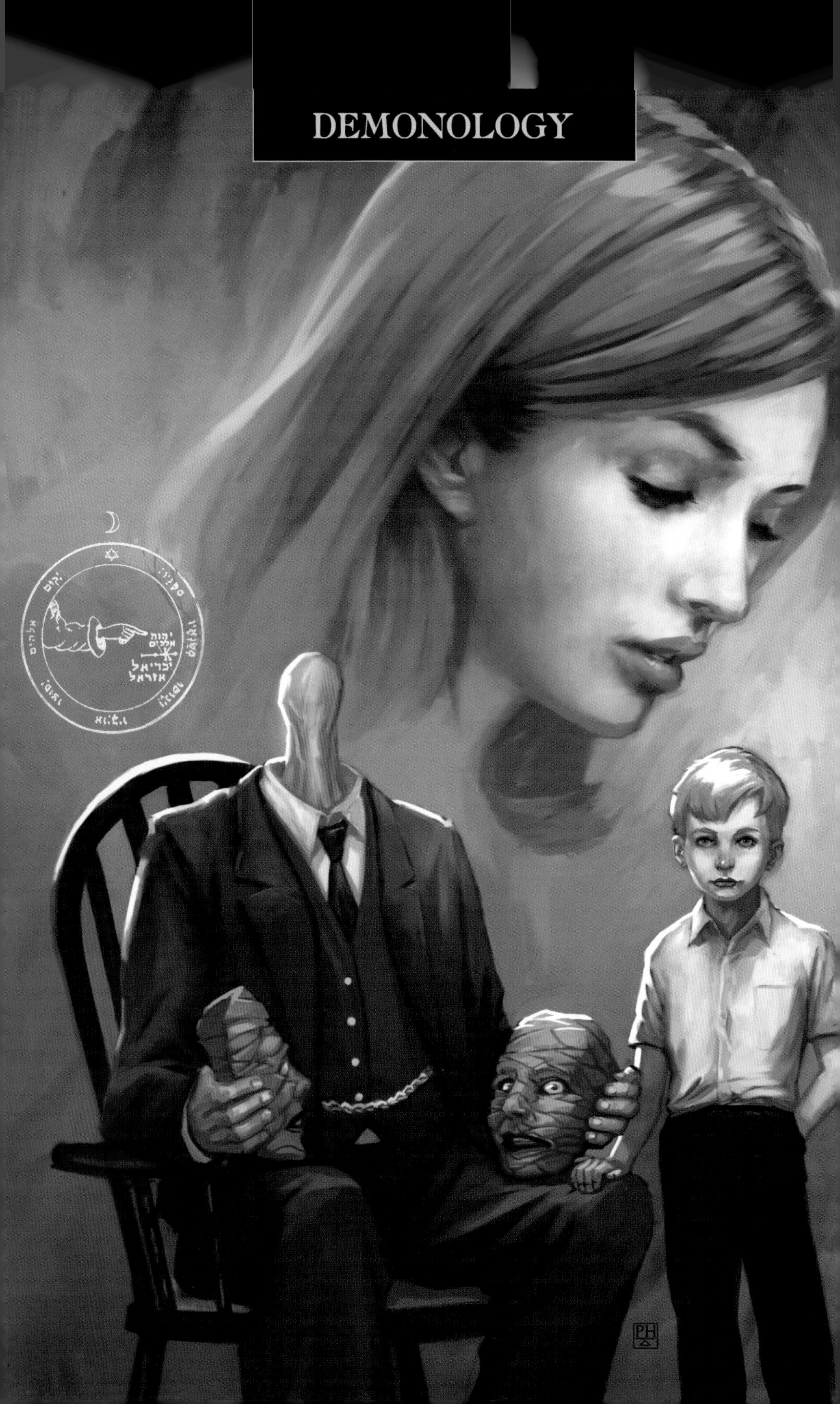

Excerpt from *The Secret Teachings of All Ages*, Manly P. Hall, 1928

While the black magician at the time of signing his pact with the elemental demon may be fully convinced that he is strong enough to indefinitely control the powers placed at his disposal, he is speedily undeceived. Before many years elapse he must turn all of his energies to the problem of self-preservation. A world of horrors to which he has attuned himself by his own covetousness looms nearer every day, until he exists upon the edge of a seething maelstrom, expecting momentarily to be sucked down into its turbid depths. Afraid to die—because he will become the servant of his own demon—the magician commits crime after crime to prolong his wretched earthly existence. Realizing that life is maintained by the aid of a mysterious universal life force which is the common property of all creatures, the black magician often becomes an occult vampire, stealing this energy from others.

Excerpts from *A Modern History of the Occult Intelligences*, ca. 1890

IDPA

Idpa, or Yadapa, an Etruscan god (and later Roman demon) of fever, appears in certain Babylonian magic, and has more recent and obscure roles in such varied histories as the papacy and vampirism.

At the end of the 12th century, the station of the Pope in Rome held final authority over all governments of Europe. France's King Philip the Fair opposed the traditional power of the Holy See, declaring his own sovereign rule over his nation. His rebellion led Pope Boniface VIII to publish his *Unam Sanctam* on 18 November 1302. With this document the Pope sought to assert his failing dictatorship over the civilized west. Philip responded by seizing the property of French bishops still loyal to Rome. This led, on 13 April 1303, to Philip's excommunication, and the threat of the impending excommunication of France, the most powerful country on the Continent. In June Philip held a national assembly to announce a list of formal charges against the Boniface. His twenty-nine accusations included adulteration of the Holy See, murder, heresy, sodomy, blasphemy, betraying the confessional, and more: "The Anti-Pope Boniface has for seven years indulged himself in sexual relations with a demon, kept as a pet in his ring."

On 6 September, six hundred horsemen and the Pontiff's fellow residents of Anagni marched on Boniface's home there. They

captured the Pope, but did not kill him; Boniface died one month later, after suffering a mental breakdown. Rumor has it that he crushed his skull against the stone wall of his chamber, after chewing the flesh from his fingers, but it has also been suggested that it was Idpa, the demon so long imprisoned in the Pope's ring, which finally killed him. Stripped of his Holy office, the Pope was no longer able to contain the creature, and it had its revenge.

Europe was soon to suffer the Black Death; in less that fifty years it would threaten to end the civilized world. Even today Catholics draw a connection between the Plague and Boniface's death—with the subsequent relocation of the papacy to Avignon. They, of course, believe the Black Death to be God's retribution for the treachery of Philip the Fair and the people of Anagni, which so weakened the Holy See. More than one occult authority, however, holds that after Idpa was freed, the coincidence is too easy to ignore—that this ancient demon of disease is responsible for the Plague, which entered Europe through Boniface's homeland, and had such a devastating effect there, and on man's faith in the church.

If the demon was not directly responsible for the Plague, it was at least there to witness its arrival in Europe, according to an Austrian seer from the 18th century. On 31 May 1725, during an experiment conducted in the ruins of Teufelstoss Manor, Lord Giedt encountered Idpa directly. The demon did not in fact claim responsibility for the Black Death, but offered a related story.

The city of Caffa, a Genoese port, was heavily contested throughout the 14th century. Italian forces and the Mongol Golden Horde fought for control of the city in bloody exchanges beginning in 1307. Fortified by two concentric walls, and built directly on the coast, the city was an ideal military and commercial port.

In 1346, Caffa had for three years been under siege by a failing Tartar force. The invaders were being devastated by the newly arrived Black Death, thousands of soldiers falling each day. As Gabriele dé Mussi wrote:

> The dying Tartars, stunned and
> stupefied by the immensity of the
> disaster brought on by the disease,
> and realizing that they had no hope
> of escape, lost interest in the siege.
> But they ordered corpses to be placed
> in catapults and lobbed into the city
> in the hope that the intolerable
> stench would kill everyone inside.
> What seemed like mountains of dead
> were thrown into the city. Soon the
> rotting corpses tainted the air and
> poisoned the water supply.

Idpa was so impressed by the inhumanity of the act that the demon reanimated the projected plague corpses as a further attack on the city, and Caffa was abandoned. Lord Giedt, in his account of his meeting with Idpa, declared this to be the origin of vampires, although of course legends date much further back, and no vampire lore comes from the region surrounding old Caffa. The vision of Idpa at Teufelstoss Manor runs contrary to the creature's original presentation; it now bore a tail instead of legs. Lord Giedt claimed that the creature had removed its legs to prevent any further indignities like those perpetrated by the Pope.

THE ERISSA JONNA

In September 1861, the Reverend Arthur Davis left his Methodist church in San Francisco, California, after a dream in which he was visited by a headless creature wearing a suit and holding in its lap two heads, hollowed out in the back. The creature praised Davis for his resourcefulness in separating even his poorest parishioners from their money, "... all in the name of god and progress." The priest was so shaken by the dream that he moved to Arizona where he joined a Franciscan monastery, embracing poverty, renouncing all wealth and possessions.

In 1891 in New Orleans, the Sacred Heart of the Blessed Mother of Christ, a church counting blacks and whites among its members, was accused by a former parishioner of worshipping the devil. During the ensuing trial, an elderly businessman, who financed the church but was not an attending member, became flustered on the witness stand and said, "We didn't worship him, we merely did business with him." The church property was confiscated and auctioned by the city. A drawing was found which matched the creature

described thirty years earlier by Reverend Davis, bearing the name "The Erissa Jonna." A handwritten manuscript found folded into a Christian bible relayed the following story. It should be noted that there is no Venice River in southeastern Texas.

In the middle years of the present century, a prospecting company founded a modest camp along the Venice River in southeastern Texas. Their search for gold was interrupted by the visit of a band of Indian warriors, claiming the river as their land. After some negotiation, the Indians agreed to let the men continue their work, as long as the whites agreed not to enter the nearby woodlands, which the Indians called their home. The miners accepted the red men's conditions, but became curious, and spied on their village. A permanent settlement in the lush forest would allow the men to bring their families to the frontier, so they seized the land. While constructing their new town, with the help of Indian servants newly educated in the Christian ways, the settlers were plagued by tragedy upon tragedy, including a series of deaths during the construction of the company bank and the church. Before completion, the town was abandoned as haunted. In the three years that the white men occupied that land, no gold was found in the river.

The record at the Sacred Heart of the Blessed Mother of Christ stated that this incident was not the work of the Erissa Jonna, as one might suspect, but the origin of the creature, meaning that it is perhaps the only demon born to the New World.

OTHER STORIES

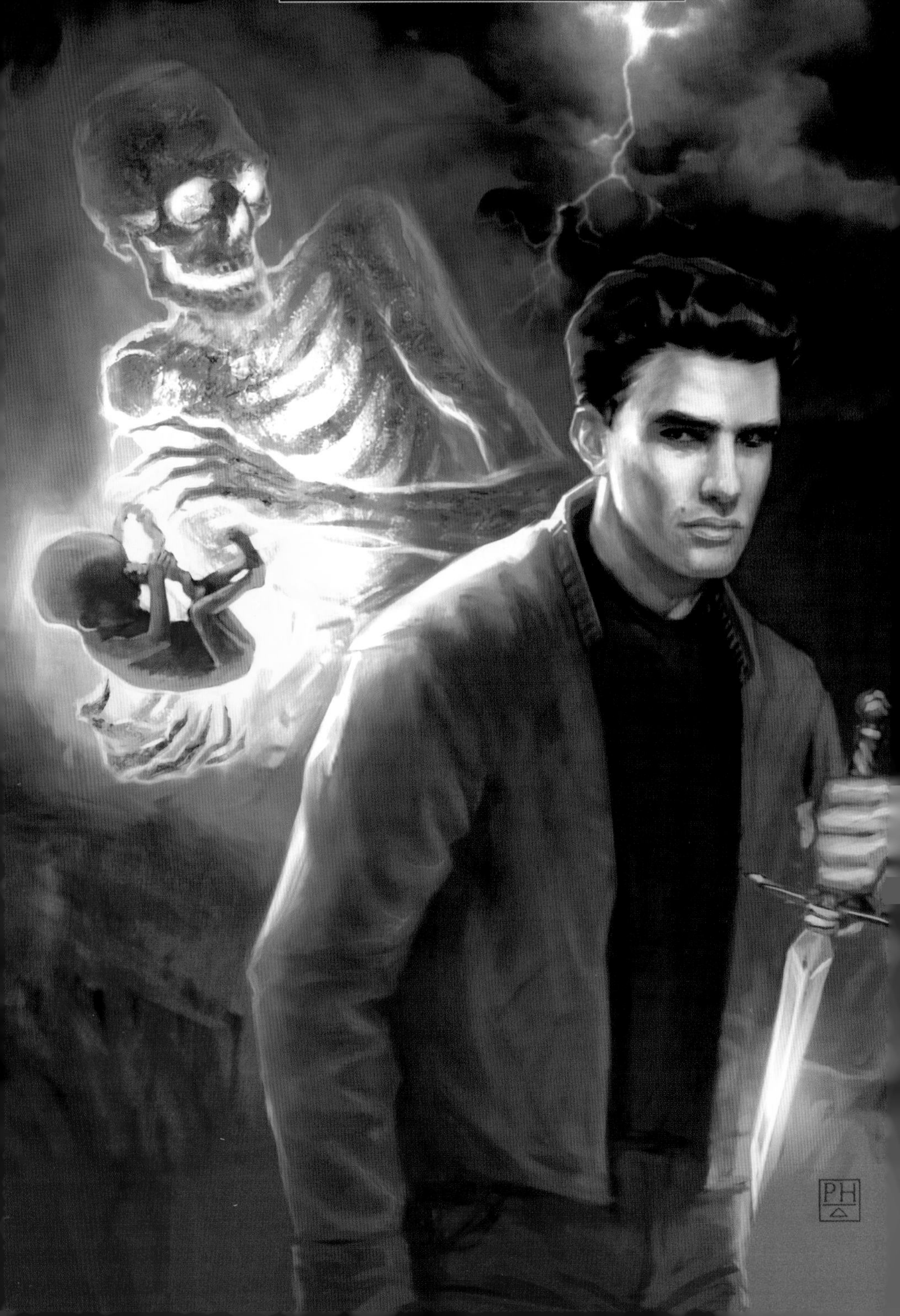
PH

The following short stories were written before the main story, as warm-ups for the world and characters important to Brandon. The artist I was originally going to do the book with, Galen Showman, drew "Worm Song" for *Dark Horse Presents* #142, an H.P. Lovecraft tribute. We wanted to get to know William a little better before tackling a major story in which he was already dead. This was back in 1999, and Galen became too busy to continue work on the series. Brian and I had talked about doing something big together, a story we could really care about. I pitched *The Devil's Footprints* to Brian, Paul, and Dave, and they signed on. We used "The Call," another homage to Lovecraft, as our trial run, and that story ran in the anthology *Reveal* in 2002. I wrote the final story presented here, "The Current," in an attempt to bring Brandon's love for Sarah to life. I needed that to make the main story work for me. It was drawn after the completion of the series, when Brian was busy with other work; Paul drew it from my rough layouts, and Dave painted over his pencil drawings. For this collection, Dave also went back and colored Galen's "Worm Song" story.

Scott Allie

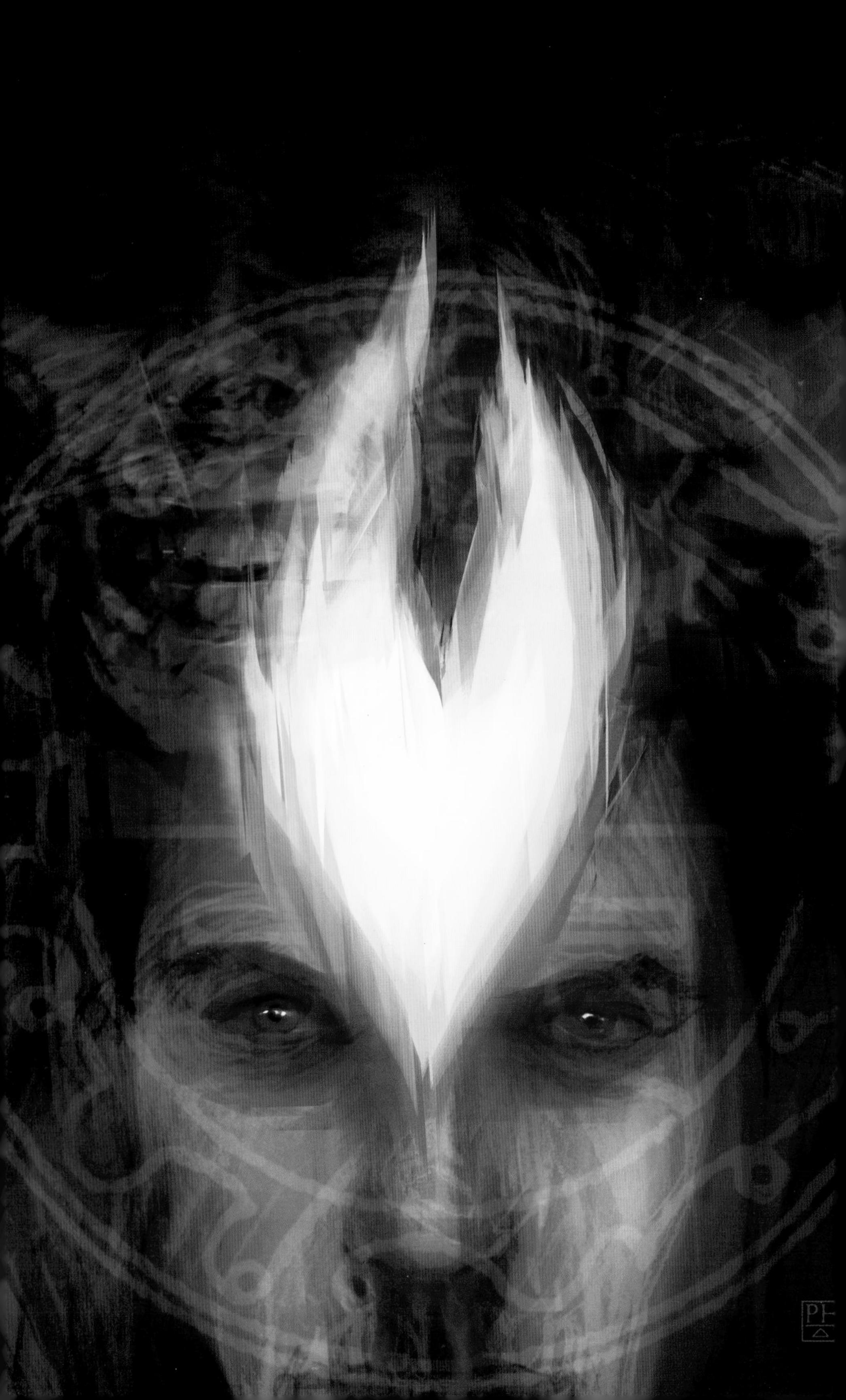

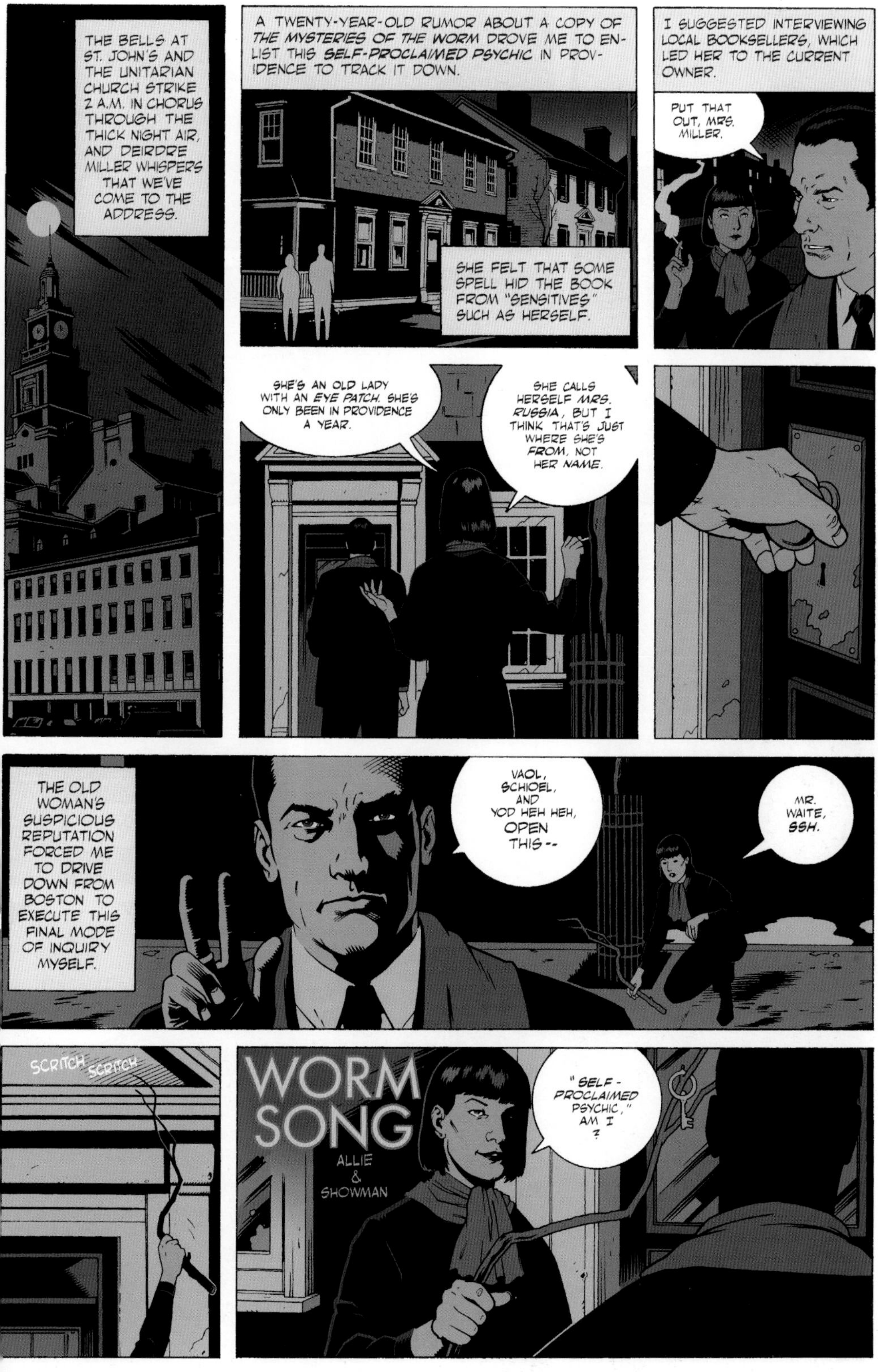

THE BELLS AT ST. JOHN'S AND THE UNITARIAN CHURCH STRIKE 2 A.M. IN CHORUS THROUGH THE THICK NIGHT AIR, AND DEIRDRE MILLER WHISPERS THAT WE'VE COME TO THE ADDRESS.
A TWENTY-YEAR-OLD RUMOR ABOUT A COPY OF *THE MYSTERIES OF THE WORM* DROVE ME TO ENLIST THIS *SELF-PROCLAIMED PSYCHIC* IN PROVIDENCE TO TRACK IT DOWN.
SHE FELT THAT SOME SPELL HID THE BOOK FROM "SENSITIVES" SUCH AS HERSELF.
I SUGGESTED INTERVIEWING LOCAL BOOKSELLERS, WHICH LED HER TO THE CURRENT OWNER.
PUT THAT OUT, MRS. MILLER.
SHE'S AN OLD LADY WITH AN *EYE PATCH*. SHE'S ONLY BEEN IN PROVIDENCE A YEAR.
SHE CALLS HERSELF *MRS. RUSSIA*, BUT I THINK THAT'S JUST WHERE SHE'S *FROM*, NOT HER *NAME*.
THE OLD WOMAN'S SUSPICIOUS REPUTATION FORCED ME TO DRIVE DOWN FROM BOSTON TO EXECUTE THIS FINAL MODE OF INQUIRY MYSELF.
VAOL, SCHIOEL, AND YOD HEH HEH, **OPEN** THIS--
MR. WAITE, ***SSH.***
SCRITCH SCRITCH
WORM SONG
ALLIE & SHOWMAN
"*SELF-PROCLAIMED* PSYCHIC," AM I ?

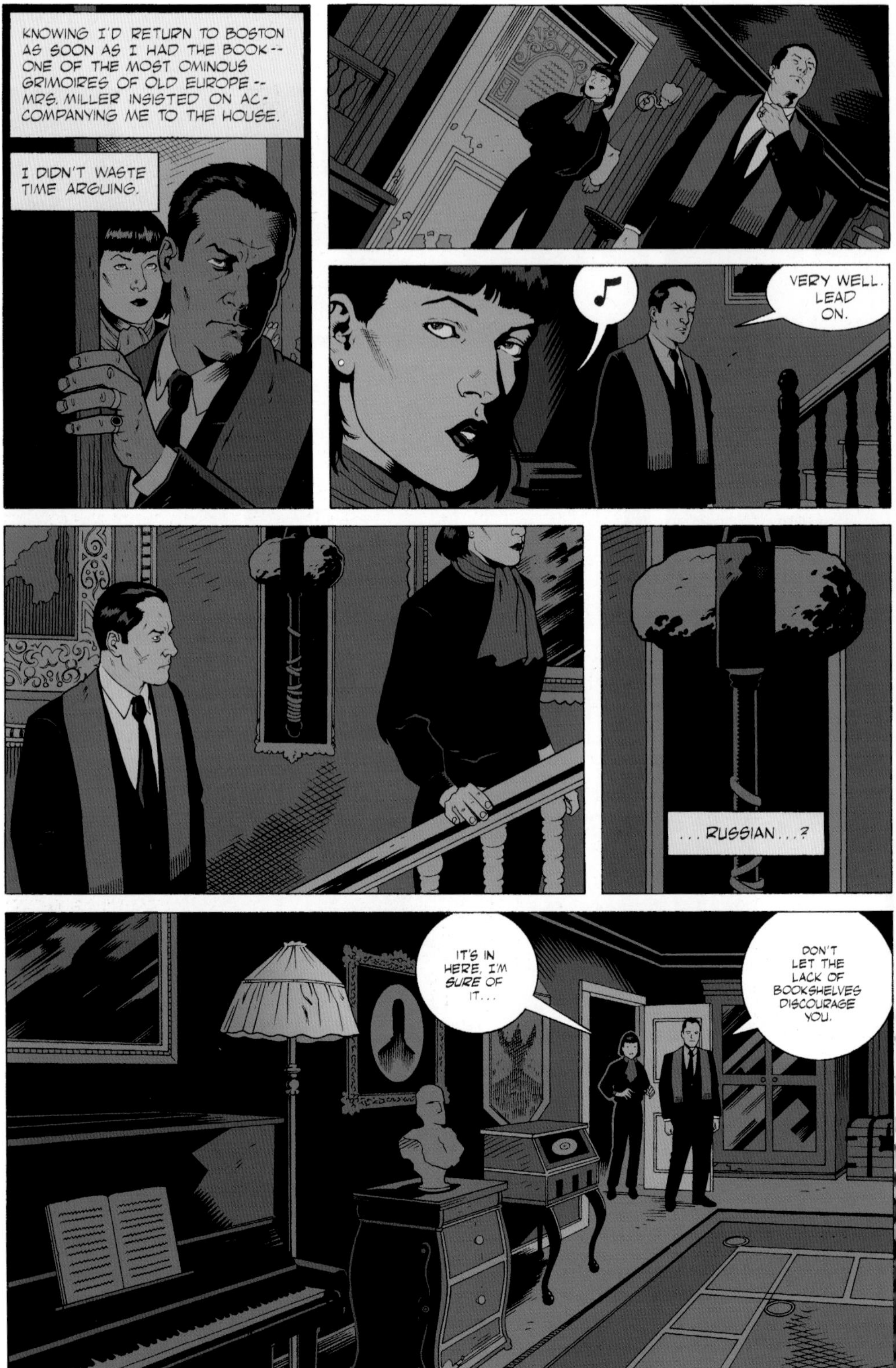
KNOWING I'D RETURN TO BOSTON AS SOON AS I HAD THE BOOK -- ONE OF THE MOST OMINOUS GRIMOIRES OF OLD EUROPE -- MRS. MILLER INSISTED ON ACCOMPANYING ME TO THE HOUSE.
I DIDN'T WASTE TIME ARGUING.
♪
VERY WELL. LEAD ON.
. . . RUSSIAN . . . ?
IT'S IN HERE, I'M SURE OF IT . . .
DON'T LET THE LACK OF BOOKSHELVES DISCOURAGE YOU.

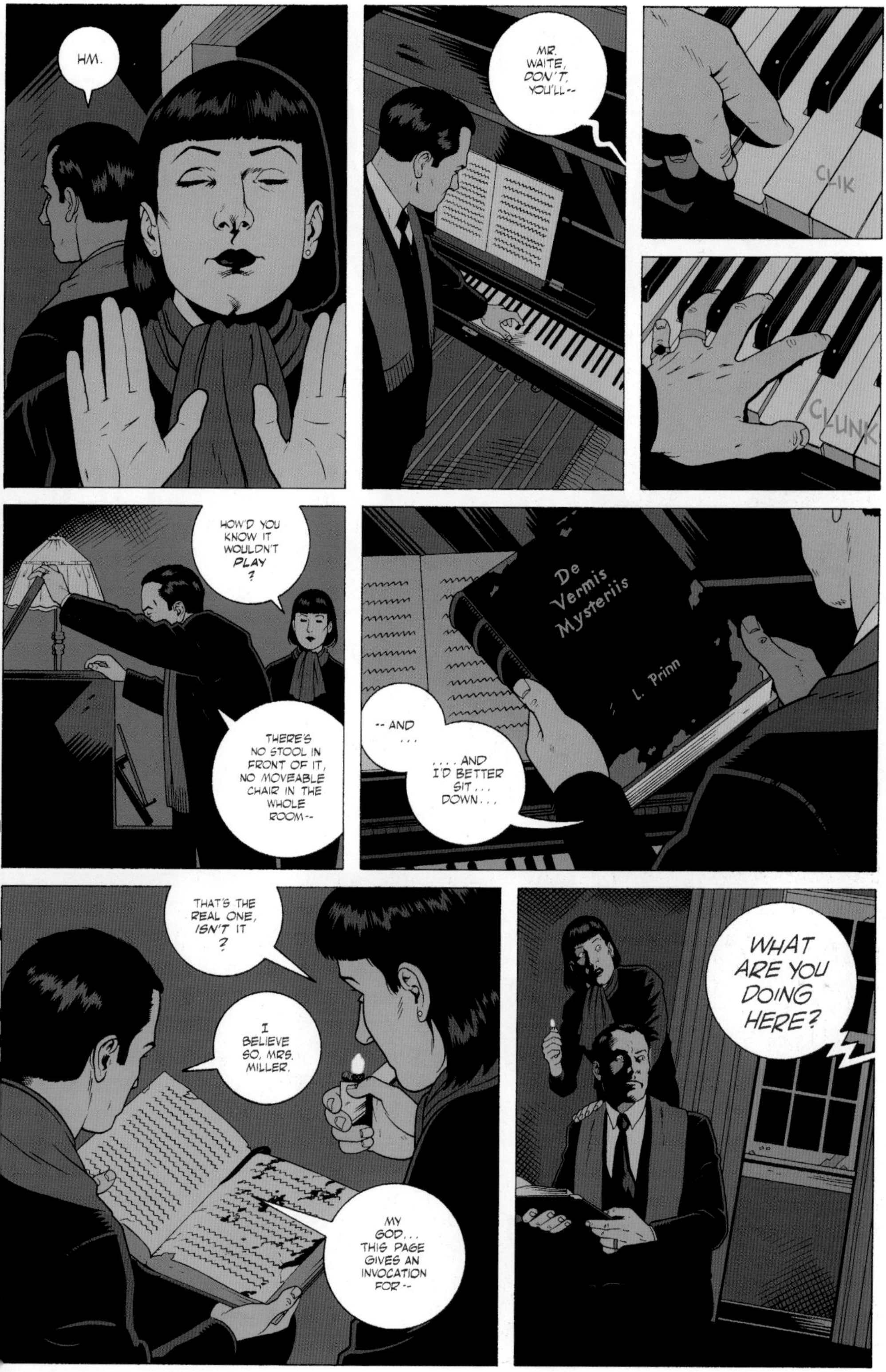

HM.
MR. WAITE, DON'T, YOU'LL--
CLIK
CLUNK
HOW'D YOU KNOW IT WOULDN'T PLAY?
THERE'S NO STOOL IN FRONT OF IT, NO MOVEABLE CHAIR IN THE WHOLE ROOM--
De Vermis Mysteriis
L. Prinn
-- AND . . .
. . . . AND I'D BETTER SIT . . . DOWN . . .
THAT'S THE REAL ONE, ISN'T IT?
I BELIEVE SO, MRS. MILLER.
MY GOD . . . THIS PAGE GIVES AN INVOCATION FOR--
WHAT ARE YOU DOING HERE?

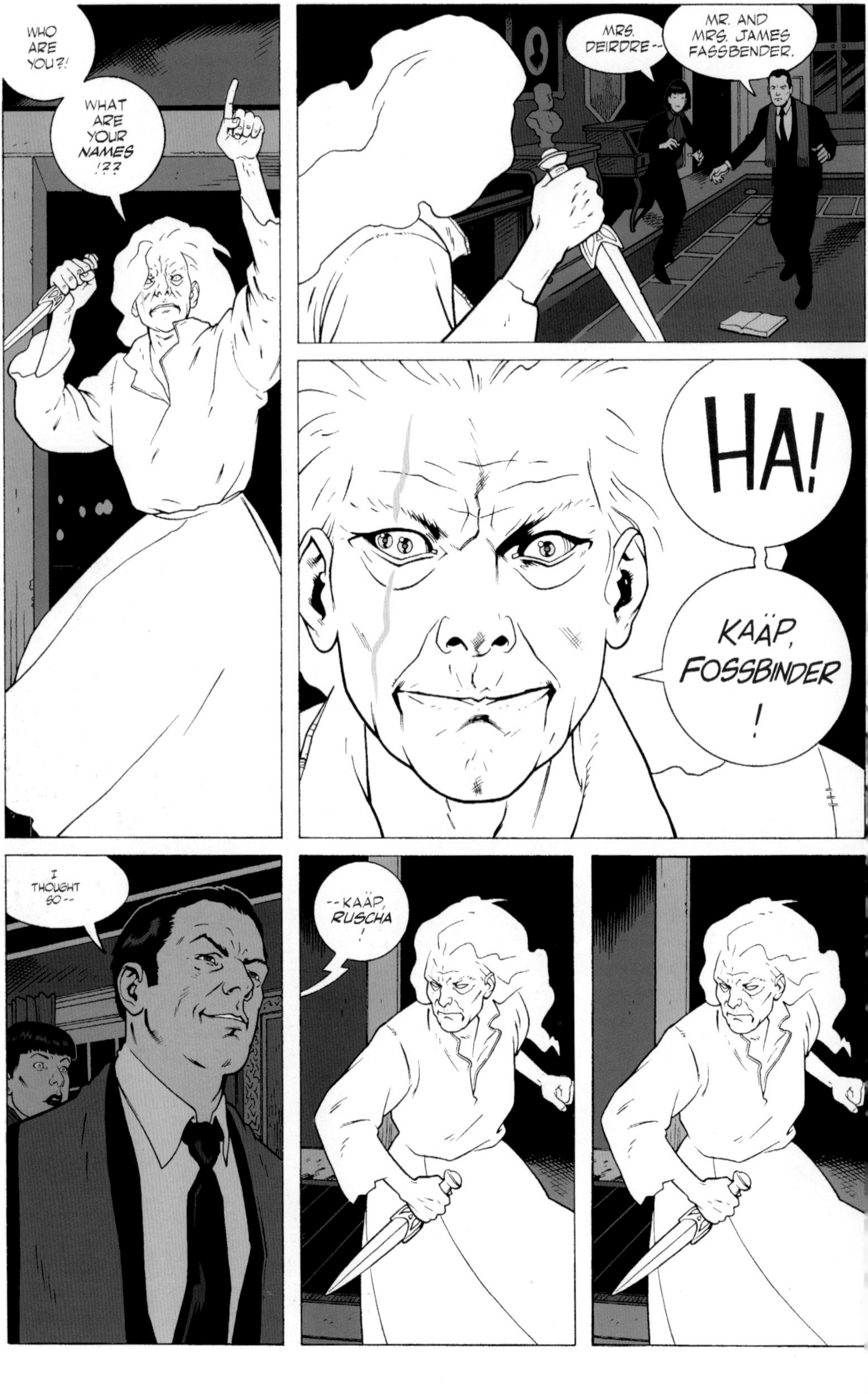
WHO ARE YOU?!
WHAT ARE YOUR NAMES !??
MRS. DEIRDRE--
MR. AND MRS. JAMES FASSBENDER.
HA!
KAÄP, FOSSBINDER !
I THOUGHT SO--
--KAÄP, RUSCHA !

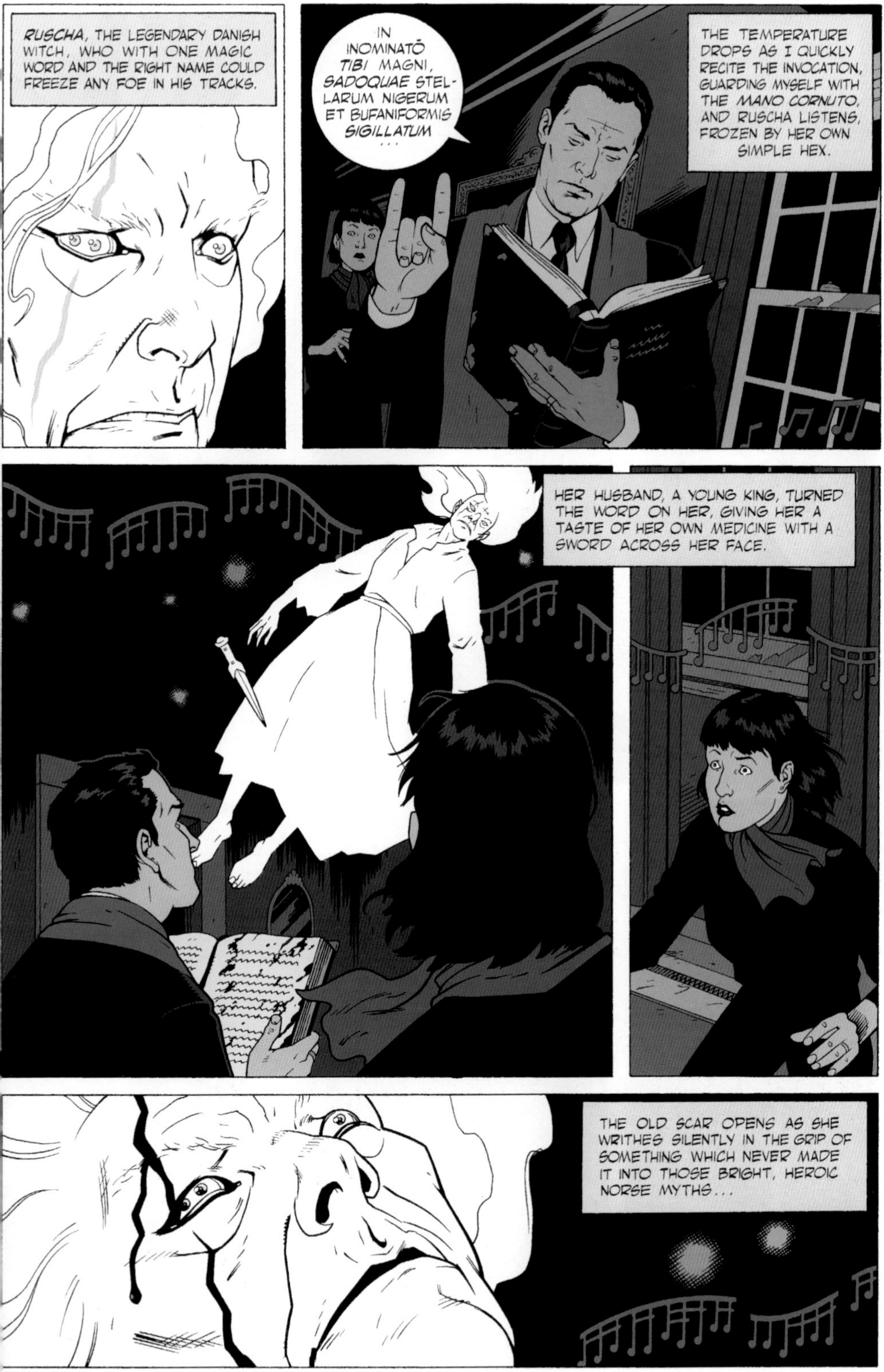
RUSCHA, THE LEGENDARY DANISH WITCH, WHO WITH ONE MAGIC WORD AND THE RIGHT NAME COULD FREEZE ANY FOE IN HIS TRACKS.
IN INOMINATŌ TIBI MAGNI, SADOQUAE STELLARUM NIGERUM ET BUFANIFORMIS SIGILLATUM...
THE TEMPERATURE DROPS AS I QUICKLY RECITE THE INVOCATION, GUARDING MYSELF WITH THE MANO CORNUTO, AND RUSCHA LISTENS, FROZEN BY HER OWN SIMPLE HEX.
HER HUSBAND, A YOUNG KING, TURNED THE WORD ON HER, GIVING HER A TASTE OF HER OWN MEDICINE WITH A SWORD ACROSS HER FACE.
THE OLD SCAR OPENS AS SHE WRITHES SILENTLY IN THE GRIP OF SOMETHING WHICH NEVER MADE IT INTO THOSE BRIGHT, HEROIC NORSE MYTHS...

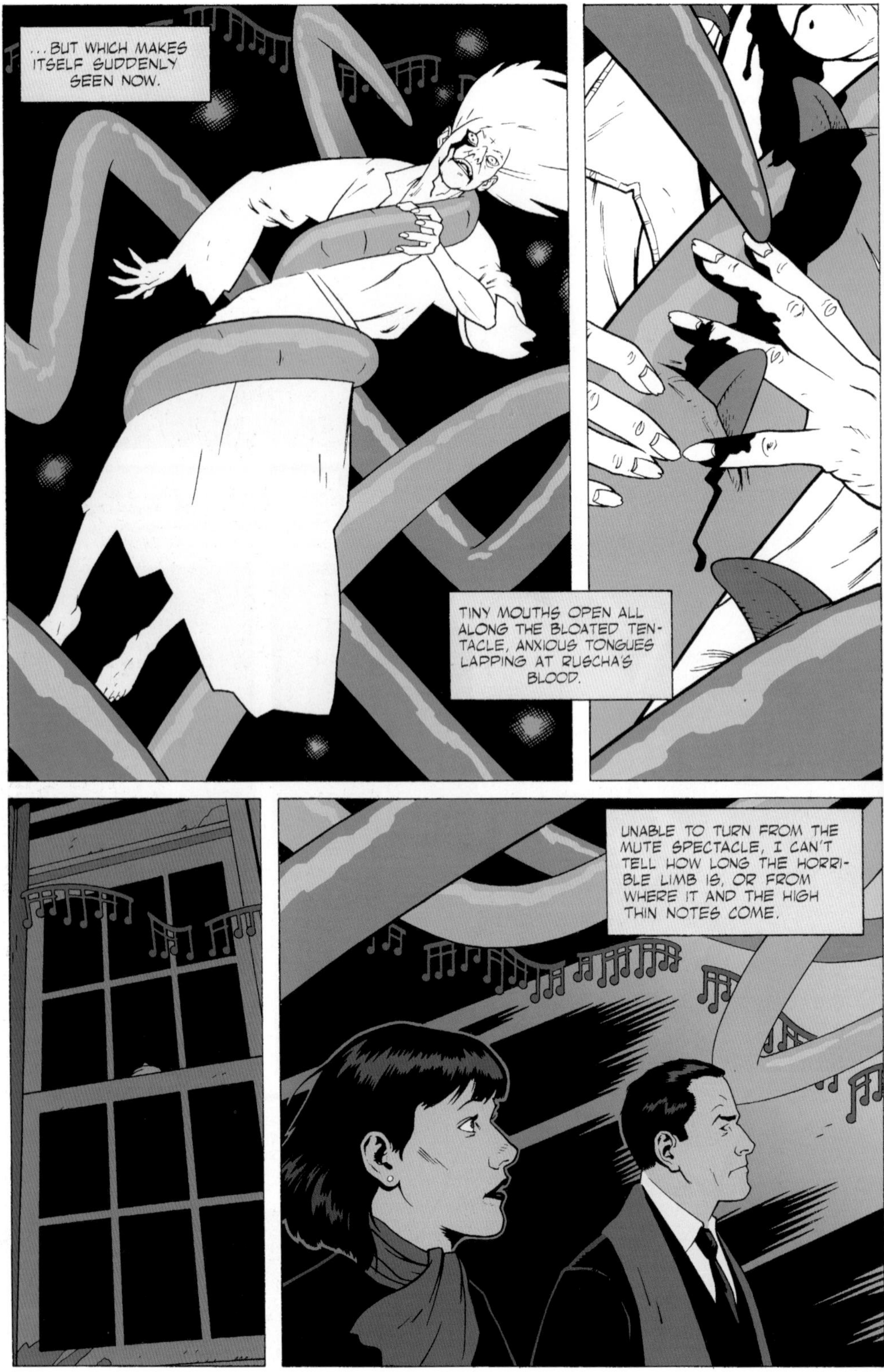
...BUT WHICH MAKES ITSELF SUDDENLY SEEN NOW.
TINY MOUTHS OPEN ALL ALONG THE BLOATED TEN-TACLE, ANXIOUS TONGUES LAPPING AT RUSCHA'S BLOOD.
UNABLE TO TURN FROM THE MUTE SPECTACLE, I CAN'T TELL HOW LONG THE HORRI-BLE LIMB IS, OR FROM WHERE IT AND THE HIGH THIN NOTES COME.

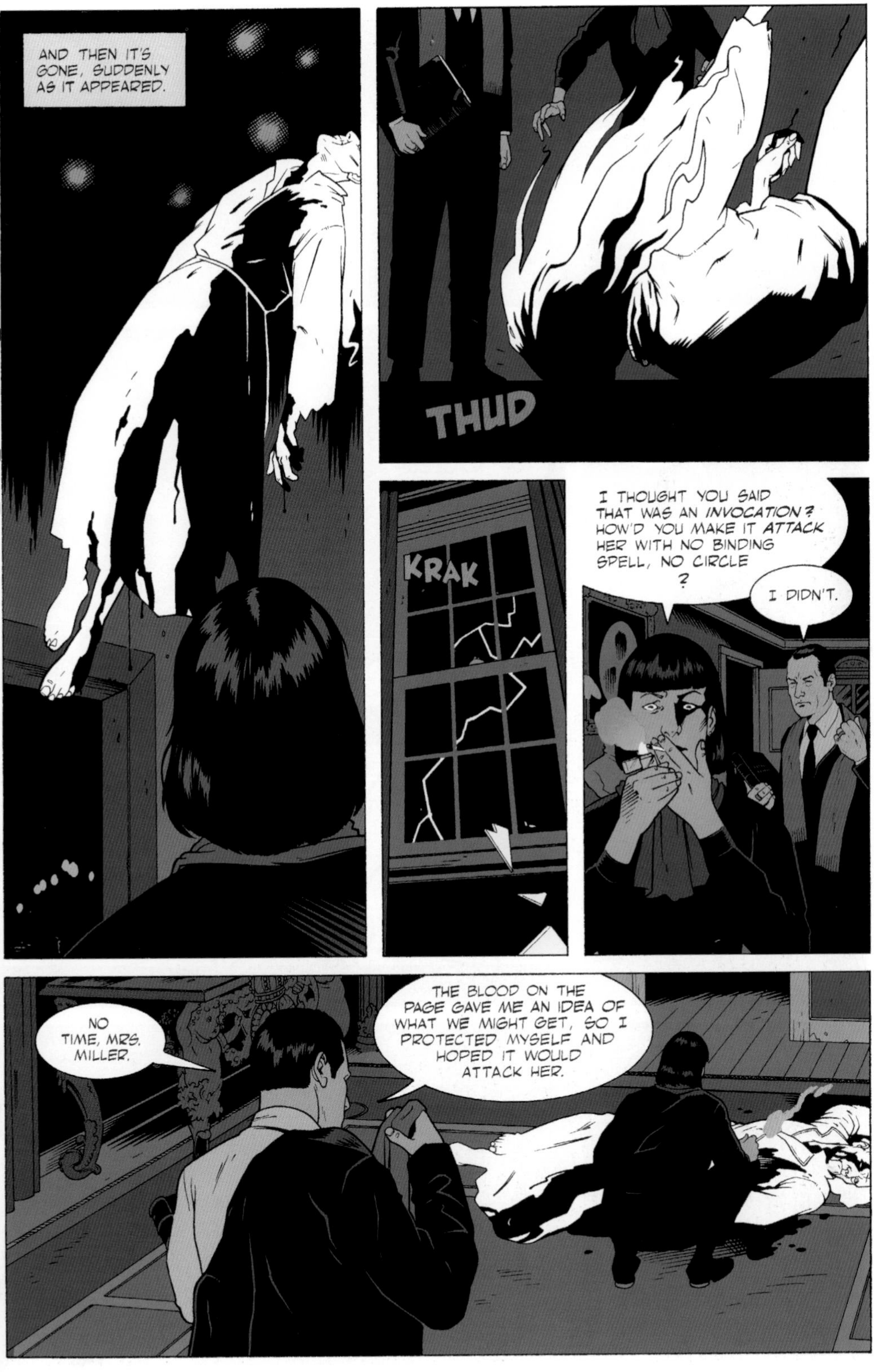
AND THEN IT'S GONE, SUDDENLY AS IT APPEARED.
THUD
KRAK
I THOUGHT YOU SAID THAT WAS AN *INVOCATION*? HOW'D YOU MAKE IT *ATTACK* HER WITH NO BINDING SPELL, NO CIRCLE ?
I DIDN'T.
NO TIME, MRS. MILLER.
THE BLOOD ON THE PAGE GAVE ME AN IDEA OF WHAT WE MIGHT GET, SO I PROTECTED MYSELF AND HOPED IT WOULD ATTACK HER.

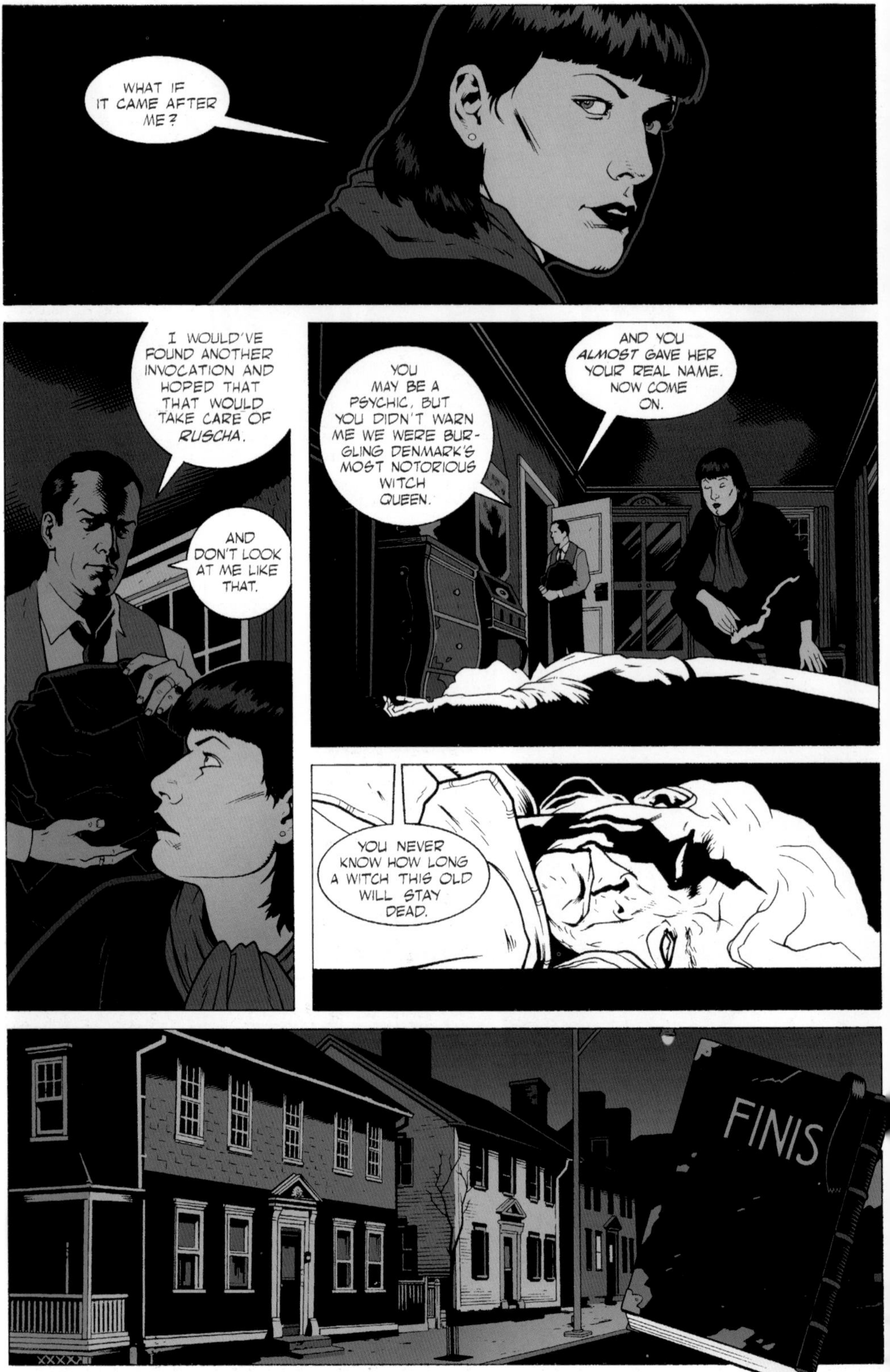
WHAT IF IT CAME AFTER ME?
I WOULD'VE FOUND ANOTHER INVOCATION AND HOPED THAT THAT WOULD TAKE CARE OF *RUSCHA*.
AND DON'T LOOK AT ME LIKE THAT.
YOU MAY BE A PSYCHIC, BUT YOU DIDN'T WARN ME WE WERE BUR-GLING DENMARK'S MOST NOTORIOUS WITCH QUEEN.
AND YOU *ALMOST* GAVE HER YOUR REAL NAME. NOW COME ON.
YOU NEVER KNOW HOW LONG A WITCH THIS OLD WILL STAY DEAD.
FINIS

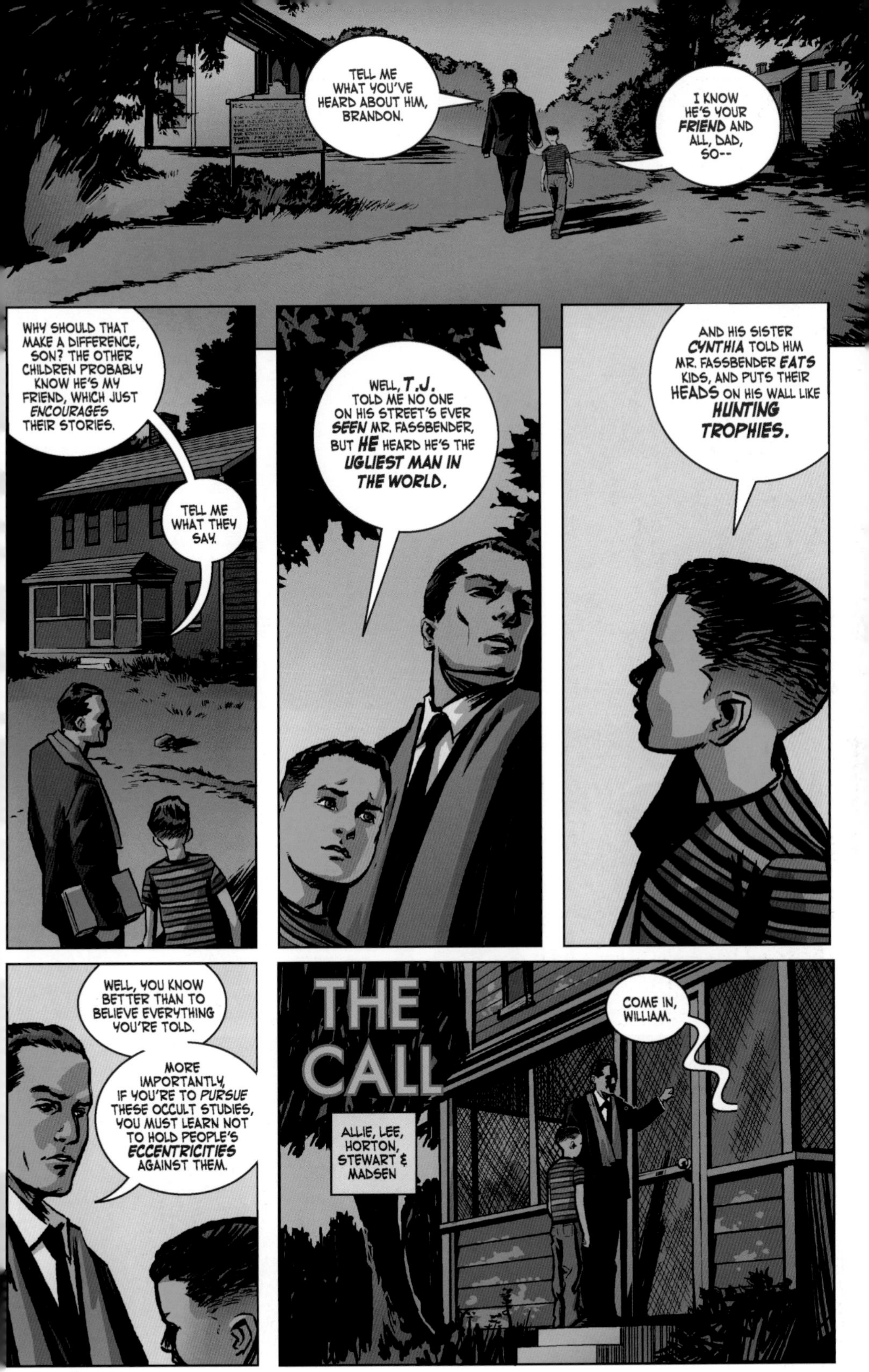
TELL ME WHAT YOU'VE HEARD ABOUT HIM, BRANDON.
I KNOW HE'S YOUR FRIEND AND ALL, DAD, SO--
WHY SHOULD THAT MAKE A DIFFERENCE, SON? THE OTHER CHILDREN PROBABLY KNOW HE'S MY FRIEND, WHICH JUST ENCOURAGES THEIR STORIES.
TELL ME WHAT THEY SAY.
WELL, T.J. TOLD ME NO ONE ON HIS STREET'S EVER SEEN MR. FASSBENDER, BUT HE HEARD HE'S THE UGLIEST MAN IN THE WORLD.
AND HIS SISTER CYNTHIA TOLD HIM MR. FASSBENDER EATS KIDS, AND PUTS THEIR HEADS ON HIS WALL LIKE HUNTING TROPHIES.
WELL, YOU KNOW BETTER THAN TO BELIEVE EVERYTHING YOU'RE TOLD.
MORE IMPORTANTLY, IF YOU'RE TO PURSUE THESE OCCULT STUDIES, YOU MUST LEARN NOT TO HOLD PEOPLE'S ECCENTRICITIES AGAINST THEM.
THE CALL
ALLIE, LEE, HORTON, STEWART & MADSEN
COME IN, WILLIAM.

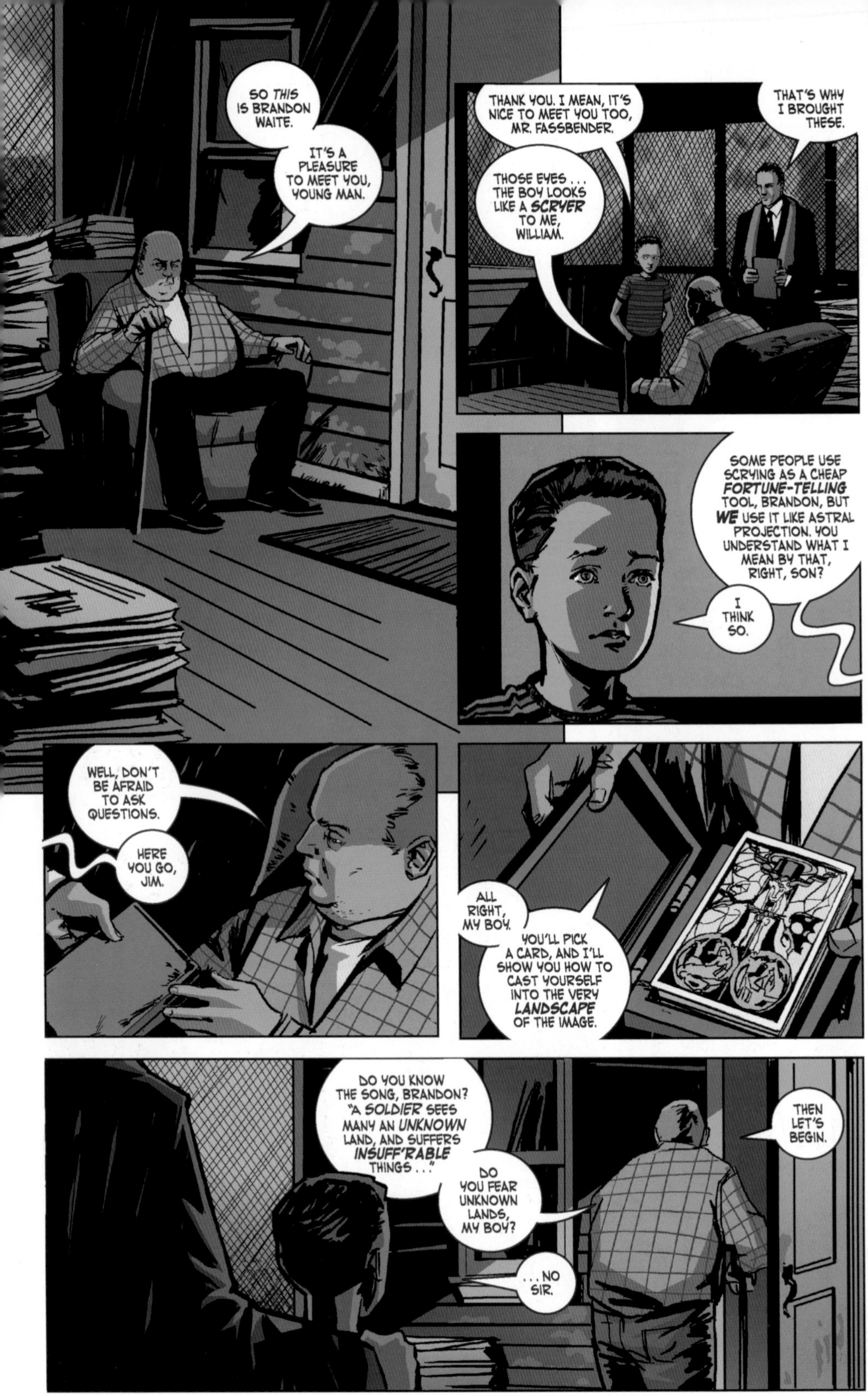
SO *THIS* IS BRANDON WAITE.
IT'S A PLEASURE TO MEET YOU, YOUNG MAN.
THANK YOU. I MEAN, IT'S NICE TO MEET YOU TOO, MR. FASSBENDER.
THOSE EYES . . . THE BOY LOOKS LIKE A ***SCRYER*** TO ME, WILLIAM.
THAT'S WHY I BROUGHT THESE.
SOME PEOPLE USE SCRYING AS A CHEAP ***FORTUNE-TELLING*** TOOL, BRANDON, BUT ***WE*** USE IT LIKE ASTRAL PROJECTION. YOU UNDERSTAND WHAT I MEAN BY THAT, RIGHT, SON?
I THINK SO.
WELL, DON'T BE AFRAID TO ASK QUESTIONS.
HERE YOU GO, JIM.
ALL RIGHT, MY BOY.
YOU'LL PICK A CARD, AND I'LL SHOW YOU HOW TO CAST YOURSELF INTO THE VERY ***LANDSCAPE*** OF THE IMAGE.
DO YOU KNOW THE SONG, BRANDON? "A ***SOLDIER*** SEES MANY AN ***UNKNOWN*** LAND, AND SUFFERS ***INSUFF'RABLE*** THINGS . . ."
DO YOU FEAR UNKNOWN LANDS, MY BOY?
. . . NO SIR.
THEN LET'S BEGIN.

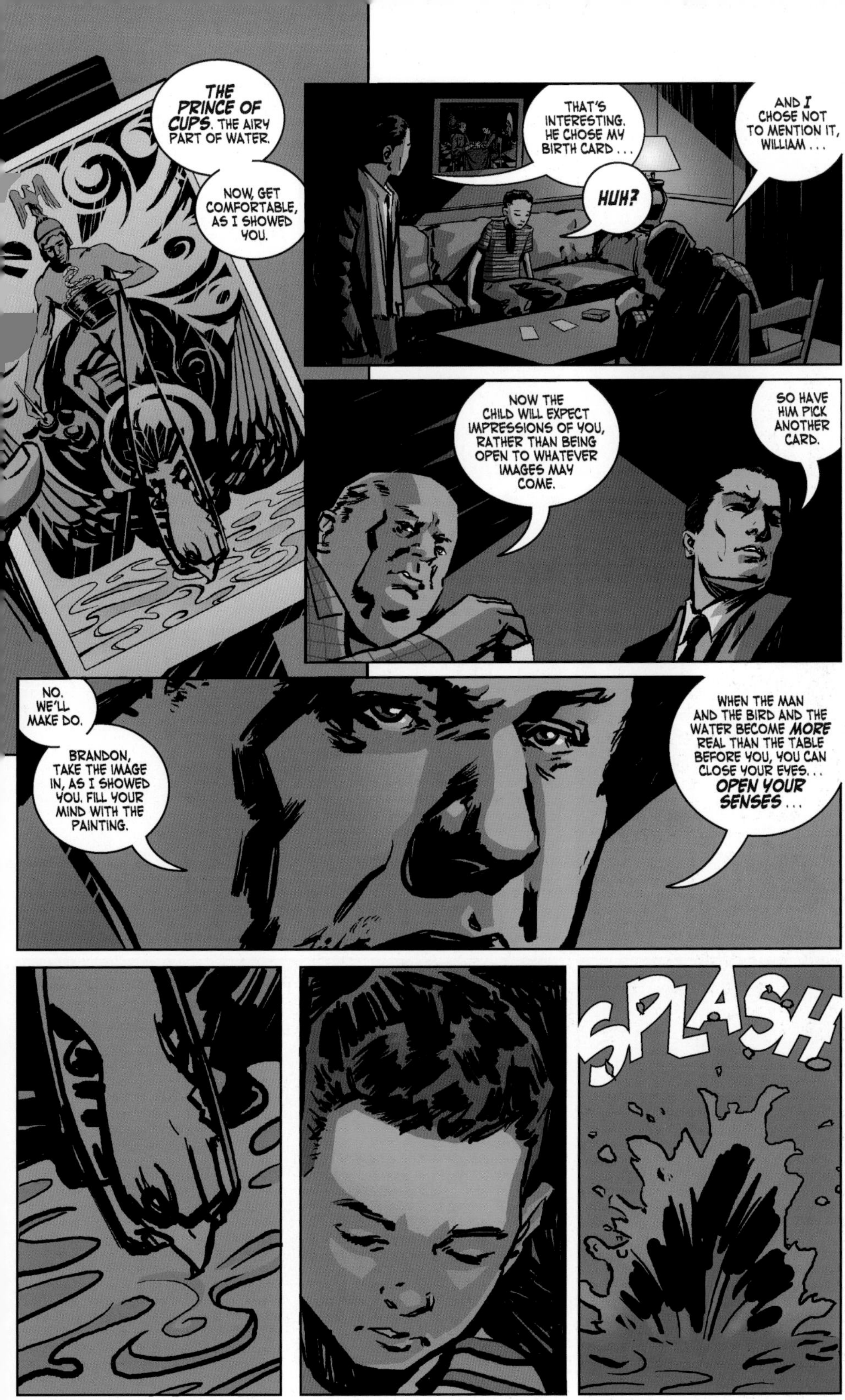
THE PRINCE OF CUPS. THE AIRY PART OF WATER.
NOW, GET COMFORTABLE, AS I SHOWED YOU.
THAT'S INTERESTING. HE CHOSE MY BIRTH CARD . . .
HUH?
AND I CHOSE NOT TO MENTION IT, WILLIAM . . .
NOW THE CHILD WILL EXPECT IMPRESSIONS OF YOU, RATHER THAN BEING OPEN TO WHATEVER IMAGES MAY COME.
SO HAVE HIM PICK ANOTHER CARD.
NO. WE'LL MAKE DO.
BRANDON, TAKE THE IMAGE IN, AS I SHOWED YOU. FILL YOUR MIND WITH THE PAINTING.
WHEN THE MAN AND THE BIRD AND THE WATER BECOME MORE REAL THAN THE TABLE BEFORE YOU, YOU CAN CLOSE YOUR EYES. . . OPEN YOUR SENSES . . .
SPLASH

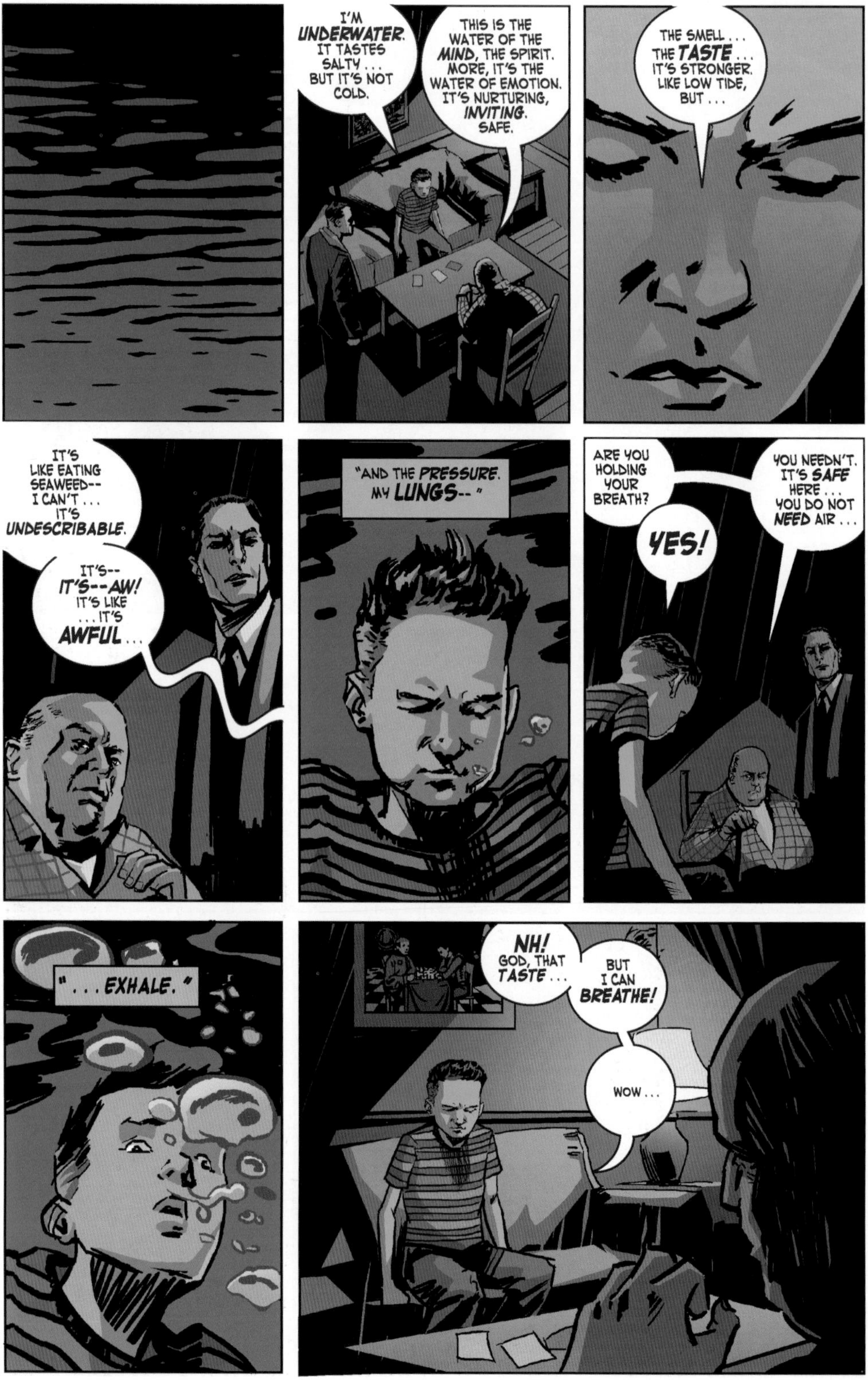
I'M UNDERWATER. IT TASTES SALTY . . . BUT IT'S NOT COLD.
THIS IS THE WATER OF THE MIND, THE SPIRIT. MORE, IT'S THE WATER OF EMOTION. IT'S NURTURING, INVITING. SAFE.
THE SMELL . . . THE TASTE . . . IT'S STRONGER. LIKE LOW TIDE, BUT . . .
IT'S LIKE EATING SEAWEED-- I CAN'T . . . IT'S UNDESCRIBABLE.
IT'S-- IT'S--AW! IT'S LIKE . . . IT'S AWFUL . . .
"AND THE PRESSURE. MY LUNGS-- "
ARE YOU HOLDING YOUR BREATH?
YES!
YOU NEEDN'T. IT'S SAFE HERE . . . YOU DO NOT NEED AIR . . .
". . . EXHALE."
NH! GOD, THAT TASTE . . .
BUT I CAN BREATHE!
WOW . . .

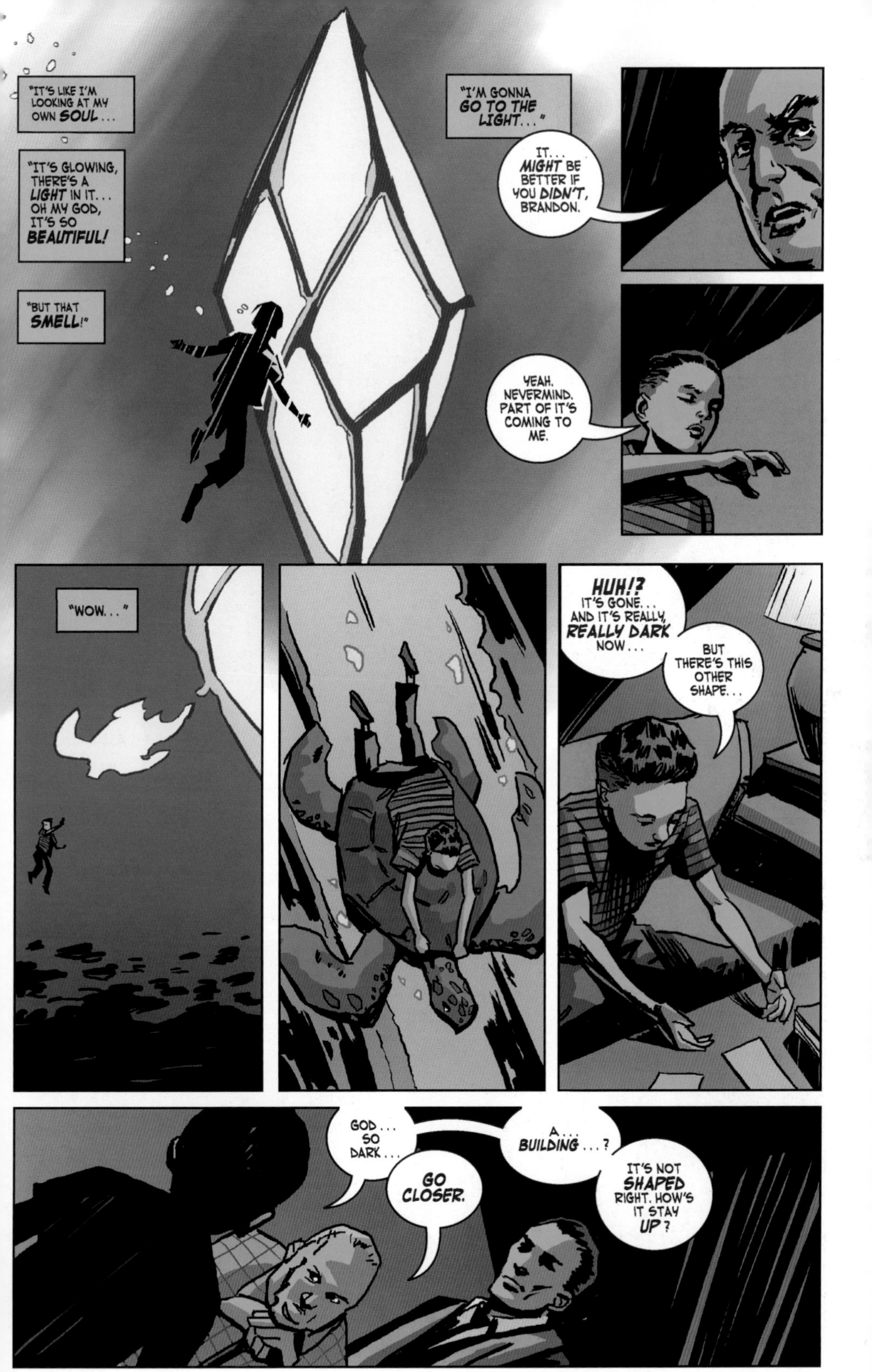
"IT'S LIKE I'M LOOKING AT MY OWN SOUL...
"IT'S GLOWING, THERE'S A LIGHT IN IT... OH MY GOD, IT'S SO BEAUTIFUL!
"BUT THAT SMELL!"
"I'M GONNA GO TO THE LIGHT..."
IT... MIGHT BE BETTER IF YOU DIDN'T, BRANDON.
YEAH. NEVERMIND. PART OF IT'S COMING TO ME.
"WOW..."
HUH!? IT'S GONE... AND IT'S REALLY, REALLY DARK NOW...
BUT THERE'S THIS OTHER SHAPE...
GOD... SO DARK...
GO CLOSER.
A... BUILDING...?
IT'S NOT SHAPED RIGHT. HOW'S IT STAY UP?

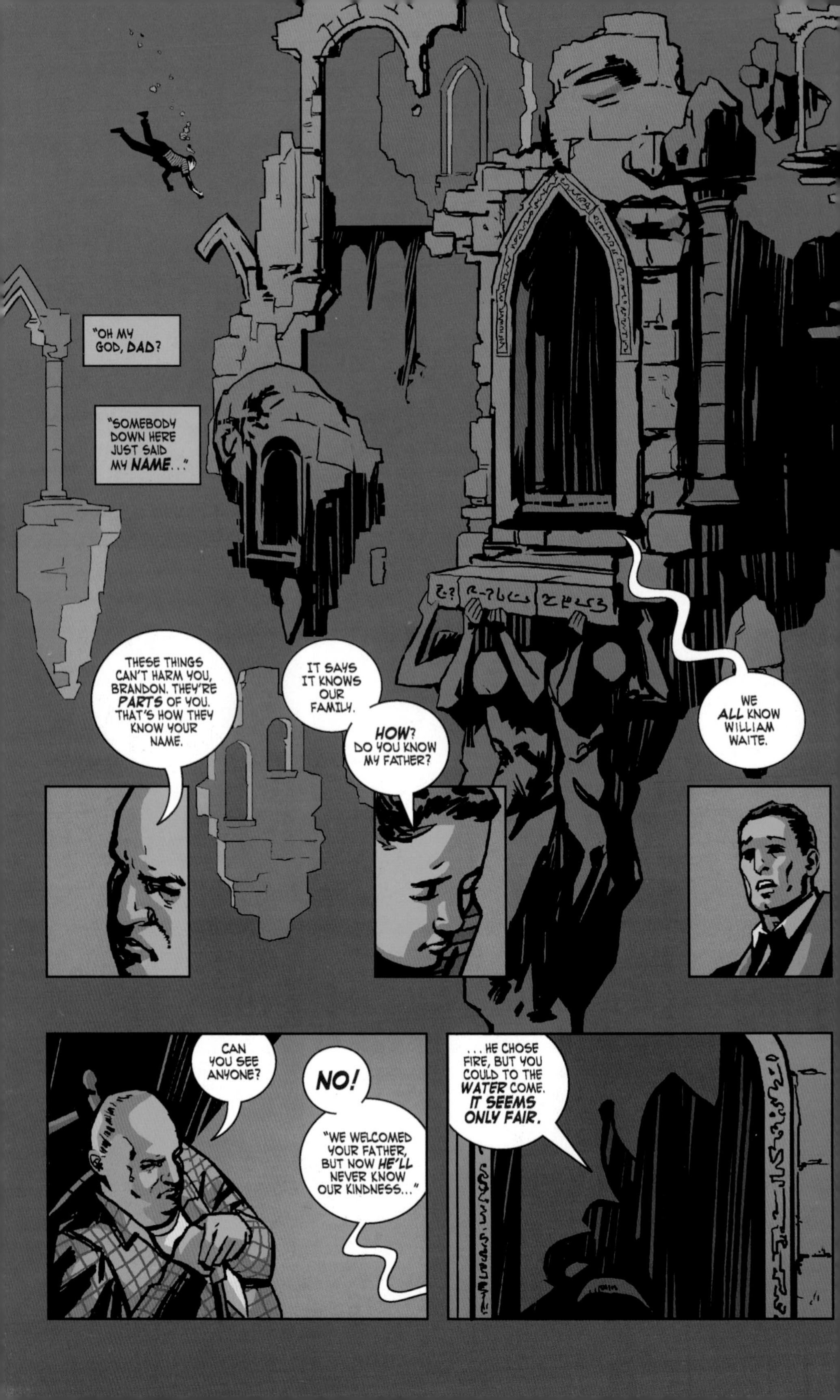
"OH MY GOD, DAD?
"SOMEBODY DOWN HERE JUST SAID MY NAME..."
THESE THINGS CAN'T HARM YOU, BRANDON. THEY'RE PARTS OF YOU. THAT'S HOW THEY KNOW YOUR NAME.
IT SAYS IT KNOWS OUR FAMILY.
HOW? DO YOU KNOW MY FATHER?
WE ALL KNOW WILLIAM WAITE.
CAN YOU SEE ANYONE?
NO!
"WE WELCOMED YOUR FATHER, BUT NOW HE'LL NEVER KNOW OUR KINDNESS..."
...HE CHOSE FIRE, BUT YOU COULD TO THE WATER COME. IT SEEMS ONLY FAIR.

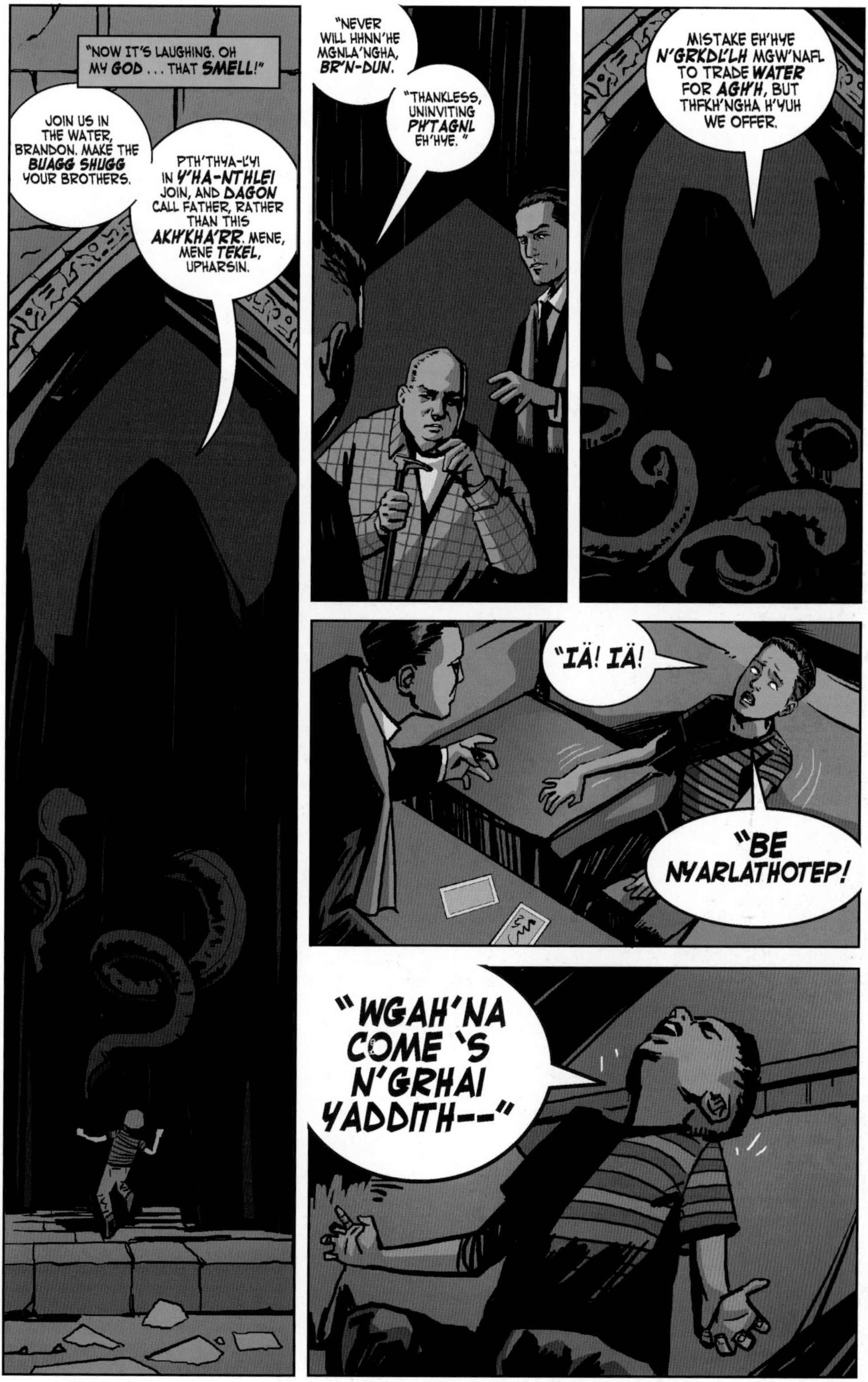
"NOW IT'S LAUGHING. OH MY GOD . . . THAT SMELL!"
JOIN US IN THE WATER, BRANDON. MAKE THE BUAGG SHUGG YOUR BROTHERS.
PTH'THYA-L'YI IN Y'HA-NTHLEI JOIN, AND DAGON CALL FATHER, RATHER THAN THIS AKH'KHA'RR. MENE, MENE TEKEL, UPHARSIN.
"NEVER WILL HHNN'HE MGNLA'NGHA, BR'N-DUN.
"THANKLESS, UNINVITING PH'TAGNL EH'HYE."
MISTAKE EH'HYE N'GRKDL'LH MGW'NAFL TO TRADE WATER FOR AGH'H, BUT THFKH'NGHA H'YUH WE OFFER.
"IÄ! IÄ!
"BE NYARLATHOTEP!
"WGAH'NA COME 'S N'GRHAI YADDITH--"

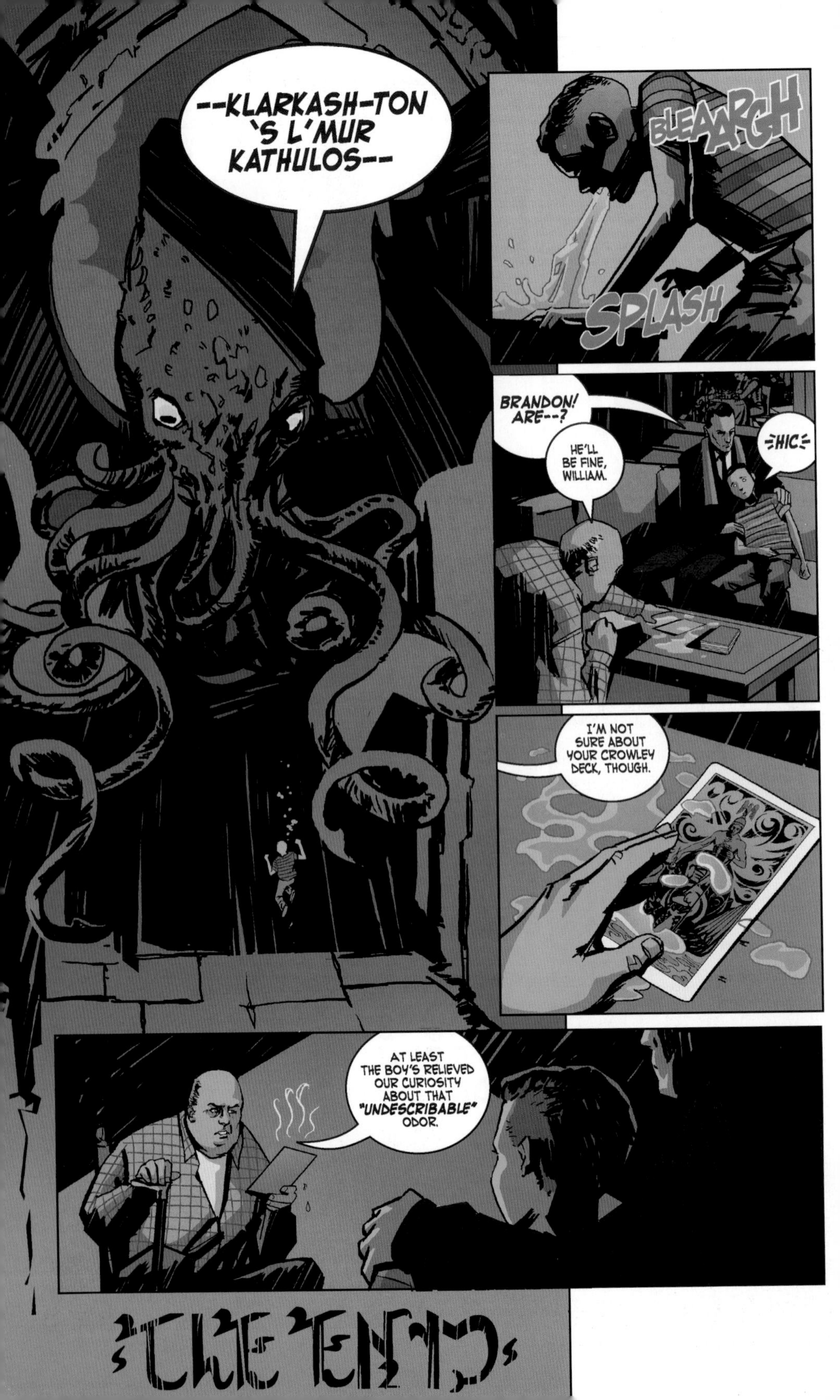
--KLARKASH-TON 'S L'MUR KATHULOS--
BLEAAARGH
SPLASH
BRANDON! ARE--?
HE'LL BE FINE, WILLIAM.
HIC
I'M NOT SURE ABOUT YOUR CROWLEY DECK, THOUGH.
AT LEAST THE BOY'S RELIEVED OUR CURIOSITY ABOUT THAT "UNDESCRIBABLE" ODOR.
THE END

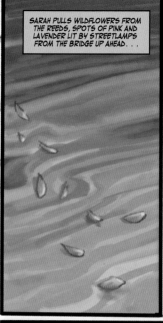

SARAH PULLS WILDFLOWERS FROM THE REEDS, SPOTS OF PINK AND LAVENDER LIT BY STREETLAMPS FROM THE BRIDGE UP AHEAD . . .

. . . AS BRIGHT AS HER EYES.

PETALS FALL IN SPIRALS TO THE WATER, MOVING FASTER THE FURTHER THEY DRIFT FROM HER.

SHE DROPS THE STEMS BETWEEN WET FOOTPRINTS, NEXT TO A FLAT ROCK, PERFECT FOR SKIPPING.

THE MUD IS COLD, AND CLINGS TO THE ROCK.

I SQUEEZE IT AS HARD AS I CAN BEFORE THROWING IT.

THE CURRENT

ALLIE, LEE, STEWART, & MADSEN

HEY, LOOK!

SPLISH

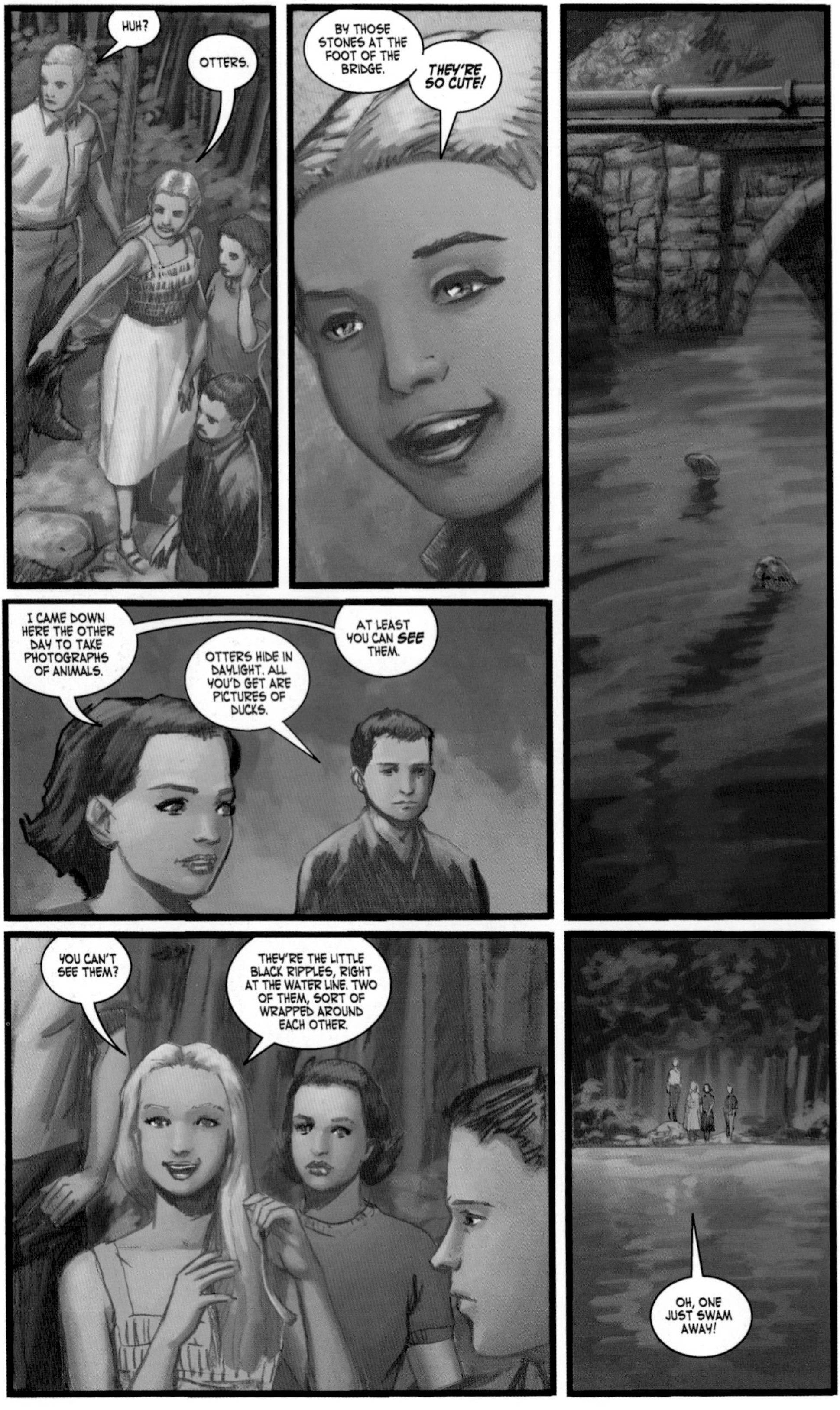
HUH?
OTTERS.
BY THOSE STONES AT THE FOOT OF THE BRIDGE.
THEY'RE SO CUTE!
I CAME DOWN HERE THE OTHER DAY TO TAKE PHOTOGRAPHS OF ANIMALS.
OTTERS HIDE IN DAYLIGHT. ALL YOU'D GET ARE PICTURES OF DUCKS.
AT LEAST YOU CAN SEE THEM.
YOU CAN'T SEE THEM?
THEY'RE THE LITTLE BLACK RIPPLES, RIGHT AT THE WATER LINE. TWO OF THEM, SORT OF WRAPPED AROUND EACH OTHER.
OH, ONE JUST SWAM AWAY!

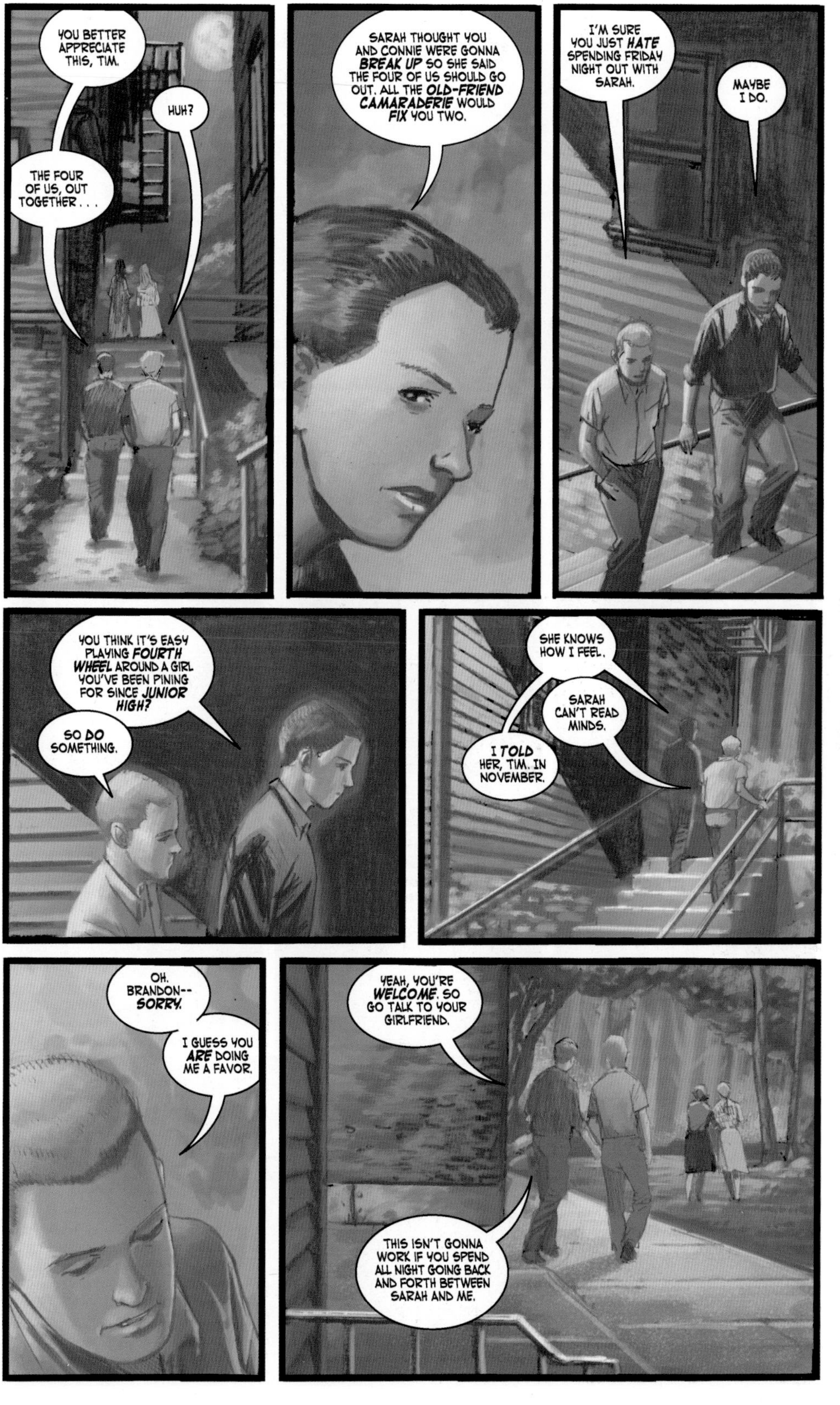
YOU BETTER APPRECIATE THIS, TIM.
THE FOUR OF US, OUT TOGETHER . . .
HUH?
SARAH THOUGHT YOU AND CONNIE WERE GONNA BREAK UP SO SHE SAID THE FOUR OF US SHOULD GO OUT. ALL THE OLD-FRIEND CAMARADERIE WOULD FIX YOU TWO.
I'M SURE YOU JUST HATE SPENDING FRIDAY NIGHT OUT WITH SARAH.
MAYBE I DO.
YOU THINK IT'S EASY PLAYING FOURTH WHEEL AROUND A GIRL YOU'VE BEEN PINING FOR SINCE JUNIOR HIGH?
SO DO SOMETHING.
SHE KNOWS HOW I FEEL.
SARAH CAN'T READ MINDS.
I TOLD HER, TIM. IN NOVEMBER.
OH. BRANDON-- SORRY.
I GUESS YOU ARE DOING ME A FAVOR.
YEAH, YOU'RE WELCOME. SO GO TALK TO YOUR GIRLFRIEND.
THIS ISN'T GONNA WORK IF YOU SPEND ALL NIGHT GOING BACK AND FORTH BETWEEN SARAH AND ME.

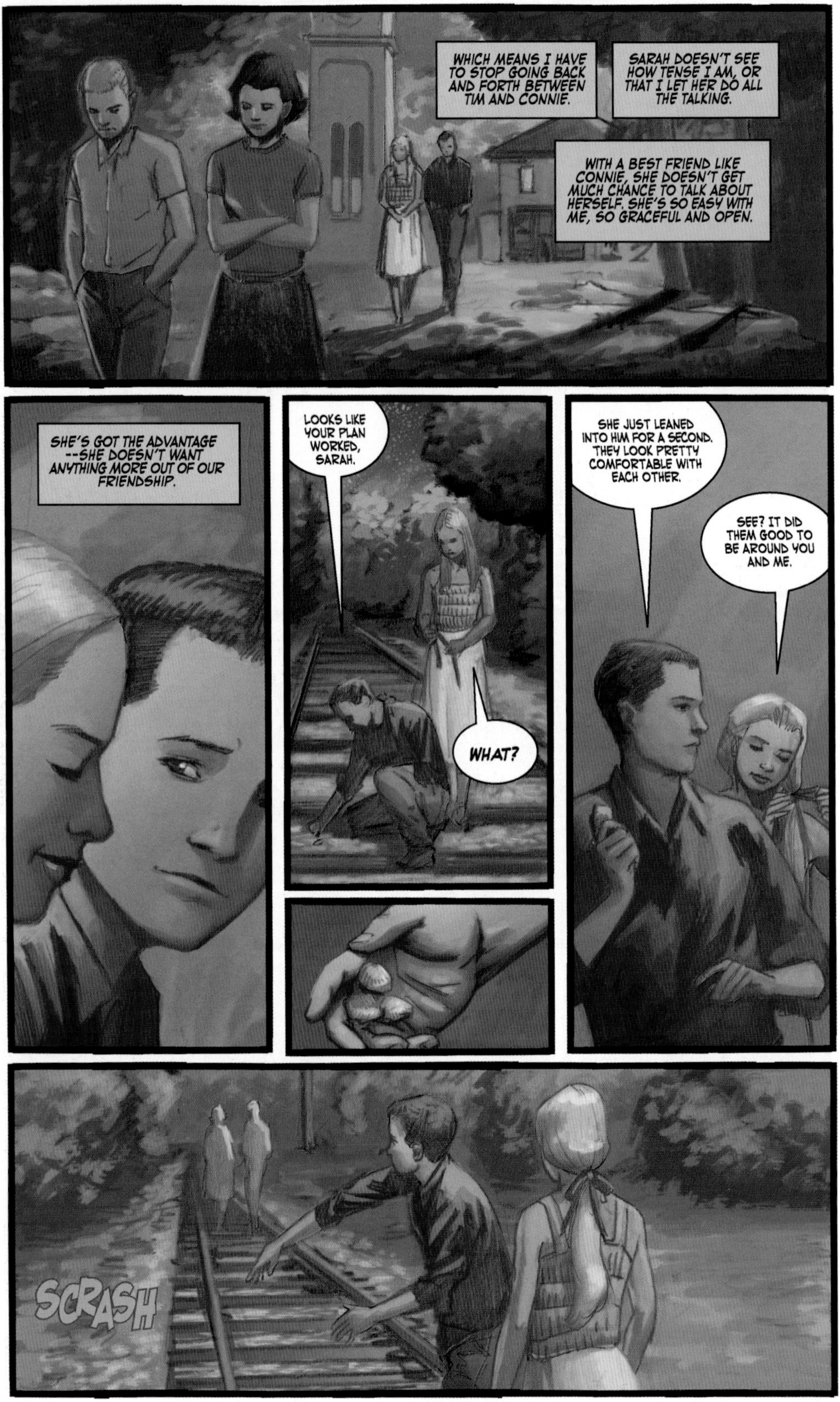
WHICH MEANS I HAVE TO STOP GOING BACK AND FORTH BETWEEN TIM AND CONNIE.
SARAH DOESN'T SEE HOW TENSE I AM, OR THAT I LET HER DO ALL THE TALKING.
WITH A BEST FRIEND LIKE CONNIE, SHE DOESN'T GET MUCH CHANCE TO TALK ABOUT HERSELF. SHE'S SO EASY WITH ME, SO GRACEFUL AND OPEN.
SHE'S GOT THE ADVANTAGE --SHE DOESN'T WANT ANYTHING MORE OUT OF OUR FRIENDSHIP.
LOOKS LIKE YOUR PLAN WORKED, SARAH.
WHAT?
SHE JUST LEANED INTO HIM FOR A SECOND. THEY LOOK PRETTY COMFORTABLE WITH EACH OTHER.
SEE? IT DID THEM GOOD TO BE AROUND YOU AND ME.
SCRASH

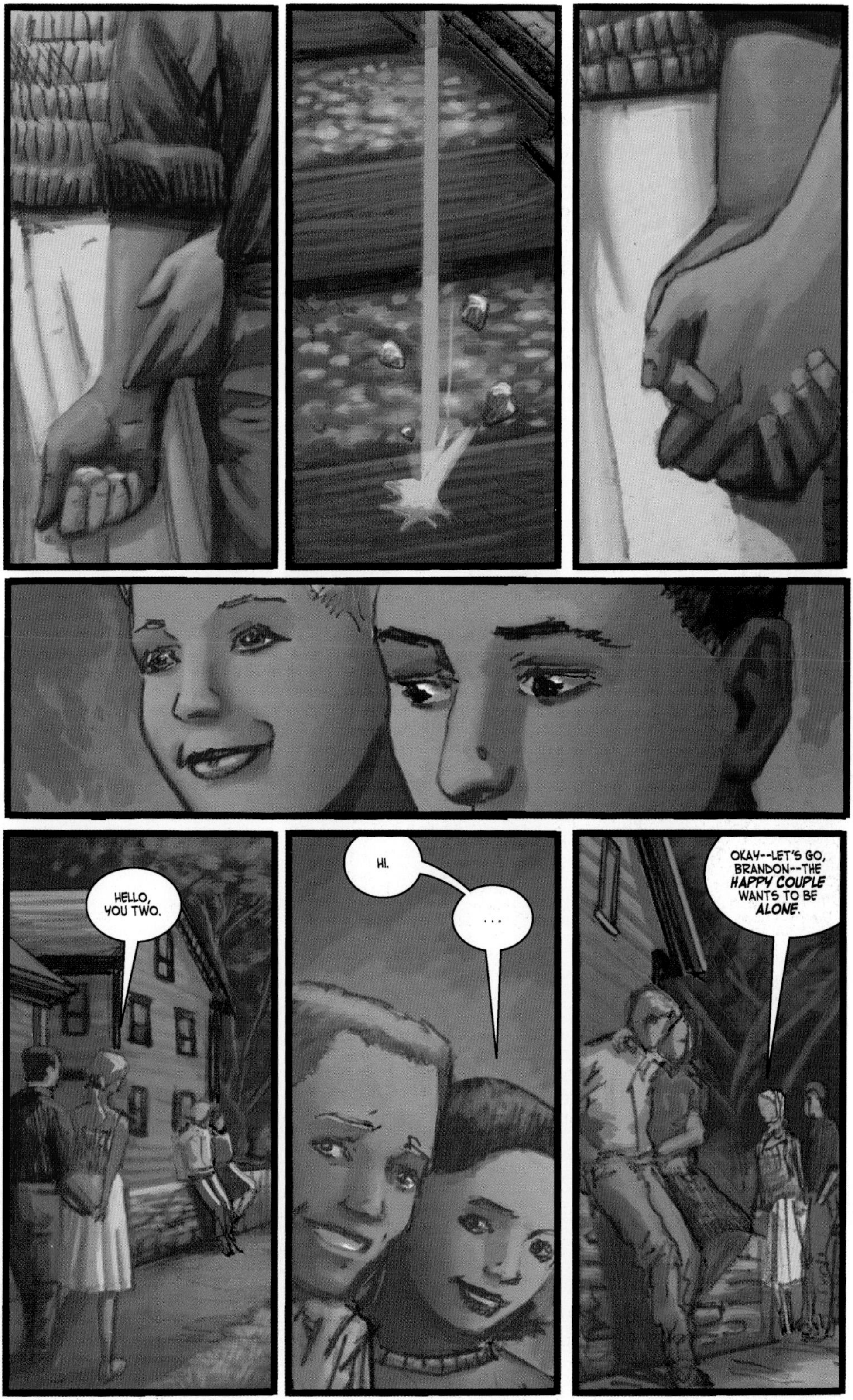
HELLO, YOU TWO.
HI.
. . .
OKAY--LET'S GO, BRANDON--THE HAPPY COUPLE WANTS TO BE ALONE.

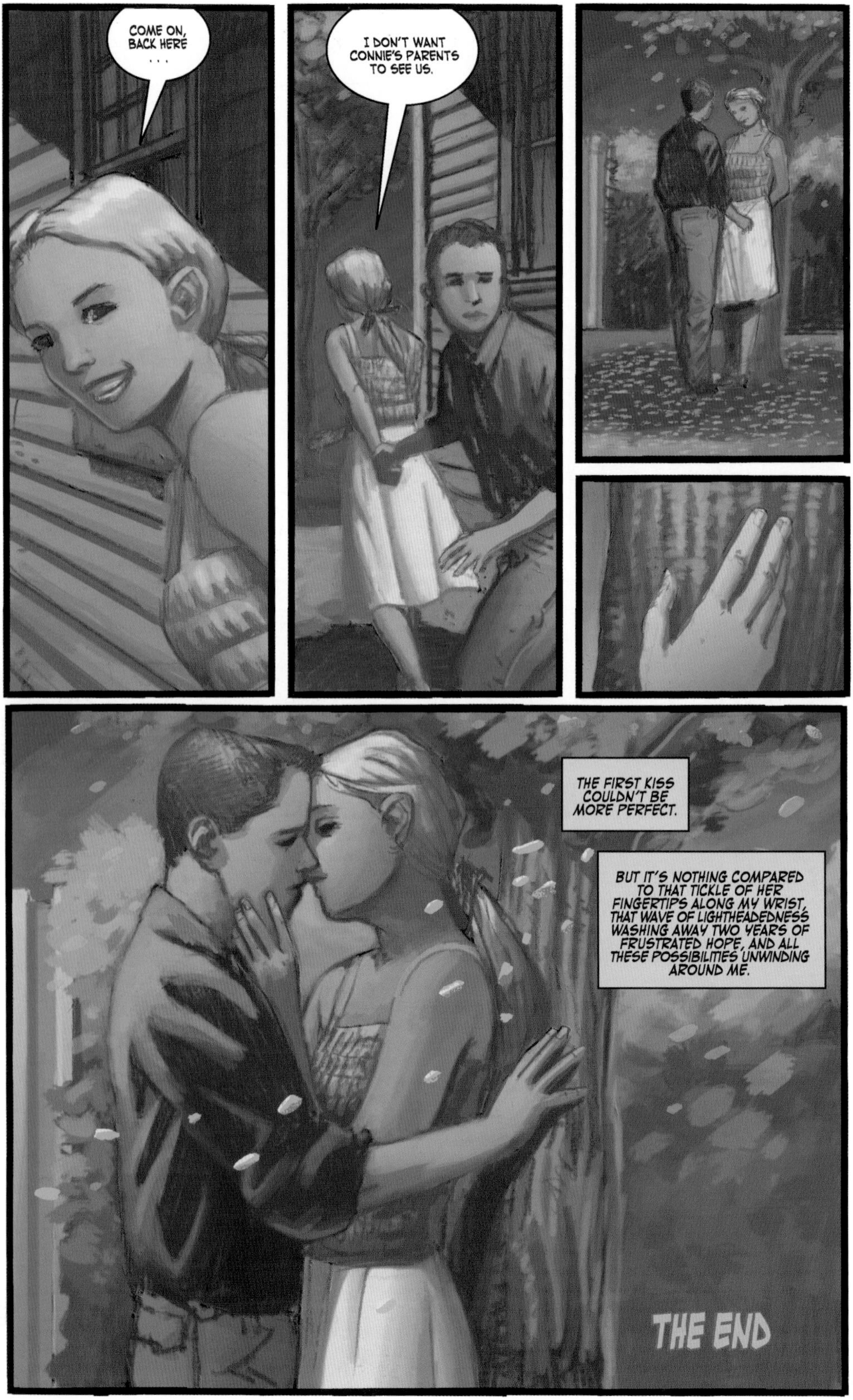
COME ON, BACK HERE . . .
I DON'T WANT CONNIE'S PARENTS TO SEE US.
THE FIRST KISS COULDN'T BE MORE PERFECT.
BUT IT'S NOTHING COMPARED TO THAT TICKLE OF HER FINGERTIPS ALONG MY WRIST, THAT WAVE OF LIGHTHEADEDNESS WASHING AWAY TWO YEARS OF FRUSTRATED HOPE, AND ALL THESE POSSIBILITIES UNWINDING AROUND ME.
THE END

SKETCH GALLERY

The following pages present concept art by Paul Lee and Brian Horton.

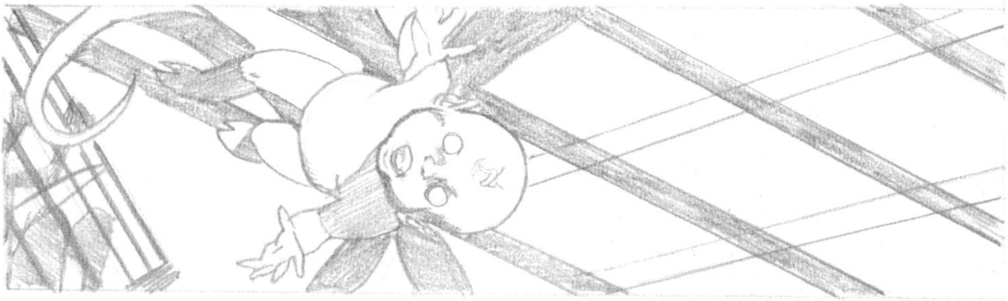

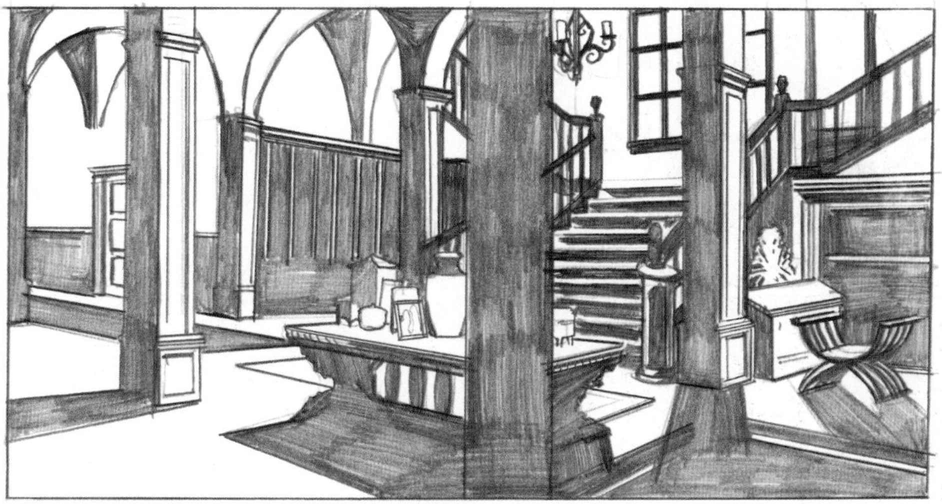

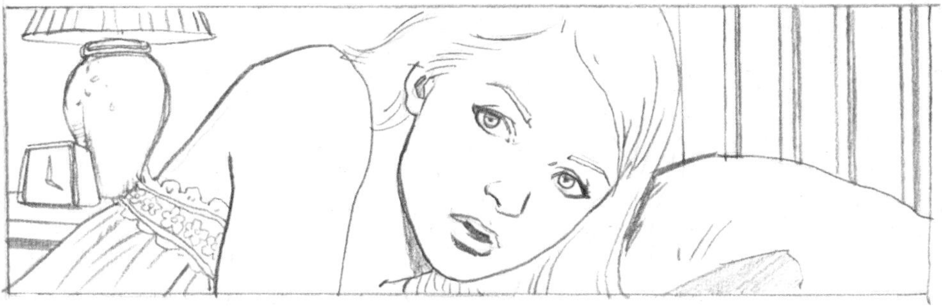

Pencils by Paul.

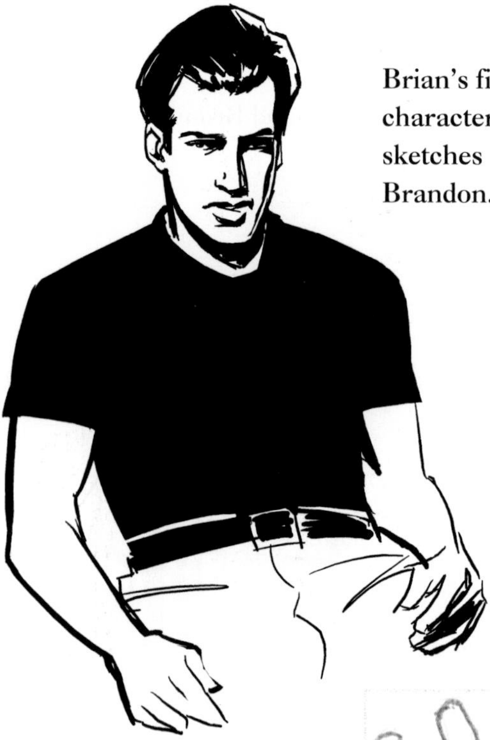

Brian's first character sketches of Brandon.

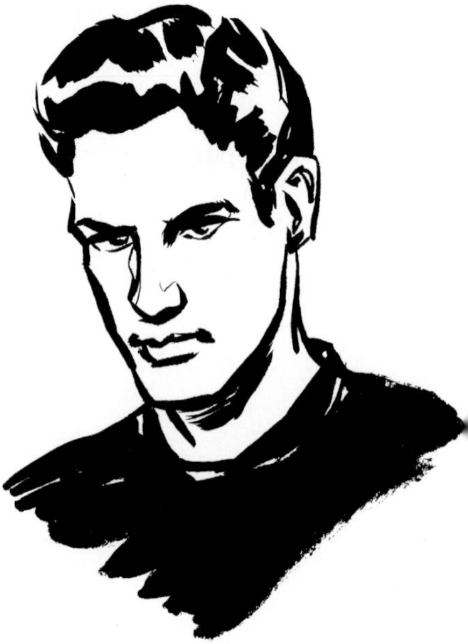

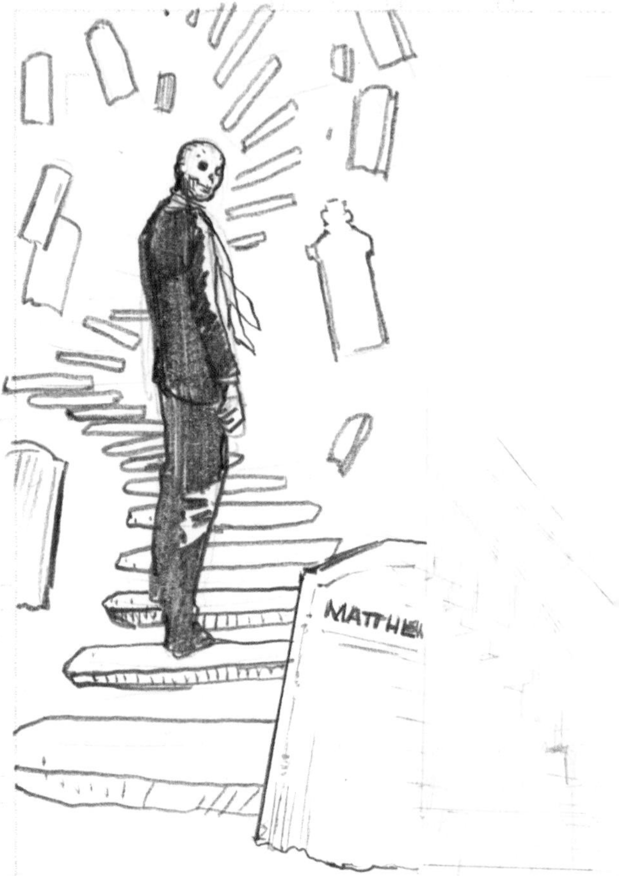
MATTHE

Paul's pencil rough of Brandon's vision preceding Sarah's accident.

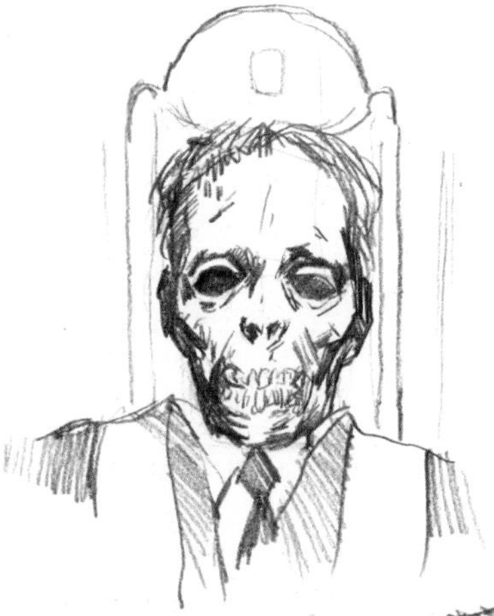

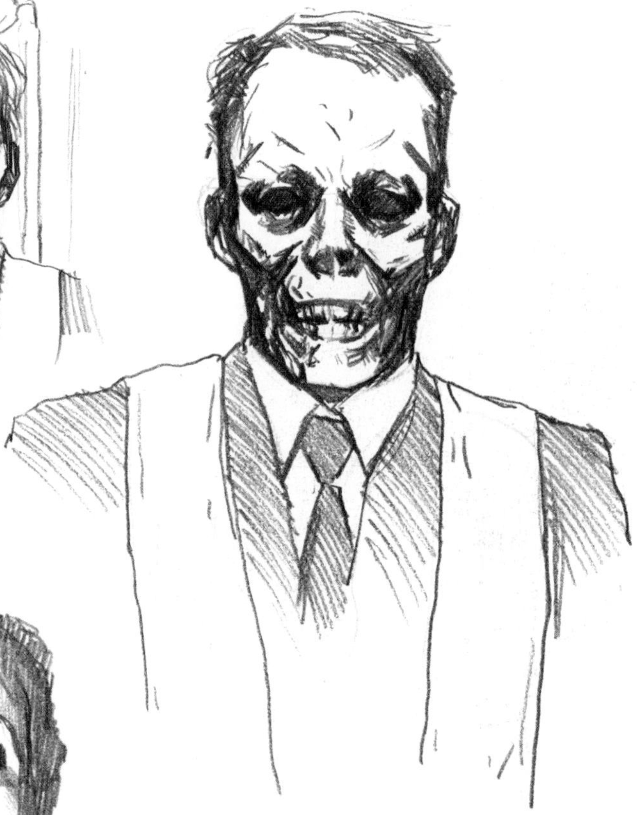

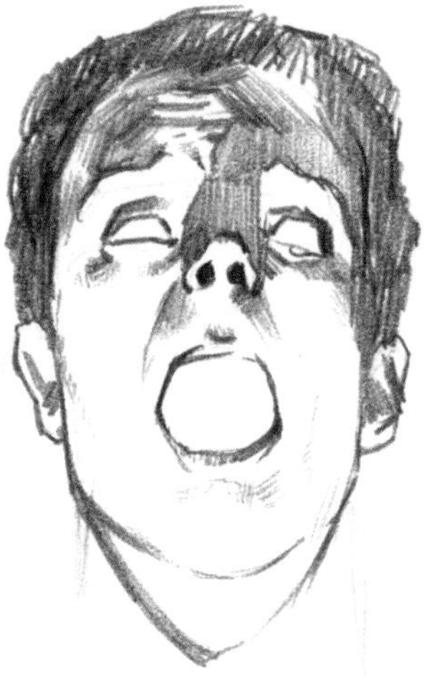

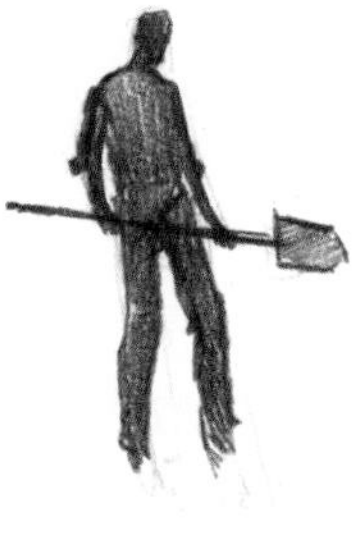

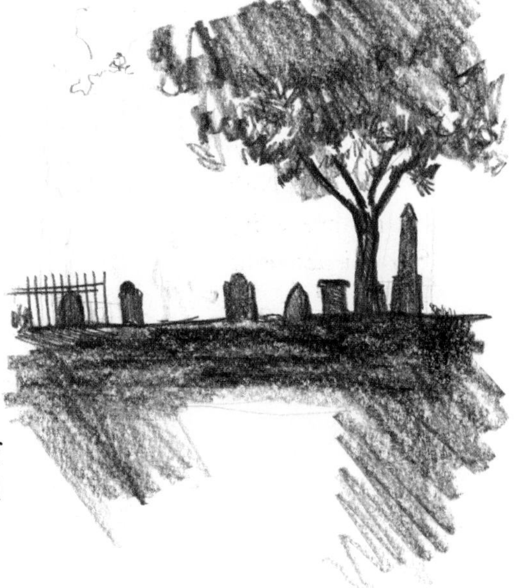

Paul's pencil studies for the covers of the original series (compare to second page and back cover of this edition).

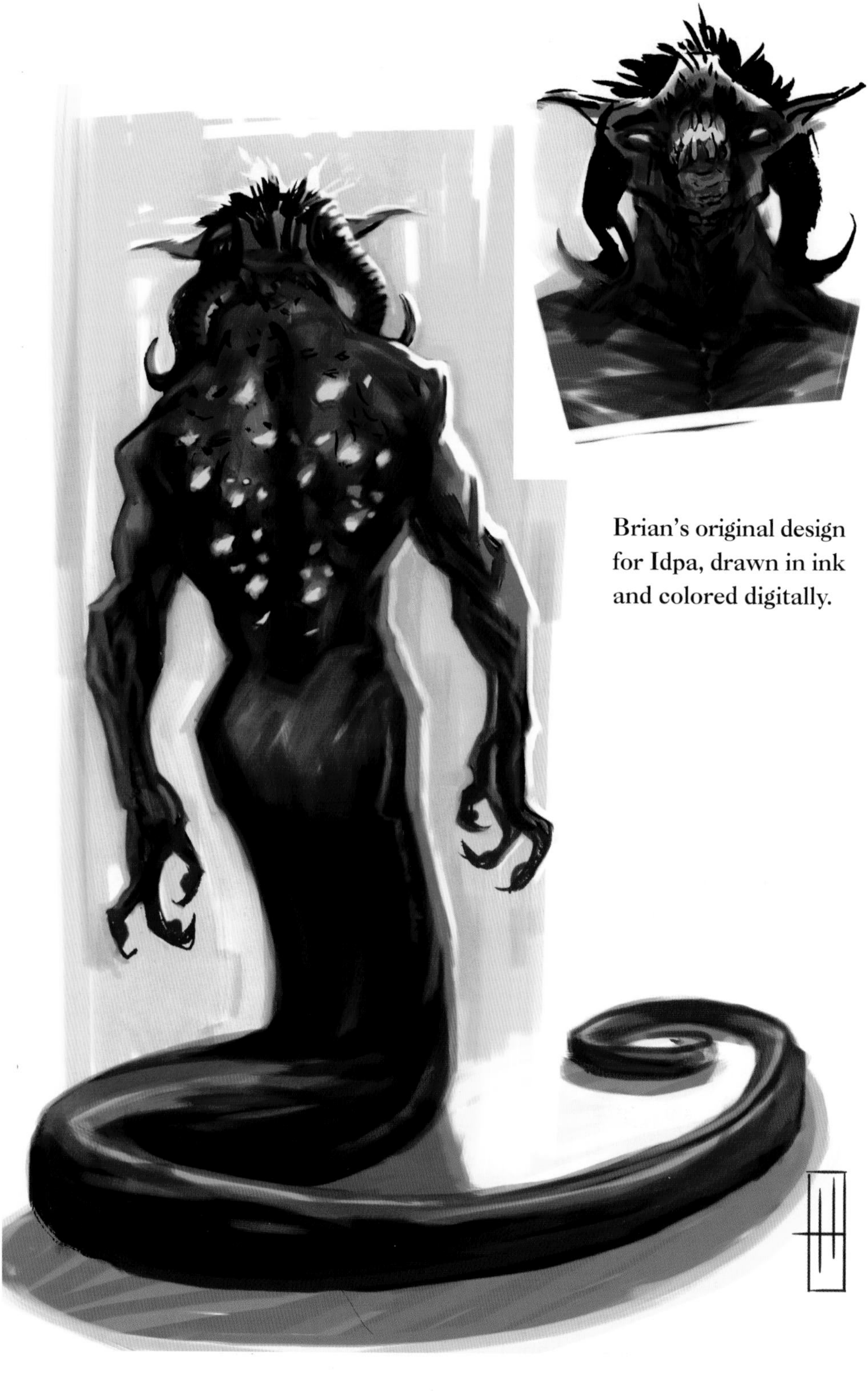

Brian's original design for Idpa, drawn in ink and colored digitally.

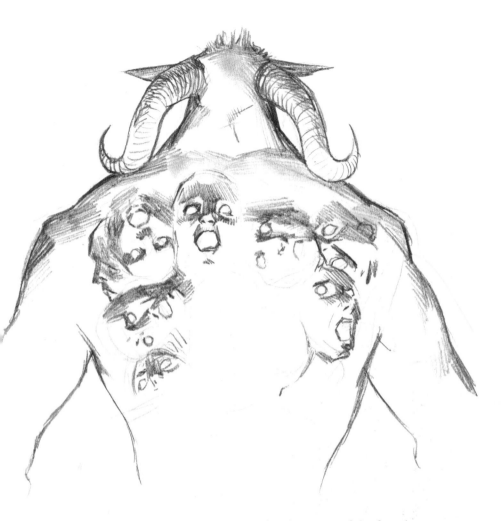

Paul's pencil studies of Idpa's back for the cover of the fourth
issue (compare to back cover of this edition).

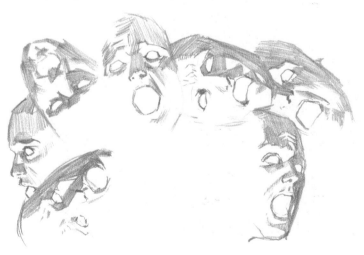

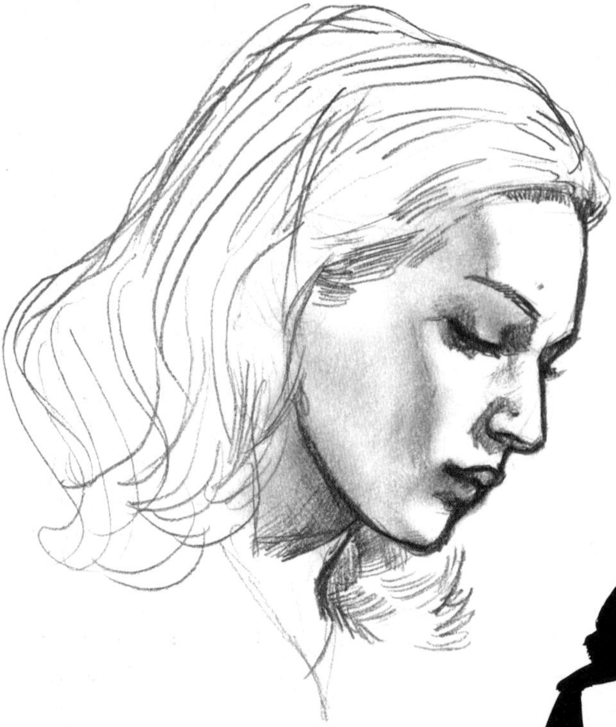

Paul's study of Sarah for the third issue cover. The face changed noticeably in Brian's final painting (compare to title page of the "Demonology" section of this book).

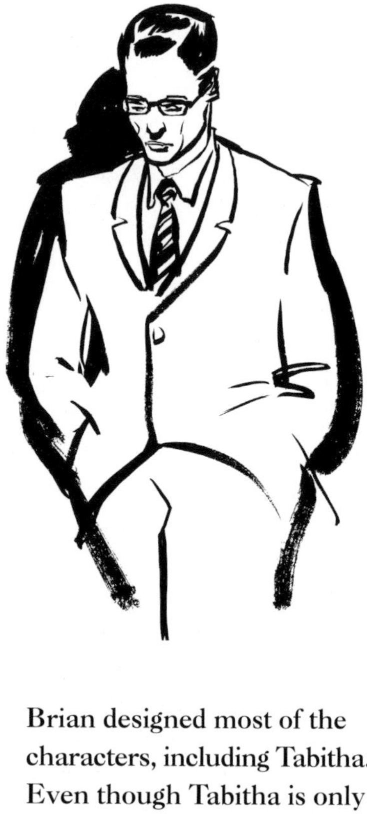

Brian's initial design for Dexter.

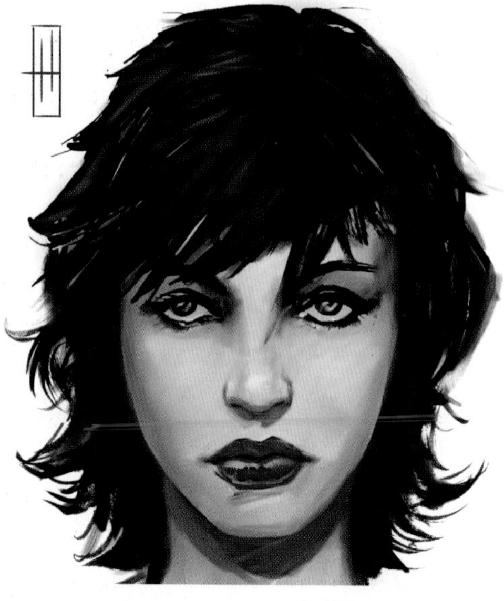

Brian designed most of the characters, including Tabitha. Even though Tabitha is only in two scenes in the book, this is the most fully realized character design Brian did; the character is based on his wife Susan.

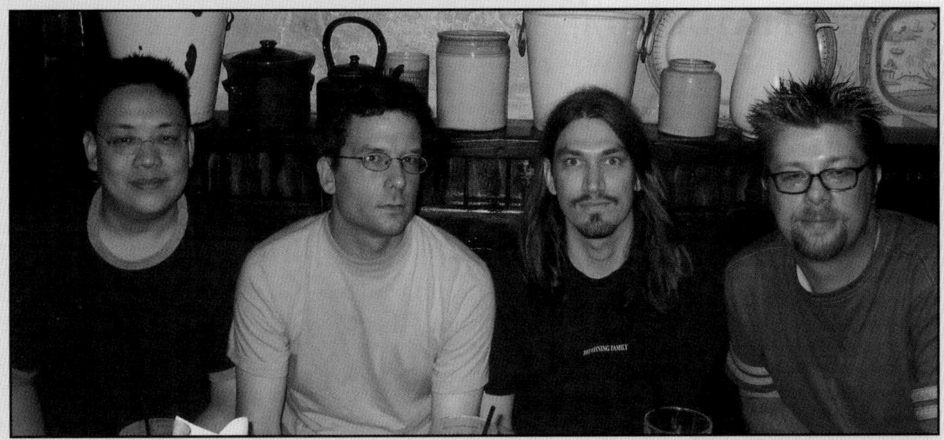

Photo credit: Shawna Ervin-Gore

PAUL LEE is a painter and freelance illustrator, the creator of the comics series *Lurid*, and co-creator of *The Devil's Footprints*. He often collaborates with Brian Horton, most notably on a long run of Dark Horse's *Buffy the Vampire Slayer* covers. He recommends fiber to promote regularity, and lives with his wife and son in Southern California.

SCOTT ALLIE writes and edits comics and stories for Dark Horse Comics and other publishers. Like Brandon, he comes from the swamplands of Ipswich, and that has made all the difference. He lives in Portland, Oregon, with his wife Melinda and their phantom cat, Shadow.

BRIAN HORTON has been an illustrator and video-game artist for ten years. He's worked for interactive companies including Disney, Dreamworks, and Electronic Arts. At EA he was the Lead Artist on *Clive Barker's Undying*, and for the past two years has been at The Collective, art directing *Indiana Jones and the Emperor's Tomb*. Brian moonlights in comics with his partners in crime, Scott and Paul, on *Buffy the Vampire Slayer*, *Star Wars*, and *The Devil's Footprints*. He shares his life with his wife Susan and son Victor in Aliso Viejo, California.

DAVE STEWART is a colorist in high demand, the first choice for such acclaimed artists as Howard Chaykin, Adam Kubert, and Mike Mignola. Like the potato, Dave is a product of Idaho. He is currently residing in Portland, Oregon, with his wife and fellow colorist, Michelle, and their young son, a Chihuahua named Spike. He works as compulsively as Brian Horton, which is saying something indeed.

Our crack team of cartoonists would like to thank Michelle Madsen, Kenneth Haugan, Jason Hvam, Galen Showman, Mike Richardson, Randy Stradley, Grosse Pointe Girl, Lee Dawson, Sara Perrin, Ring, Jeff Macey, Amy Huey, Lia Ribacchi, Mike Mignola, Gary Gianni, Alan Moore, Natalie Berry, Jamie S. Rich, Jim Pascoe, Jonell Napper, Elizabeth Kushman, Christopher Wold, Mike Conlon, Jesse Thompson, Casey Seijas, Aaron Weisbrod, Allen Spiegel, Ellen Shefi, Paul Allen, Mark Ricketts, Dario Gulli, Kristy Bratton, Matt Brady, James Baker, Mike Conroy, Randy Lander, Greg McElhatton, Joel Meadows, Faith Tomei, and Dinah Cardin.

LLIE, LEE, HORTON, AND STEWART

Mike Mignola
P. Craig Russell
Jill Thompson
Evan Dorkin
Paul Chadwick
Gary Gianni
and others
The Dark Horse Book of
HAUNTINGS

The Dark Horse Book Of Hauntings

ISBN 1-56971-958-6 $14.95

Enter the world of spooky specters and other mysterious beings in this full-color, hardcover collection of short stories, including an all-new chapter in *The Devil's Footprints* saga by Allie, Lee, Horton, and Stewart, and stellar contributions from Mike Mignola, P. Craig Russell, Paul Chadwick, and others.

Buffy
the vampire slayer
creatures
of habit
TOM FASSBENDER & JIM PASCOE
BRIAN HORTON & PAUL LEE

Buffy The Vampire Slayer
Creatures of Habit

ISBN 1-56971-563-7 $17.95

A walk on the wild side lures Buffy's sister into the dance-club scene, where a drug targeted at vampires has made a night on the town more dangerous than ever. Authors Tom Fassbender and Jim Pascoe craft a hip *Buffy* novel featuring spot illustrations and full-page paintings by Lee and Horton.

STAR WARS
EMPIRE
VOLUME ONE
BETRAYAL

Star Wars
Empire Volume I, Betrayal

ISBN 1-56971-964-0 $12.95

This acclaimed *Star Wars* graphic novel revolves around a plot by high-ranking Imperial generals to assassinate the Emperor and Darth Vader. Vader's own loyalties are called into question in this story by Allie, Horton, and Stewart, and penciled by Ryan Benjamin.

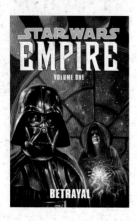